Fodor's 92 Cancún, Cozumel, Yucatán Peninsula

Erica Metzler

D1305994

Fodor's Travel Publications, Inc.
New York and London

Fodor's Cancún, Cozumel, Yucatán Peninsula

Editor: Alison Hoffman
Editorial Contributors: Wendy Ashmore, Suzanne E. De Galan, Judith Glynn, Mary Ellen Schultz, Frank "Pancho" Shiell, Todd Whitley
Art Director: Fabrizio LaRocca
Cartographer: David Lindroth
Illustrator: Karl Tanner
Cover Photograph: Pasley/Stock Boston

Design: Vignelli Associates

About the Author

Yucatán was where freelance writer and translator Erica Meltzer first set foot on Mexican soil, back in 1967. She lived in Mexico City for three years, and gets back to the country as often as possible from her base in New York.

Special Sales

Contents

Foreword

The author acknowledges, with warm thanks, those who helped her in researching this guide: the Mexican Government Tourism Office, New York; Mexicana Airlines; Hoteles Camino Real; Meliá Hoteles; Ramada Inns; Del Prado Hotels; Quality Inns International; the Posada del Capitán Lafitte, and the Stouffer Presidente Cozumel. The hotel associations of Cancún and Cozumel and the hard-working staff at the tourist offices of Campeche and Mérida were also helpful, as were GCI Group, Jeanne Westphal Associates, Rita Glassman Public Relations, Inc., and RY&P.

While every care has been taken to ensure the accuracy of the information in this guide, the passage of time will always bring change, and consequently the publisher cannot accept responsibility for errors that may occur.

All prices and opening times quoted here are based on information supplied to us at press time. Hours and admission fees may change, however, and the prudent traveler will avoid inconvenience by calling ahead.

Fodor's wants to hear about your travel experiences, both pleasant and unpleasant. When a hotel or restaurant fails to live up to its billing, let us know and we will investigate the complaint and revise our entries where the facts warrant it.

Send your letters to the editors of Fodor's Travel Publications, 201 E. 50th Street, New York, NY 10022.

Highlights'92 and Fodor's Choice

Highlights '92

The Yucatán peninsula is undergoing two opposing trends that mirror what is happening in other tourism destinations worldwide: a continued explosion of development and a growing concern for the environment. **Tour operators** are capitalizing on these trends by selling packages that focus on the Mayan ruins, wildlife, and natural beauty for which the peninsula is famous.

The **Ruta Maya,** a five-country venture to develop impoverished regions and promote low-impact tourism to the Mayan sites in Mexico, Belize, Guatemala, Honduras, and El Salvador, should be operating by 1992.

Also of interest to travelers to Yucatán is the 1992 opening of government-funded **bilingual medical clinics** in Cancún and Cozumel. These facilities will provide 24-hour emergency medical care free of charge.

Campeche Until recently, the modest State of Campeche offered little to tourists aside from its flourishing wildlife and the genial, pleasant attitude of its native population. But thanks to a massive international restoration effort, the ruined Mayan city of **Edzná** has put the state on the tourist map. Unfortunately, work at the site, where modern-day Mayan refugees from Guatemala were employed, has been temporarily halted because of a lack of funds.

Cancún Almost since its inception, Cancún has been Mexico's most popular destination, hosting more than 1.8 million foreign visitors in 1990. Judging by the numbers of package-tour takers, college students, and weekend vacationers who flock to its white Caribbean beaches and warm turquoise waters, Cancún is now almost synonymous with Mexican tourism.

The devastation caused by Hurricane Gilbert in 1988 is far in the past. Countless hotels have been made over, and new ones are springing up, although as the authorities become more concerned that Cancún is approaching the saturation point, the growth rate is slowing down. Among the deluxe international properties to have opened recently are the **Conrad Cancún** and the **Marriott Casa Magna.** The **Ritz Carlton** and the **Aoki-Westin** will round out the list of new openings by 1993. The all-inclusive fad has also arrived at Cancún, offering yet another alternative vacation concept.

As the hotel inventory plateaus, however, **time-share condominiums** are going up at a feverish pitch—not just in Cancún, but all along the Caribbean coast and on Isla Mujeres as well. In an effort to keep pace with the nearly constant flow of visitors, the vast majority of whom are North Americans, **regularly scheduled and charter airlines** have been boosting their service to Cancún and Cozumel from a growing number of gateways.

To attract a more diversified clientele, in 1991 Cancún launched an annual **Jazz Festival,** and the first such event promises to be a sell-out. In addition, two megaprojects—comprising an "eco-archaeological" park, aquariums, yacht marinas, golf courses, hotels, and commercial space—are in the works in and around Cancún.

Cozumel The offshore island of Cozumel, Mexico's largest cruise-ship port and a favorite among honeymooners and scuba divers, has also been struck by the **ecology craze.** Development of several deluxe hotels has been halted; the island museum has embarked on a serious save-the-turtle campaign; and Isla de Pasión—a tiny island off the west coast, previously used for picnic cruises—has been made into a state reserve. Negative publicity from diving accidents has resulted in the formation of the **Cozumel Association of Dive Operators (CADO)** to raise safety standards. Cozumel's hotels—which together offer about 3,500 rooms—now count on the **Cozumel Central Reservation Service** to boost the ranks of foreign visitors, who numbered more than 137,000 in 1990.

Isla Mujeres Fans of Isla Mujeres (an offshore island much smaller and less developed than Cozumel) can be reassured that it has seen relatively little change, either physically or temperamentally. A quiet place with beaches and fishing similar to Cozumel's, Isla Mujeres has only about 600 hotel rooms. Still, there have been some new additions, including the **Condominio Playa Norte Nautibeach,** the **Cristalmar** condohotel, and the cozy little **Na-Balam,** as well as the makeover of the island's largest luxury hotel, the **Costa Azul,** into an all-inclusive property. The **Cabañas María del Mar** and the **Mesón del Bucanero** have also been renovated and expanded.

Although there is talk of rebuilding the town dock to accommodate cruise ships and of operating an air charter service to Florida, Mérida, Chichén Itzá, and the Guatemalan ruins of Tikal, actual planning has not begun. In the meantime, Isla remains a backwater, beloved by backpackers and other budget travelers.

Mérida and the Mérida, the charming and understated capital of the State **State of Yucatán** of Yucatán, will not soon become a mass-tourism destination. But **Progreso,** a town on the Gulf of Mexico and Mérida's closest access to the sea, is another story. A **new pier** designed to berth cruise ships there seems likely to bring a new onslaught of tourists to the interior of the peninsula and the celebrated Mayan ruins. Hotel development near Progreso, at **Yucalpetén** and **Nuevo Yucatán,** proceeds at a steady pace. The face of northern Yucatán is also being altered by the proliferating in-bond (foreign-owned assembly plants) manufacturing plants and the burgeoning offshore oil industry. And if Cuba succeeds in garnering international tourists, many of them will pass through Mérida, a gateway for flights to Havana.

By late 1991, amateur archaeologists will be able to visit the recently excavated Mayan site of **Oxkintok,** about 51 kilometers (31 miles) south of Mérida.

Mexico's Caribbean Coast The Caribbean coast—generally known as the Cancún–Tulum Corridor—is attracting growing numbers of independent travelers. **Ecotourism** is on the rise here as well, thanks to the exotic birds, marine life, and lagoons of the **Sian Ka'an Biosphere Reserve.** The Boca Paila peninsula, virtually all of which is contained in that reserve, is earning a glowing reputation for flatfishing, fly-fishing, and bonefishing. At the same time, resorts and time-share complexes are making their inevitable appearance on this vast, sparsely inhabited, and beautiful region (which extends all the way to the border with Belize), particularly at Akumal and Puerto Aventuras.

By contrast, the sleepy coastal towns of **Playa del Carmen** and **Puerto Morelos** have not changed, although Playa, which now receives cruise ships, is positioned to become the next Cozumel. The beaches in these two destinations draw more and more Europeans each year; access to the Mayan ruins of Yucatán has been facilitated by stepped-up air service.

Fodor's Choice

No two people will agree on what makes a perfect vactation, but it's fun and helpful to know what others think. We hope you'll have a chance to experience some of Fodor's Choices yourself in Cancún, Cozumel, and the Yucatán peninsula. For detailed information about each entry, refer to the appropriate chapter.

Archaeological Sites

Chichén Itzá (Mérida)

Cobá (Mexico's Caribbean Coast)

Edzná (Campeche)

Kohunlich (Mexico's Caribbean Coast)

Tulum (Mexico's Caribbean Coast)

Uxmal (Mérida)

Attractions

Historical Buildings and Churches

Calkiní (Campeche)

Casa de Montejo (Mérida)

Ermita de Santa Isabel (Mérida)

Ex-Templo de San José and Cathedral (Campeche)

Mansión Carvajal (Campeche)

Museums

Hecelchakán (Campeche)

City Museum (Mérida)

Museum of Anthropology and History (Mérida)

Regional Museum (Campeche)

Beaches

Akumal (Mexico's Caribbean Coast)

Boca Paila peninsula (Mexico's Caribbean Coast)

Chemuyil and Paamul (Mexico's Caribbean Coast)

Isla del Carmen (Campeche)

Playa Cocoteros (Isla Mujeres)

Punta Chiqueros and Punta Celerain (Cozumel)

Boat Trips

Alacranes Reef (Mérida)

Isla Contoy (Isla Mujeres)

Isla de Pájaros (Mexico's Caribbean Coast)

Isla Holbox (Mérida)

Dining

Bogart's, Cancún *(Very Expensive)*

Chez Magaly, Isla Mujeres *(Very Expensive)*

Alberto's Continental Patio, Mérida *(Expensive)*

Arrecife, Cozumel *(Expensive)*

La Habichuela, Cancún *(Expensive)*

El Mexicano, Cancún *(Expensive)*

La Cabaña del Pescador, Cozumel *(Moderate)*

Café Amsterdam, Cancún *(Moderate)*

El Capi Navegante, Cozumel *(Moderate)*

Gypsy's, Cancún *(Moderate)*

La Peña, Isla Mujeres *(Moderate)*

El Pescador, Cancún *(Moderate)*

Rosa Mexicana, Cancún *(Moderate)*

Jalapeños, Cancún *(Inexpensive)*

El Moro, Cozumel *(Inexpensive)*

Festivals and Special Events

Billfish Tournaments (Cancún, Cozumel)

Cancún Jazz Festival (Cancún)

Carnaval (Campeche, Mexico's Caribbean Coast, Cozumel, Isla Mujeres, Mérida)

Equinox at Chichén Itzá (Mérida)

Fiesta of San Román (Campeche)

Mérida en Domingo (Mérida)

Sol a Sol International Regatta (Cozumel, Isla Mujeres)

Lodging

Caphe-Ha, Mexico's Caribbean Coast *(Very Expensive)*

Meliá Cancún, Cancún *(Very Expensive)*

Sol Pez Maya, Mexico's Caribbean Coast *(Very Expensive)*

Villas Tacul, Cancún *(Very Expensive)*

Cancún Playa, Cancún *(Expensive)*

Na-Balam, Isla Mujeres *(Expensive)*

Posada del Capitán Lafitte, Mexico's Caribbean Coast *(Expensive)*

Albatros, Mexico's Caribbean Coast *(Moderate)*

Casa Mexilio, Mérida *(Moderate)*

Gran Hotel, Mérida *(Inexpensive)*

Mesón San Miguel, Cozumel *(Inexpensive)*

Sports

Bird-watching Celestún (Mérida)

Punta Celerain and Colombia Lagoon (Cozumel)

Río Lagartos (Mérida)

Fishing Billfishing (Cozumel, Isla Mujeres)

Bonefishing (Mexico's Caribbean Coast, Cozumel)

Deep-sea fishing (Cancún, Cozumel, Isla Mujeres)

Flatfishing, fly-fishing (Mexico's Caribbean Coast)

Sportfishing (Cozumel, Mérida)

Scuba Diving and Akumal (Mexico's Caribbean Coast)
Snorkeling
Banco Chinchorro (Cozumel)

Laguna de Bacalar (Mexico's Caribbean Coast)

Palancar Reef (Cozumel)

Nature Reserves and Natural Beauty

Celestún (Mérida)

Cenote Dzitnup (Mérida)

Chankanaab (Cozumel)

Laguna de Bacalar (Mexico's Caribbean Coast)

Río Lagartos (Mérida)

Sian Ka'an Biosphere Reserve (Mexico's Caribbean Coast)

Xcaret (Mexico's Caribbean Coast)

Nightlife

Dady'O (Cancún)

Express (Mérida)

Restaurante La Peña (Isla Mujeres)

Rutilio's y Chimbo's (Isla Mujeres)

Shopping

Bazar García Rejón (Mérida)

Halachó (Campeche)

Fernando Huertas (Mérida)

La Loma (Isla Mujeres)

Los Cinco Soles (Cozumel)

Taste Treats

Huevos motuleños (Isla Mujeres, Mérida)

Ixtabentún and *licuados* (Mérida)

Lebanese cuisine (Mérida)

Poc chuc (throughout Yucatán)

Pozole at La Palapa del Paisa (Campeche)

Tik in chik (Isla Mujeres)

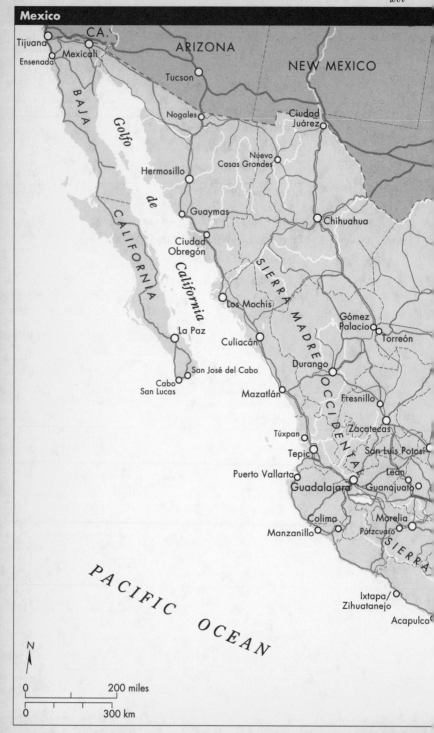

Mexico

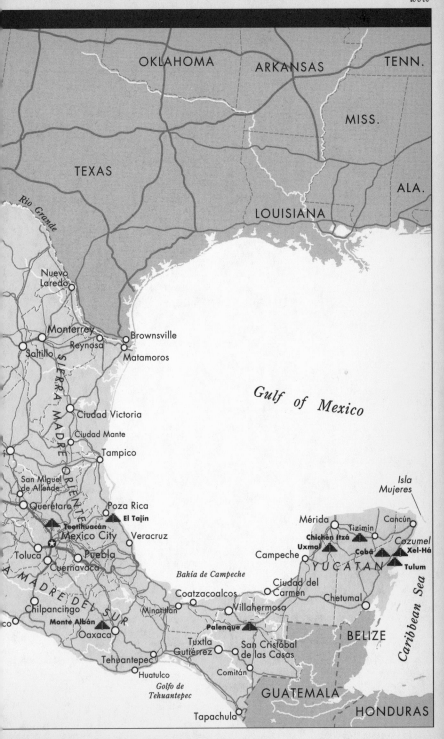

OKLAHOMA

ARKANSAS

TENN.

MISS.

TEXAS

ALA.

LOUISIANA

Rio Grande

Nuevo
Laredo

Monterrey
Reynosa
Saltillo
Brownsville
Matamoros

SIERRA MADRE ORIENTE

Ciudad Victoria

Ciudad Mante

Tampico

San Miguel
de Allende

Querétaro

Poza Rica
El Tajín

Teotihuacán
Mexico City
Toluca
Cuernavaca
Puebla

Veracruz

Gulf of Mexico

Isla
Mujeres

Mérida
Tizimín
Cancún

Chichén Itzá
Uxmal
Cobá
Cozumel
Xel-Há

Campeche
YUCATÁN
Tulum

Bahía de Campeche

Ciudad del
Carmen

Caribbean Sea

SIERRA MADRE DEL SUR

Chilpancingo

Monte Albán

co
Oaxaca

Coatzacoalcos

Minatitlán
Villahermosa

Chetumal

BELIZE

Palenque

Tehuantepec

Tuxtla
Gutiérrez

San Cristóbal
de las Casas

Comitán

Huatulco

*Golfo de
Tehuantepec*

GUATEMALA

Tapachula

HONDURAS

Golfo de México

Dzilam de Bravo

Santa Clara

Dzilan González

Progreso

Yucalpetén

Motul

Tema

Punta Baz

Dzibilchaltún

25

261

Tekantó

80

Celestún

Mérida

Citilcúm

Izamal

281

Umán

180

Hoctún

Punta Nimun

Holca

Maxcanú

Mayapán

18

YUCAT

Muna

Santa Cruz

Uxmal

Ticul

184

Ozkutzcab

Kabah

Sayil

Labná

Tzucacab

Tenabó

261

Campeche

Tinúm

180

261

Hopelchén

Punta Seybaplaya

Edzná

QUI

La Joya

Champoton

CAMPECHE

Río Champotón

Sabancuy

180

Escárcega

186

E

Río

Xpujil

186

186

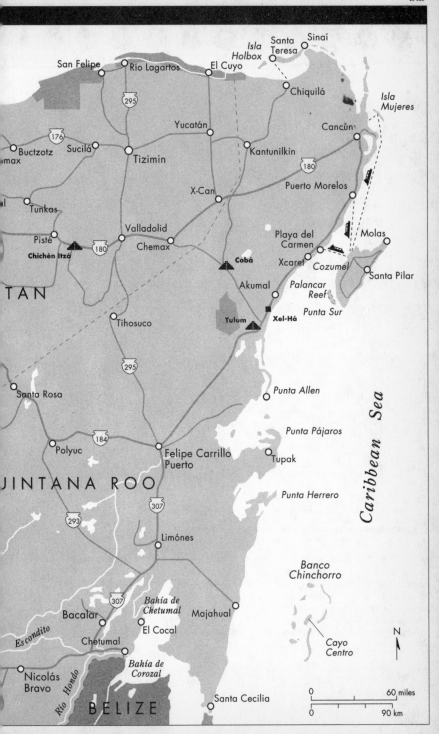

San Felipe
Río Lagartos
El Cuyo
Isla Holbox
Santa Teresa
Sinaí
295
Chiquilá
Isla Mujeres
Yucatán
Cancún
176
Buctzotz
Sucilá
Tizimin
Kantunilkin
max
180
Puerto Morelos
Tunkas
X-Can
Valladolid
Playa del Carmen
Molas
Pisté
Chichén Itzá
180
Chemax
Cobá
Xcaret
Cozumel
Santa Pilar
TAN
Akumal
Palancar Reef
Tihosuco
Tulum
Xel-Há
Punta Sur
295
Santa Rosa
Punta Allen
Caribbean Sea
184
Punta Pájaros
Polyuc
Felipe Carrillo Puerto
Tupak
JINTANA ROO
Punta Herrero
307
293
Limónes
Banco Chinchorro
307
Bahía de Chetumal
Majahual
Bacalar
El Cocal
Escondido
Chetumal
Cayo Centro
N
Nicolás Bravo
Río Hondo
Bahía de Corozal
BELIZE
Santa Cecilia

0   60 miles
0   90 km

World Time Zones

Numbers below vertical bands relate each zone to Greenwich Mean Time (0 hrs.).
Local times frequently differ from these general indications,
as indicated by light-face numbers on map.

Algiers, **29**
Anchorage, **3**
Athens, **41**
Baghdad, **46**
Bangkok, **50**
Beijing, **54**

Berlin, **34**
Bogotá, **19**
Budapest, **37**
Buenos Aires, **24**
Caracas, **22**
Chicago, **9**
Copenhagen, **33**
Dallas, **10**

Delhi, **48**
Denver, **8**
Djakarta, **53**
Dublin, **26**
Hong Kong, **56**
Honolulu, **2**

Istanbul, **40**
Jerusalem, **42**
Johannesburg, **44**
Lima, **20**
Lisbon, **28**
London (Greenwich), **27**
Los Angeles, **6**
Madrid, **38**
Manila, **57**

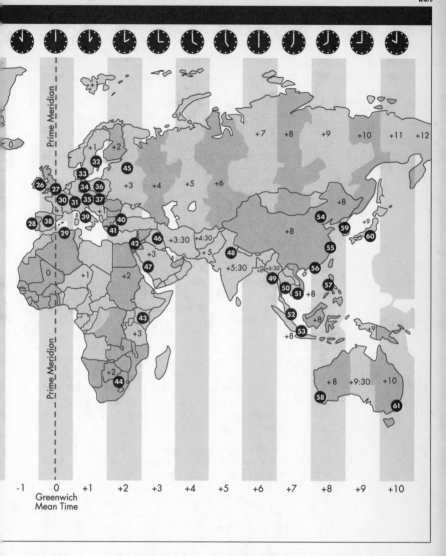

Introduction

By Erica Meltzer

The Yucatán peninsula has captivated travelers since the early Spanish explorations. "A place of white towers, whose glint could be seen from the ships . . . temples rising tier on tier, with sculptured cornices" is how the expeditions' chroniclers described the peninsula, then thought to be an island. Rumors of a mainland 10 days west of Cuba were known to Columbus, who obstinately hoped to find "a very populated land," and one that was richer than any he had yet discovered. Subsequent explorers and conquistadores met with more resistance there than in almost any other part of the New World, and this rebelliousness continued for centuries.

The Yucatecáns of today as a whole are honest and generous, perhaps more than their countrymen in other parts of Mexico. Largely because of their geographic isolation, they tend to preserve ancient traditions more than many other indigenous groups in the country. This can be seen in such areas as housing (the use of the ancient Maya thatched hut, or *na*); dress (*huipiles* have been made and worn by Maya women for centuries); occupation (most modern-day Maya are farmers, just as their ancestors were); language (while the Maya language has evolved considerably, basically it is very similar to that spoken at least 500 years ago); and religion (ancient deities persist particularly in the form of gods associated with agriculture, such as the *chacs* or rain gods, and festivals to honor the seasons and benefactor spirits maintain the traditions of old).

This vast peninsula encompasses 113,000 square kilometers (43,630 square miles) of a flat limestone table covered with sparse topsoil and scrubby jungle growth. Geographically, it comprises the states of Yucatán, Campeche, and Quintana Roo, as well as Belize and a part of Guatemala, though the latter two countries are not discussed in this book. Long isolated from the rest of Mexico and still one of the least Hispanicized (or Mexicanized) regions of the country, Yucatán catapulted into the tourist's vocabulary with the creation of its most precious man-made asset, Cancún.

Mexico's most popular resort destination owes its success to its location on the superb eastern coastline of Yucatán, which is washed by the exquisitely colored and translucent waters of the Caribbean and endowed with a semitropical climate, unbroken stretches of beach, and the world's fifth-longest barrier reef, which separates the mainland from Cozumel. Cancún, along with Cozumel and to a lesser extent Isla Mujeres, incarnates the success formula for sun-and-sand tourism: luxury hotels, sandy beaches, water sports, nightlife, and restaurants that specialize in international fare.

Cancún has several advantages over its Caribbean neighbors: It is less expensive; it can be reached via more nonstop flights; and it offers a far richer culture. With the advent of Cancún, the peninsula's Mayan ruins—long a mecca for archaeology enthusiasts—have become virtual satellites of that glittering star. The proximity of such compelling sites as Chichén Itzá, Uxmal, and Tulum allows Cancún's visitors to explore the vestiges of one of the most brilliant civilizations in the ancient world without having to journey too far from their base.

Yucatán offers a breathtaking diversity of other charms, too. The waters of the Mexican Caribbean are clearer and more turquoise than those of the Pacific; many of the beaches are unrivaled. Scuba diving (in natural sinkholes and along the barrier reefs), snorkeling, deep-sea fishing, and other water sports attract growing numbers of tourists. They can also go birding, help save sea turtles, camp, spelunk, and shop for Yucatán's splendid handicrafts. There is a broad spectrum of settings and accommodations to choose from: the high-rise, pricey strip of hotels along Cancún's Paseo Kukulcán; the less showy properties on Cozumel, beloved by partying college-age scuba divers from Texas; and the relaxed ambience of Isla Mujeres and Playa del Carmen, where most lodgings consist of rustic bungalows with ceiling fans and hammocks.

There are also the cities of Yucatán. Foremost is Mérida, wonderfully unaltered by time, where Moorish-inspired, colonnaded colonial architecture blends handsomely with turn-of-the-century pomposities. In Mérida, café living is still an art and Indians still rule the streets. Campeche, one of the few walled cities in North America, possesses an eccentric charm; it is slightly out of step with the rest of the country and not the least bothered by the fact. Down on the border with Belize stands Chetumal, a ramshackle place of wood-frame houses that is pervaded by the hybrid culture of coastal Central America and the pungent smell of the sea. Progreso, at the other end of the peninsula on the Gulf of Mexico, is Chetumal's northern counterpart, an overgrown fishing village turned commercial port. Hotels in these towns, while for the most part not as luxurious as the beach resort properties, range from the respectable if plain 1970s commercial buildings to the undated fleabags so popular with detective novelists (one thinks especially of Raymond Chandler) and movie makers.

Wildlife is another of Yucatán's riches. Iguanas, lizards, tapir, jaguars, deer, armadillos, and wild boars thrive on this alternately parched and densely foliaged plain. Flamingos and herons, manatees and sea turtles, their once dwindling numbers now rising in response to Mexico's newly awakened ecological consciousness, find idyllic watery habitats in and above the coastline's mangrove swamps, lagoons, and sandbars, acres of which have been made into national parks. Both Río Lagartos and the coast's Sian Ka'an biosphere reserve sparkle with Yucatán's natural beauty. Orchids, bougainvillea, and poinciana are ubiquitous; dazzling reds and pinks and oranges and whites spill over into countless courtyards—effortless hothouses. And while immense palm groves and forests of precious hardwood trees slowly succumb to forest fires and disease, the region's edible tropical flora—coconuts, papaya, bananas, and oranges—remain succulent ancillaries to the celebrated Yucatecán cuisine.

It is the colors of Yucatán that are most remarkable. From the stark white, sun-bleached sand, the sea stretches out like some immense canvas painted in bands of celadon greens, pale aquas, and deep dusty blues. At dusk the sea and the horizon meld in the sumptuous glow of a lavender sunset, the sky just barely tinged with periwinkle and violet. Inland, the beige, gray, and amber stones of ruined temples are set off by riotous greenery. The colors of newer structures are equally intoxicating: Tawny, gray-brown thatched roofs sit atop white oval huts. Colonial mansions favor creamy pastels of bisque, salmon, and coral tones, again highlighted by elegant white: white arches, white balustrades, white rococo porticos. Brilliant colors glimmer in carved hardwood doors, variegated tile floors, brown and green pottery and rugs affixed to walls, and snatches of bougainvillea rushing down the sides of buildings.

But for all of Yucatán's fine attributes, the peninsula faces grave danger, especially in the state of Quintana Roo. Coastlines are being polluted, coral reefs destroyed, tropical rain forests razed to make way for farms and ranches. Public services for the state's booming population, which—at 16%—has the highest growth rate in the country, have become woefully inadequate. The gap between rich and poor is widening, and as the laws governing foreign ownership of coastal lands are eased, time-share condominium developers are making more and more of the peninsula's land off-limits to its Mexican residents. On the up side, however, the government is beginning to realize that in the long run unbridled development can only hurt the country. Consequently, hotel construction in both Cancún and Cozumel has been slowed. The biggest areas of growth at present are the so-called Cancún–Tulum Corridor and the northern gulf coast, east of Progreso.

Yucatán's color extends beyond the physical to the historical. From the conquistadores' first landfall off Cape Catoche in 1517 to the bloody skirmishes that wiped out most of the Indians to the razing of Mayan temples and burning of their sacred books, the peninsula was a battlefield. Pirates wreaked havoc off the coast of Campeche for centuries. Half the Indian population was killed during the 19th-century uprising known as the War of the Castes, when the enslaved indigenous population rose up and massacred thousands of Europeans; Yucatán was attempting to secede from Mexico, and dictator Porfirio Díaz sent in his troops. These events, like the towering Mayan civilization, have left their mark throughout the peninsula: in its archaeological museums, its colonial monuments, and the opulent mansions of the hacienda owners who enslaved the natives to cultivate their henequen.

But years after all the violent conflicts with foreigners, the people of Yucatán treat today's visitors with genuine hospitality and friendliness. Once you leave the beach resorts, you are likely to enjoy spontaneous, honest interaction with the locals. They appreciate any attempts you make to communicate with them in Spanish, and their native tongue will give you a better understanding of the people of this region.

1 Essential Information

Before You Go

Government Tourist Offices

In the United States 405 Park Ave., New York, NY 10022, tel. 212/755–8233; 1911 Pennsylvania Ave., Washington, DC 20006, tel. 202/728–1750; 70 E. Lake St., Chicago, IL 60601, tel. 312/565–2778; 10100 Santa Monica Blvd., Los Angeles, CA 90067, tel. 213/203–8191; 2707 North Loop W, Suite 450, Houston, TX 77008, tel. 713/880–5153; 11522 S.W. 81st St., Miami, FL 33156, tel. 305/252–1440. All offices can be reached toll-free at 800/262–8900.

In Canada 1 Place Ville Marie, Suite 2409, Montreal, Quebec H3B 3M9, tel. 514/871–1052; 2 Bloor St. W, Suite 18011, Toronto, Ontario M4W 3E2, tel. 416/925–0704.

In the United Kingdom 60-61 Trafalgar Sq., London WC2N 5DS, tel. 071/734–1058 or 071/734–1059.

Tour Groups

The vast majority of travelers who are bound for Yucatán—whether their destination is the sun and sand of Cancún and Cozumel or the archaeological sites farther inland—opt for independent packages. Group tours of the Mexican Caribbean are scarce, for good reason. If your goal is to relax and get away from it all, you probably won't want to crowd your itinerary with many activities other than swimming, snorkeling, sailing, and perhaps a trip to the nearby Mayan ruins. A number of packages are available from tour operators, airlines, travel agencies, and hotels. Some are land only; others include round-trip airfare. Your choice of a package will depend mostly on your pocketbook. Accommodations range from modest hotels to superglitzy resorts. As usual, you get what you pay for.

When you are evaluating a package, be sure to find out exactly what expenses are included (particularly transfers, tips, hotel taxes and service charges, meals, and entertainment); the hotel's rating and the facilities offered; cancellation policies for both you and the tour operator; and, if you are traveling alone, the cost of a single supplement. Listed below is a sampling of operators and packages to give you an idea of what is available. For additional resources, contact your travel agent or the nearest Mexican Government Tourism Office (*see* above). Most tour operators request that bookings be made through a travel agent; there is no additional charge for doing so.

General-Interest Tours
U.S.-based Tour Operators **American Express Vacations** (Box 5014, Atlanta, GA 30302, tel. 404/368–5100 in GA or 800/241–1700 outside GA) has a variety of tours available, or one can be designed for you. **GoGo Tours** (69 Spring St., Ramsey, NJ 07446, tel. 201/934–3500 or 800/821–3731) offers a wide selection of tours at an equally wide range of prices. **Friendly Holidays** (1983 Marcus Ave., Lake Success, NY 11042, tel. 516/358–1200 or 800/221–9748) runs regional tours.

U.K.-based Tour Operators **Club Med** (110 Brompton Rd., London SW3 1JJ, tel. 071/581–1161) offers seven- and 14-night packages to its Cancún resort, which features water sports, tennis, and other activities as well as optional deep-sea-fishing trips and excursions to the ruins. **Esplanade Tours** (581 Boylston St., Boston, MA 02116, tel. 617/

266–7465) is marketing a 20-day tour of Mayan sites and archaeological museums that begins in Mexico City and goes on to Palenque, Yucatán, Guatemala, and Honduras. **Hayes and Jarvis Ltd.** (Hayes House, 152 King St., London W6 OQU, tel. 081/748–5050) features a two-week tour of Mexico's ancient Indian ruins, beginning in Mexico City and ending in Cancún, with an optional seven-night extension in the latter. **Mexican Tours** (61 High St., Barnet, Herts EN5 5UR, tel. 081/440–7830), which specializes in the Cancún area and the archaeological sites of Yucatán, will arrange individualized tours, including flights, accommodations, and all ground arrangements. **Speedbird Holidays** (Pacific House, Hazelwick Ave., Three Bridges, Crawley, West Sussex RH10 1NP, tel. 0293/611611) offers a 14-day "Mexican Discovery" tour that ends in Cancún, with an optional four-night extension there. **Sunset Travel Ltd.** (306 Clapham Rd., London SW9 9AE, tel. 071/622–5466) has air and hotel packages to Cancún.

Special-Interest Tours   **Maya-Caribe Travel** (87 Wolfs La., Pelham, NY 10803, tel. 914/738–8254 or 800/223–4084) offers customized tour service to Yucatán that include hotels, airport transfers, ground transportation, and guide services. A West Coast tour operator specializing in archaeology, ecology, and birding trips to Yucatán and the southeast is **Mayan Adventure Tours** (Box 15204, Seattle, WA 98105, tel. 206/523–5309). **Questers Worldwide Nature Tours'** (257 Park Ave. S, New York, NY 10010, tel. 212/673–3120 or 800/468–8668) 15-day Mexico land-only program includes stops in Uxmal and Chichén Itzá. **Rothschild Travel Consultants** (900 West End Ave., Suite 1B, New York, NY 10025, tel. 212/662–4858 or 800/359–0747) runs eight-day dive packages to Akumal, including accommodations, two boat dives daily, rental car, taxes, and service charges. **Special Expeditions** (720 5th Ave., New York, NY 10019, tel. 212/765–7740 or 800/762–0003 outside NY) operates 8-, 11-, and 15-day cruises from the Panama Canal to the "Maya Coast," stopping at Belize, Banco Chinchorro, Tulum, Cozumel, Isla Contoy, Alacrán Reef, and Progreso. **Tropical Travel** (720 Worthshire, Houston, TX 77008, tel. 713/688–1985 or 800/451–8017) has put together an eight-day all-inclusive "Mexico–Maya Caribbean Adventure" program, an 11-day tour highlighting Yucatán's wildlife and archaeological sites, and a 14-day cultural tour, "Ancient Maya Kingdoms of the Yucatán," beginning in Mexico City. Hotel, scuba, and fishing packages are also available. **Universal Destinations** (5065 Westheimer, Suite 725E, Houston, TX 77056, tel. 713/961–1257 or 800/627–3483) offers golf and tennis packages to Cancún.

Package Deals for Independent Travelers

Cancún   **GoGo Tours** (69 Spring St., Ramsey, NJ 07446, tel. 201/934–3500) gives you a choice of nearly three dozen of Cancún's hotels and resorts in its three-, five-, and seven-night packages; extra nights are available. All packages include round-trip airport transfers. "Cancún Sun Splash" from **Friendly Holidays** (1983 Marcus Ave., Lake Success, NY 11042, tel. 516/358–1200 or 800/221-9748) includes round-trip air transportation and airport transfers; three- and seven-night packages to more than two dozen hotels are available. **American Express Vacations** (300 Pinnacle Way, Norcross GA 30071, tel. 800/282–0800 in GA or 800/241–1700 outside GA) gives you either four or eight days in Cancún, including round-trip air transportation. **M. I. Travel** (450 7th Ave., Suite 1805, New York, NY 10123, tel. 212/967–6565) has a seven-night package at a choice of six of Cancún's hotels, including round-trip air transportation, transfers, and airport and hotel gratuities on arrival and departure. Round-trip airfare is also included in the three-night Cancún packages offered by **Continental's Grand Destinations** (tel. 800/634–5555) and **American Airlines' Fly AAway Vacations** (tel. 817/355–1234 or 800/321–2121), as well as in **Globetrotters'** (139 Main St., Cambridge, MA 02142, tel. 617/621–9911 or 800/999–9696) three- to seven-night packages. **Mexicana Airlines** (3201 Cherry Ridge, Suite 200, San Antonio, TX 78230-4852, tel. 512/525–8505 or 800/533–7935; fax 800/533–7945) offers four-day, three-night packages at your choice of 17 hotels and including round-trip airfare, hotel tax, transfers, and U.S. departure tax.

Other reliable operators include **American Leisure** (9800 Centre Pkwy., Suite 800, Houston, TX 77036, tel. 713/988–57777 or 800/777–1980), **Asti Tours** (21 E. 40th St., New York, NY 10016, tel. 800/535–3711 in NY or 800/327–4390 outside NY), **GWV International** (300 1st Ave., Needham, MA 02194, tel. 617/449–5460 or 800/CALL–GWV), **Magnatours** (325 E. 75th St., New York, NY 10021, tel. 212/517–7770 or 800/223–0476), **Mexico Travel Consultants** (246 S. Robertson Blvd., Beverly Hills, CA 90211, tel. 213/854–8500 or 800/252–0100), **Travel Impressions** (465 Smith St., Farmingdale, NY 11735, tel. 516/845–8000, 800/284–0044 in the northeastern U.S., 800/284–0077 in the rest of the U.S.), and **Universal Destinations** (5065 Westheimer, Suite 725E, Houston, TX 77056, tel. 713/961–1257 or 800/627–3483).

Cozumel For travelers to Cozumel, **Barbachano Tours' Cozumel Central Reservations** (1570 Madruga Ave., Ph #1, Coral Gables, FL 33146, tel. 800/327–2254) offers three-night packages at a choice of 20 hotels, including round-trip airfare, transfers, departure tax, and hotel tax, with optional scuba add-ons. In addition, several of the internationally affiliated chain hotels in Cancún and Cozumel offer air and hotel packages in cooperation with the airlines.

When to Go

High season along the Mexican Caribbean runs from mid-December through Easter week. Seasonal price changes are less pronounced in Mérida and other inland regions than at the beach resorts, but it may be difficult to find a room during Christmas, Easter, and the last week of July and first three weeks of August.

Climate Spring and summer are usually pleasant along the coast, although you may experience some afternoon rain and evening breezes; in autumn, storms are common. The steamiest time of year inland is late spring, just before the May–October rainy season. What follows are the average daily maximum and minimum temperatures for Mérida. The rest of Yucatán follows the same general pattern.

Mérida	Jan.	83F	28C	May	94F	40C	Sept.	90F	32C
		62	17		72	22		73	23
	Feb.	85F	29C	June	92F	33C	Oct.	87F	31C
		63	17		73	23		71	22
	Mar.	89F	37C	July	92F	33C	Nov.	85F	29C
		66	19		73	23		67	19
	Apr.	92F	41C	Aug.	91F	33C	Dec.	82F	28C
		69	21		73	23		64	18

Current weather information for more than 750 cities around the world may be obtained by calling **WeatherTrak** information service at 900/370–8728 (cost: 95¢ per minute). A taped message will tell you to dial the three-digit access code for the destination in which you're interested. The code is either the area code (in the United States) or the first three letters of the foreign city. For a list of all access codes, send a stamped, self-addressed envelope to Cities (9B Terrace Way, Greensboro, NC 27403). For more information, call 800/247–3282.

A similar service operated by **American Express** can be accessed by dialing 900/WEATHER (900/932–8437). In addition to supplying a three-day weather forecast for 600 cities worldwide, this service provides international travel information at a cost of 75¢ per minute.

Festivals and Seasonal Events

Traditional religious and patriotic festivals rank among Yucatán's most memorable activities. Towns throughout the region host a number of additional annual fairs, shows, and local celebrations.

Jan. 1: New Year's Day is celebrated throughout the region.
Feb.–Mar.: Carnaval (Mardi Gras) festivities take place the week before Lent, with parades, floats, outdoor dancing, music, and fireworks, and are especially spirited in Mérida, Cozumel, Isla Mujeres, Campeche, and Chetumal.
Mar. 21 and Sept. 21: At the **Equinoxes** Kukulcán, the plumed serpent deity, appears to emerge from his temple atop El Castillo Pyramid at Chichén Itzá and slither down to earth. The phenomenon happens through a fascinating interplay of light and shadow (sunshine is necessary, however). It attracts large crowds; be sure to make hotel reservations well in advance.
Apr.–May: The Sol a Sol International Regatta, launched from St. Petersburg, Florida, arrives in Isla Mujeres and Cozumel, sparking regional dances and a general air of festivity.
Late Apr.–early June: Isla Mujeres Regattas bring a fleet of sailboats from Florida and Texas for a series of races.
Late Apr.–June: Billfish Tournaments take place in Cozumel and Cancún.
Apr. 28–May 3: Holy Cross Fiestas in Chumayel, Celestún, Hopelchén—all in Yucatán state—include cockfights, dances, and fireworks.
Memorial Day Weekend: The Cancún Jazz Festival, an annual event as of 1991, has featured top musicians, such as Wynton Marsalis and Chick Corea.
Last week in May: Hammock Festival, hailing the furnishing that originated here, is held in Tecoh, on the southern outskirts of Mérida.
Last week of July: Fiesta de San Ignacio takes place in Chetumal

and features reggae and calypso rhythms and traditional Mexican music.

Sept. 14: *Vaquerías* (traditional cattle-branding feasts) attract pilgrims who gather for bullfights, fireworks, and music.

Sept. 14–28: Fiesta of San Román attracts 50,000 people to Campeche to view the procession carrying the Black Christ of San Román—the city's most sacred patron saint—through the streets.

Sept. 15–16: Independence Day is celebrated throughout Mexico with fireworks and parties.

Sept. 27: Fiesta of Our Lord of the Blisters (El Señor de las Ampollas), Mérida's biggest festival, begins two weeks or more of processions, dances, bullfights, and fireworks.

Oct. 18–25: Fiesta of the Christ of Sitilpech in Izamal, near Mérida, begins a week of daily processions in which the image of Christ is carried from Sitilpech village to Izamal; dances and fireworks accompany the processions.

Oct. 23–Nov. 2: Cancún Fair serves as a nostalgia trip for provincials who now live along the Caribbean shore but still remember the small-town fiestas back home.

Nov. 1–2: Day of the Dead, or All Saints' Day, is celebrated throughout the peninsula with graveside picnics. Bakers herald the annual return of the departed from the spirit world with pastry skulls and candy.

Nov. 13–20: Fiesta de Santiago, in Tekax, Yucatán, features a week of bullfights, cockfights, dancing, and fireworks.

Nov. 31–Dec. 8: Fiesta of the Virgin of the Conception is held each year in Champotón, Campeche.

Dec. 1–8: Fiesta of Isla Mujeres honors the island's patron saint, as members of various guilds stage processions, dances, and bullfights.

Dec. 3–9: Day of the Immaculate Conception, celebrated for six days in the village of Kantunilkin, Quintana Roo, with processions, folkloric dances, fireworks, and bullfights.

Dec. 8: The **Aquatic Procession** highlights festivities at the fishing village of Celestún, west of Mérida.

Dec. 16–25: Christmas is celebrated in the Yucatán villages of Espita and Temax with processions culminating in the breaking of candy-filled piñatas.

National Holidays Banks, government offices, and many businesses close on these days, so plan your trip accordingly: January 1, New Year's Day; Febuary 5, Constitution Day; March 21, Benito Juárez's birthday; May 1, Labor Day; September 16, Independence Day; November 20, Revolution Day; December 25, Christmas Day.

Banks and government offices close during Holy Week, especially the Thursday and Friday before Easter; on May 5, anniversary of the Battle of Puebla; May 10, Mother's Day; September 1, opening of Congress; October 12, Día de la Raza; November 2, Day of the Dead; December 12, Feast of the Virgin of Guadalupe; December 25–January 2, Christmas week.

What to Pack

Pack light, because you may want to save space for purchases: Yucatán is filled with bargains on clothing, leather goods, jewelry, pottery, and other crafts.

Clothing Resort wear is all you will need for the Caribbean beach towns: Bring lightweight sports clothes, sundresses, bathing suits, sun visors, and cover-ups for the beach and a jacket or sweater to wear in the chilly, air-conditioned restaurants. If you plan to visit any ruins, bring comfortable walking shoes with rubber soles. Lightweight rain gear is a good idea during the rainy season. Cancún is the dressiest spot on the peninsula, but even fancy restaurants don't require men to wear jackets. Women may wear shorts at the ruins, on the beaches, and in the beach towns, but should not do so in the cities.

Miscellaneous Insect repellent, sunscreen, and umbrellas are a must for Yucatán. A spare pair of eyeglasses and sunglasses and an adequate supply of prescription drugs are essentials on any trip. You can probably find over-the-counter drugs in pharmacies, but in some cases a local doctor's prescription is required. Other handy items—especially if you will be traveling on your own or camping—include toilet paper, facial tissues, and a flashlight (for occasional power outages or use at campsites). Snorkelers should consider bringing their own equipment unless traveling light is a priority; shoes with rubber soles for rocky underwater surfaces are also advised. For long-term stays in remote rural areas, *see* Staying Healthy, below.

Customs will allow you to bring one still and one movie or video camera, with 12 rolls of film for each; bring the limit, because film is expensive in Mexico. Electrical converters are not necessary, because the country operates on the 60-cycle, 120-volt system. However, adapters come in handy since most Mexican outlets have not been updated to accommodate safety (polarized) plugs.

Carry-on Luggage Airlines generally allow each passenger on international flights from the United States one piece of carry-on luggage. The bag cannot exceed 45 inches (length x width x height) and must fit under the seat or in the overhead luggage compartment.

Checked Luggage Passengers are generally allowed to check two pieces of luggage, neither of which can exceed 62 inches (length x width x height) or weigh more than 70 pounds. Baggage allowances vary slightly among airlines, so check with your carrier or your travel agent before departure.

Taking Money Abroad

Traveler's checks and major U.S. credit cards are accepted in larger cities and resorts, although American Express is accepted somewhat less often than MasterCard and Visa. Many stores will take your credit cards but tack on a surcharge of about 6%, claiming that this is what they will have to pay the credit card companies. Whether or not this is true, or even legal, is a moot point in Mexico. The general rule is that you get a better deal with cash or traveler's checks. However, there is some risk involved in carrying cash, and even traveler's checks are not always that convenient to replace, so you will have to weigh the trade-off yourself.

In smaller towns and rural areas, you may need cash. You won't get as good an exchange rate at home as abroad, but it's wise to change a small amount of money into pesos before you go: Lines at airport currency-exchange booths can be very long, and in any event they are not always open when flights arrive late at night or on Sundays. Banks charge the lowest commissions, but their hours (weekdays 9–1:30, in most cases) may not suit you;

you should also avoid the 15th and 30th of the month, when Mexicans are paid. Next best are probably the exchange houses (*casas de cambio*), and your last resort should be the hotel cashier's desk. Changing money on the street is not a good idea.

If your local bank at home can't change your currency, you can exchange money through **Thomas Cook Currency Services.** To find the office nearest you, contact the headquarters at 29 Broadway, New York, NY 10006 (tel. 212/635–0515). For safety and convenience, it's always best to take traveler's checks. The most recognized traveler's checks are **American Express, Barclay's, Thomas Cook,** and those issued through major commercial banks, such as **Citibank** and **Bank of America.** Some banks will issue the checks free to established customers, but most charge a 1% commission fee. Buy part of the traveler's checks in small denominations to cash toward the end of your trip. This will save you from having to cash a large check and ending up with more foreign currency than you need. (There is no limit on the amount of pesos that can be changed back into dollars. However, coins are not accepted.) Remember to take the addresses of offices where you can get refunds for lost or stolen traveler's checks. The *American Express Traveler's Companion,* a directory of worldwide offices to contact in case of loss or theft of American Express Traveler's Checks, is available at most travel service locations.

Getting Money from Home

There are at least three ways to get money from home:

1) Have it sent through a large commercial bank with a correspondent bank in the town where you're staying. The only drawback is that you must have an account with the bank; if not, that bank will have to go through your own bank and the process will be slower and more expensive.

2) Have it sent through **American Express,** which has offices in Cancún and Cozumel. If you are a cardholder, you can cash a personal check or a counter check at an American Express office for up to $1,000 ($2,500 for holders of gold cards) in cash or traveler's checks. There is a 1% commission on traveler's checks. If you have an Express Cash personal identification number, you can withdraw funds from your checking account without actually using a check; there is a transaction fee of 2% with a minimum charge of $2 and a maximum of $6. Call 800/CASH-NOW for an application.

American Express also provides another service that you don't have to be a cardholder to use: the **American Express Money-Gram.** You will have to call home and have someone go to an American Express office or MoneyGram agent and fill out the necessary form. The amount sent must be in increments of $50 and must be paid for with cash, a MasterCard or Visa, or the Optima card. The American Express MoneyGram agent authorizes the transfer of funds to an American Express office in the town where you're staying. You'll need to show identification when you pick up the money. You'll also need to know the transaction reference number, so remember to get it from the person at home. In most cases, the money will be available in 15 minutes. Fees vary according to the amount sent: For sending $300, the fee is $35; for $1,000, $70; for $5,000, $170. For the American Express MoneyGram location nearest your home, call 800/543–4080. The service has offices in Mérida and Cozumel, through Banamex, but not in Cancún.

3) Have it sent through **Western Union** (tel. 800/325–6000). If you have a MasterCard or Visa, you can have money sent for any amount up to your credit limit. If not, have someone take cash or a certified cashier's check to a Western Union office; the funds will be delivered in one to three business days to a tele-communications office in Mexico. Fees vary with the amount of money being sent: For $1,000, the standard fee is $57 if you use a credit card, $45 if you pay in cash.

Cash Machines Virtually all U.S. banks belong to a network of ATMs (Auto-matic Teller Machines, called *cajas permanentes* in Mexico), which dispense cash 24 hours a day in cities throughout the country. There are some eight major networks in the United States, the largest of which are **Cirrus** (tel. 800/4–CIRRUS), owned by MasterCard, and **Plus** (tel. 800/THE-PLUS), affili-ated with Visa. Some banks belong to more than one network. To receive a card for one of these systems you must apply for it. Cards issued by Visa and MasterCard can also be used in the ATMs, but the fees are usually higher than the fees on bank cards. There is also a daily interest charge on credit-card "loans," even if monthly bills are paid on time. Each network has a toll-free number you can call to locate machines in a given city, but these numbers work only for the United States and Canada. Check with your bank for information on fees, on the amount of cash you can withdraw on any given day, and on loca-tions in Yucatán. At press time (January 1991), The Plus had two ATMs in Mérida, at **Bancomer** (Calle 56, No. 4, at Paseo de Montejo, and Calle 65, No. 506), but none in Cancún or Cozumel. Cirrus operates five ATMs in the region, through the following Banamex offices: in Cancún, at Avenida Tulum 19; in Mérida, at Calle 56-A between Calles 27 and 29; Calle 59, no. 485; Calle 60, no. 277; and Calle 63, no. 506.

Currency

The unit of currency in Mexico is the peso, subdivided into 100 centavos. Mexicans use the dollar sign, often accompanied by the initials M.N. (for *moneda nacional*, or national currency), although banks and international financiers favor the prefix "P$." Because of inflation, centavos are rarely used; bills are issued in denominations of 10,000, 20,000, 50,000, and 100,000 pesos. Coins come in 1,000-, 2,000-, and 5,000-peso denomina-tions, although some coins in lesser denominations are still cir-culating. The peso is devalued daily to keep pace with inflation. At press time (January 1991), the official exchange rate was 2,936 pesos to the U.S. dollar, 3,367 pesos to the Canadian dol-lar, and 5,603 pesos to the pound sterling.

Dollars are widely accepted in many parts of Mexico, particu-larly near the border and in Cozumel. Many tourist shops and market vendors, as well as virtually all hotel service personnel, take them, too.

What It Will Cost

Mexico has a reputation for being inexpensive, particularly compared with other North American vacation spots such as the Caribbean. Cancún, however, is probably the most expensive destination in Mexico, with Cozumel running a close second. In Mérida and the other cities in Yucatán, which are considerably less expensive, you will find the best value for your money. For obvious reasons, if you stay at international chain hotels and eat at restaurants geared to tourists (especially hotel restaurants), you may not find Yucatán such a bargain.

Rates in Yucatán decrease in the off-season by as much as 30%. Speaking Spanish is helpful in bargaining and when asking for dining recommendations. As a general rule, the less that English is spoken in a region, the cheaper things will be (*see also* Language, below).

Sample costs are as follows: cup of coffee, P$2,000; bottle of beer, P$4,000; plate of tacos, P$5,000; 2-km taxi ride, P$5,000.

Off-season, Cancún hotels cost one-third to one-half what they cost during the peak season. Cozumel is less costly than Cancún, and Isla Mujeres is slightly less costly than Cozumel. In Mérida and the rest of Yucatán state, as well as in Campeche and Chetumal, a couple might manage to spend $200 a day, as opposed to $450 in Cancún.

Taxes Mexico has a value-added tax, or I.V.A. (*impuesto de valor agregado*) of 15%, which is occasionally (and illegally) waived for cash purchases. Other taxes and charges apply for phone calls, dining, and lodging. An air departure tax of US$12 or the peso equivalent must be paid at the airport for international flights from Mexico, and there is a domestic air departure tax of US$4.86. Traveler's checks and credit cards are not accepted as payment for these taxes.

Passports and Visas

Americans U.S. citizens can enter Mexico with a tourist card and proof of citizenship. The only acceptable proof of citizenship is either a valid passport or an original birth certificate plus a photo ID. Tourist cards are available from any Mexican consulate or tourism office and from most airlines serving Mexico. They are valid for a single entry for up to three months. For more information, contact the **Embassy of Mexico** (1019 19th St., NW, Suite 810, Washington, DC 20036, tel. 202/293–1710). To obtain a new passport, apply in person; renewals can be obtained in person or by mail. First-time applicants should apply to one of the 13 U.S. Passport Agency offices at least five weeks in advance of their departure date. In addition, local county courthouses, many state and probate courts, and some post offices accept passport applications. Necessary documents include (1) a completed passport application (Form DSP-11); (2) proof of citizenship (a birth certificate with a raised seal or naturalization papers); (3) proof of identity (a current driver's license, employee ID card, military ID, student ID, or any other document with your photograph and signature); (4) two recent, identical, two-inch-square photographs (black and white or color); and (5) a $42 application fee for a 10-year passport (those under 18 pay $27 for a five-year passport). Passports are mailed to you in about 10–15 working days. If you are paying in cash, you must have exact change; no change is given.

To renew your passport by mail, send a completed Form DSP-82; two recent, identical passport photographs; your current passport (less than 12 years old); and a check or money order for

$35 to your U.S. Passport Agency. If your passport is lost or stolen abroad, report it immediately to the nearest U.S. embassy or consulate and to the local police. If you can provide the consular officer with the information contained in the passport, they will usually be able to issue you a new passport. For this reason, it is a good idea to keep a copy of the data page of your passport in a separate place, or to leave the passport number, date, and place of issuance with a relative or friend in the United States.

Canadians Canadian citizens also need a tourist card and proof of citizenship to enter Mexico. The only acceptable proof is a valid passport or an original birth certificate plus a photo ID. (Tourist cards are available from travel agents, airlines, or local Mexican consulates.) To acquire a passport, send a completed application (available at any post office or passport office) to the Bureau of Passports (Suite 215, West Tower, Guy Favreau Complex, 200 René Lévesque Blvd. W, Montreal, Quebec H2Z 1X4). Include $25, two photographs, the name of a guarantor, and proof of Canadian citizenship. Applications can be made in person at regional passport offices in many locations, including Edmonton, Halifax, Montreal, Toronto, Vancouver, and Winnipeg. Passports are valid for five years and are nonrenewable.

Britons British citizens need a valid 10-year passport to enter Mexico (£15 for a standard 32-page passport, £30 for a 94-page passport). A British Visitors Passport is not acceptable. Application forms are available from most travel agents and major post offices and from the Passport Office (Clive House, 70 Petty France, London SW1 H 9HD, tel. 071/279–3434 for recorded information or 071/279–4000). You do not need a visa; however, a tourist card, available from your travel agent, airline, or the Mexican Embassy (8 Halkin St., London SW1, tel. 071/235–6393), is required.

Customs and Duties

Americans on Arrival Entering Mexico, you may bring in (1) 200 cigarettes or 50 cigars or 250 grams of tobacco, (2) up to 3 liters of wine and spirits, (3) one photographic camera and one 18mm film or video camera and 12 rolls of film for each, and (4) gift items not exceeding a combined value of $300. You are not allowed to bring meat, vegetables, plants, fruit, or flowers into the country.

On Departure If you are bringing any foreign-made equipment, such as cameras, with you from home, it's wise to carry the original receipt or register it with Customs before your trip (U.S. Customs Form 4457). Otherwise, you may end up paying duty on your return.

U.S. Customs You may bring home up to $400 worth of foreign goods duty-free as long as you have been out of the country for at least 48 hours and you haven't claimed that exemption in the past 30 days. Each member of the family is entitled to the same exemption, regardless of age, and exemptions may be pooled. A flat 10% rate is assessed for the next $1,000 worth of goods; above $1,400, duties vary with the merchandise. Included in the allowances for travelers 21 or older are 1 liter of alcohol, 100 cigars (non-Cuban), and 200 cigarettes. Only one bottle of perfume trademarked in the United States may be imported. There is no duty on antiques or works of art over 100 years old. Anything exceeding these limits will be taxed at the port of entry and may be taxed additionally in the traveler's home state. Gifts valued at under $50 may be mailed duty-free to friends or relatives at home, but you may not send more than one package per day to a single addressee and packages may not include perfumes costing more than $5, tobacco, or liquor.

Because Mexico is considered a developing country, many arts and handicrafts may be brought back into the United States duty-free as part of the U.S. Generalized System of Preferences (GSP). These allowances are in addition to the $400 limit, but you will still need to declare the items and state their value and purpose. For a list of exempt items, write the U.S. Customs Service (Room 201, 6 World Trade Center, New York, NY 10048) for a copy of *GSP and the Traveler*. The leaflet is also available at the customs desks of many airports.

Canadians Exemptions for returning Canadians range from $20 to $300, depending on the length of stay outside the country. For the $300 exemption, you must have been out of the country for one week. In any given year you are allowed only one $300 exemption. You may bring in up to 50 cigars, 200 cigarettes, 2.2 pounds of tobacco, and 40 ounces of liquor duty-free, provided they are declared in writing to customs on arrival. Personal gifts labeled "Unsolicited Gift–Value under $40" may be mailed home. Obtain a copy of the Canadian Customs brochure "I Declare" for further details.

Britons Returning to the United Kingdom, a traveler 17 or over can take home (1) 200 cigarettes or 100 cigarillos or 50 cigars or 250 grams of tobacco; (2) 1 liter of alcohol over 22% volume, 2 liters of alcohol under 22% volume, or 2 liters of fortified or sparkling wine; (3) 2 liters of still table wine; (4) 60 milliliters of perfume and 250 milliliters of toilet water; and (5) other goods to a value of £32 but no more than 50 liters of beer or 25 mechanical lighters.

Traveling with Film

If your camera is new, shoot and develop a few rolls before you leave home. Pack some lens tissue and an extra battery for your built-in light meter. Invest about $10 in a skylight filter; it will protect the lens and reduce haze.

Film doesn't like hot weather, so if you're driving in summer, don't store film in the glove compartment or on the shelf under the rear window. Put it on the floor behind the front seat, on the side opposite the exhaust pipe.

On a plane trip, never pack unprocessed film in checked luggage; if your bags get x-rayed, you can say goodbye to your pictures. Always carry undeveloped film through security with you and ask to have it inspected by hand. (It helps to keep your film in a plastic bag, ready for quick inspection.) Inspectors at U.S. airports are required by law to honor requests for hand inspection.

The newer airport scanning machines used in all U.S. airports are safe for anything from five to 500 scans, depending on the speed of your film. The effects are cumulative; you can put the same roll of film through several scans without worry. After five scans, though, you're asking for trouble.

If your film gets fogged and you want an explanation, send it to the National Association of Photographic Manufacturers (550 Mamaroneck Ave., Harrison, NY 10528). They will try to determine what went wrong. The service is free.

Language

Spanish is the official language of Mexico, although Indian languages are spoken by approximately 20% of the population, many of whom speak no Spanish at all. This is the case in Mérida and much of the State of Yucatán, where Mayan dialects are spoken. In the beach resorts of Cancún and Cozumel, English is understood by most people employed in tourism; at the very least, shopkeepers will know the numbers for bargaining purposes. Mexicans welcome even the most halting attempts to use their language, and if you are in Mérida, you may even be introduced to a few Mayan words and phrases. For a rudimentary vocabulary of terms that travelers are likely to encounter in Yucatán, *see* the Spanish Vocabulary and Menu at the end of this book.

The Spanish most North Americans learn in high school is based on Castilian Spanish, which is different from Latin American Spanish. In terms of grammar, Mexican Spanish ignores the *vosotros* form of the second person. As for pronunciation, the lisped Castilian "c" or "z" is dismissed in Mexico as a sign of affectation. The most obvious differences are in vocabulary: Mexican Spanish has thousands of Indian words, and the use of *¿mande?* instead of *¿cómo?* (excuse me?) is a dead giveaway that one's Spanish was acquired in Mexico. Words or phrases that are harmless or commonplace in one Spanish-speaking country can take on salacious or otherwise offensive meanings in another. Unless you are lucky enough to be briefed on these nuances by a native coach, the only way to learn is by trial and error.

Staying Healthy

The major health risk in Yucatán, as elsewhere in Mexico, is posed by the contamination of drinking water and fresh fruit and vegetables by fecal matter, which causes the intestinal ailment known facetiously as Montezuma's Revenge, more mundanely as traveler's diarrhea. It usually lasts only a day or two. A good antidiarrheal agent is paregoric, which dulls or eliminates abdominal cramps, but you will need a doctor's prescription to get it in Mexico. Three drugs recommended by the National Institutes of Health for mild cases of diarrhea can, however, be purchased over the counter: Pepto-Bismol, diphenoxylate hydrochloride (Lomotil), and loperamide (Imodium). If you come down with the malady, rest as much as possible; drink lots of fluids (such as tea without milk—camomile is quite common in Mexico, and a good folk remedy for diarrhea); in severe cases, rehydrate yourself with a salt-sugar mixture added to purified water. The best defense against food- and water-borne diseases is a careful diet. Stay away from unbottled or unboiled water, ice, raw food, and unpasteurized milk and milk products.

According to the Centers for Disease Control (CDC), there is a limited risk of malaria, hepatitis B, dengue fever, and rabies in certain rural areas of Mexico. Travelers to the beach resorts need have no worries. However, if you plan to visit remote regions, to do serious spelunking, or to stay for more than six weeks, check with the CDC's **International Travelers Information hotline** (tel. 404/332–4559). The hotline recommends chloroquine (Analen) as an antimalarial agent. Malaria-bearing mosquitoes bite at night, so travelers to susceptible regions should take mosquito nets, wear clothing that covers the body, and carry repellent containing Deet and a spray against flying insects for living and sleeping areas. There is currently no vaccine against dengue fever, so travelers should use aerosol insecticides indoors as well as repellents against the mosquito, which bites in daytime.

If you have a health problem that may require you to purchase a prescription drug, have your doctor write a prescription using the drug's generic name, because brand names vary from country to country. The **International Association for Medical Assistance to Travelers** (IAMAT) is a worldwide organization that offers a list of approved physicians and clinics whose training or facilities meet British and American standards. For a list of Mexican physicians and clinics that are part of this network, contact IAMAT (417 Center St., Lewiston, NY 14092, tel. 716/754–4883; in Canada, 40 Regal Rd., Guelph, Ontario N1K 1B5, tel. 519/836–0102, or 1287 St. Clair Ave. W, Toronto M6E 1B8, tel. 416/652–0137; in Europe, 57 Voirets, 1212 Grand-Lancy, Geneva, Switzerland, no phone). Membership is free.

Insurance

Travelers may seek insurance coverage in three areas: health and accident, lost luggage, and trip cancellation. Your first step is to review your existing health and homeowner policies; some health insurance plans cover health expenses incurred while traveling, some major medical plans cover emergency transportation, and some homeowner policies cover the theft of luggage.

Health and Accident Several companies offer coverage designed to supplement existing health insurance for travelers. If you plan to do any scuba diving, inquire as to whether scuba-related injuries are covered.

Carefree Travel Insurance (Box 310, 120 Mineola Blvd., Mineola, NY 11501, tel. 516/294–0220 or 800/323–3149) provides coverage for emergency medical evacuation and accidental death or dismemberment. It also offers 24-hour medical advice by phone.

International SOS Assistance (Box 11568, Philadelphia, PA 19116, tel. 215/244–1500 or 800/523–8930), a medical assistance company, provides emergency evacuation services, worldwide medical referrals, and optional medical insurance.

Travel Assistance International (1133 15th St. NW, Suite 400, Washington, DC 20005, tel. 202/331–1609 or 800/821–2828) provides emergency evacuation services and 24-hour medical referrals.

Travel Guard International, underwritten by Transamerica Occidental Life Companies (1145 Clark St., Stevens Point, WI 54481, tel. 715/345–0505 or 800/782–5151), offers reimbursement for medical expenses (with no deductibles or daily limits) and emergency evacuation services.

Wallach and Company, Inc. (243 Church St. NW, Suite 100D, Vienna, VA 22180, tel. 703/281–9500 or 800/237–6615) offers comprehensive medical coverage, including emergency evacuation services worldwide.

WorldCare Travel Assistance Association (1150 S. Olive St., Suite T-233, Los Angeles, CA 90015, tel. 213/749–0909 or 800/666–4993) provides unlimited emergency evacuation, 24-hour medical referral, and an emergency message center.

Lost Luggage On international flights, airlines are responsible for lost or damaged property of up to $9.07 per pound (or $20 per kilo) for checked baggage and up to $400 per passenger for unchecked baggage. If you're carrying valuables, either take them with you on the plane or purchase additional insurance for lost luggage. Some airlines will issue extra luggage insurance when you check in, but many do not. Before you go, itemize the contents of each bag in case you need to file an insurance claim. Be certain to put your home or business address on each piece of luggage, including carry-on bags. If your luggage is lost or stolen and later recovered, the airline will deliver the luggage to your home free of charge.

Insurance for lost, damaged, or stolen luggage is available through travel agents or directly through various insurance companies. Luggage-loss coverage is usually part of a comprehensive travel-insurance package that includes personal accident, trip cancellation, and sometimes default and bankruptcy. Two companies that issue luggage insurance are **Tele-Trip** (Box 31685, 3201 N. Farnam St., Omaha, NE 68131, tel. 800/228–9792), a subsidiary of Mutual of Omaha, and **The Travelers Corporation** (Ticket and Travel Dept., 1 Tower Sq., Hartford, CT 06183, tel. 203/277–0111 or 800/243–3174). Tele-Trip operates sales booths at airports and issues insurance through travel agents. Rates vary according to the length of the trip. The Travelers Corporation will insure checked or hand luggage at $500–$2,000 valuation per person for a maximum of 180 days. Rates for 1–5 days at $500 valuation are $10; for 180 days, $85. Other companies with comprehensive policies include **Access America Inc.** (Box 11188, Richmond, VA 23230, tel. 800/334–7525 or 800/284–8300), a subsidiary of Blue Cross–Blue Shield; **Near Services** (450 Prairie Ave., Suite 101, Calumet City, IL 60409, tel. 708/868–6700 or 800/654–6700); **Travel Guard International;** and **Carefree Travel Insurance** (*see* Health and Accident Insurance, above).

Trip Cancellation Flight insurance is often included in the price of a ticket when paid for with American Express, Visa, and other major credit cards. It is usually included in the combination travel-insurance packages available from most tour operators, travel agents, and insurance agents.

Car Rentals

To rent a car in Mexico, you'll need a valid driver's license from your country of residence. You must leave a deposit, usually a blank, signed credit card voucher. Without a credit card, you may not be able to rent a car.

When you drive in Cancún or anywhere in the Yucatán area, it is necessary to carry proof of Mexican auto insurance, which can be purchased through car rental agencies, with you. If you don't carry proof of insurance and happen to injure someone— whether it's your fault or not—you stand the risk of being jailed. Purchase enough Mexican automobile insurance to cover the length of your trip; insurance is sold by the day or by the week. Car insurance purchased outside Mexico is not valid here.

Daily car-rental rates vary from about $20 to $120. Not included in the daily rate are a per-kilometer charge, insurance, gasoline, and a 15% tax. Weekly package rates including unlimited free mileage cost about $150–$700. Think twice before you rent a car in one location to drop off in another: Drop-off charges can be hefty, at about 33¢ per kilometer between the rental city and the drop-off city. The following international car rental firms have offices in Yucatán: **Avis** (tel. 800/331–1212), **Budget** (tel. 800/527–0700), **Hertz** (tel. 800/654–3131), and **National** (tel. 800/227–7368).

Student and Youth Travel

An **International Youth Hostel Federation** (IYHF) membership card is the key to inexpensive dormitory-style accommodations at more than 5,000 hostel locations in 68 countries around the world. Hostels provide separate sleeping quarters for men and women at rates ranging from $7 to $20 a night per person, and many have family accommodations. Youth Hostel memberships, which are valid for 12 months from the time of purchase, are available in the United States through **American Youth Hostels** (AYH, Box 37613, Washington, DC 20013, tel. 202/783–6161), in Canada through the **Canadian Hostelling Association** (CHA, 1600 James Naismith Dr., Suite 608, Gloucester, Ontario K1B 5N4, tel. 613/748–5638), and in the United Kingdom through the **Youth Hostel Association of England and Wales** (Trevelyan House, 8 St. Stephen's Hill, St. Albans, Hertsfordshire AL1 2DY, tel. 0727/55215). By joining one of the national (American, Canadian, or British) youth hostel associations, you automatically become part of the International Youth Hostel Federation and are entitled to special reductions on rail and bus travel around the world. Handbooks listing these benefits are available from the associations. The cost of a first-year membership is $25 for adults 18–54. Renewals thereafter are $15. For youths (17 and under) the rate is $10, and for senior citizens (55 and older), $15. Family membership is available for $35.

Council Travel, a subsidiary of the **Council on International Educational Exchange** (CIEE), is the foremost U.S. student travel agency, specializing in low-cost charters and serving as the exclusive U.S. agent for many airfare bargains and tours for students. CIEE's 80-page *Student Travel Catalog* and "Council Charter" brochures are available free from any Council Travel office in the United States (enclose $1 postage if ordering by mail). In addition to CIEE headquarters (205 E. 42nd St., New York, NY 10017, tel. 212/661–1450) and a branch office at 356 W. 34th Street, New York, there are Council Travel offices in California (Berkeley, La Jolla, Long Beach, Los Angeles, San Diego, San Francisco, and Sherman Oaks); Colorado (Boulder); Connecticut (New Haven); Washington, DC; Georgia (Atlanta); Illinois (Chicago and Evanston); Louisiana (New Orleans); Massachusetts (Amherst, Boston, and Cambridge); Minnesota (Minneapolis); North Carolina (Durham); Oregon (Portland);

Rhode Island (Providence); Texas (Austin and Dallas); Washington (Seattle); and Wisconsin (Milwaukee).

The **Educational Travel Center** (438 N. Frances St., Madison, WI 53703, tel. 608/256–5551) is another student-travel specialist worth contacting for information on student tours, bargain fares, and bookings.

Students who would like to work abroad should contact CIEE's **Work Abroad Department** (206 E. 42nd St., New York, NY 10017, tel. 212/661–1414, ext. 1130). The council arranges paid and voluntary work experiences overseas for up to six months. CIEE also sponsors study programs in Europe, Latin America, Asia, and Australia and produces several books of interest to the student traveler. These books include *Work, Study, Travel Abroad: The Whole World Handbook* ($10.95 plus $1 book-rate postage or $2.50 first-class postage); *Volunteer! The Comprehensive Guide to Voluntary Service in the U.S. and Abroad* ($6.95 plus $1 book-rate postage or $2.50 first-class postage); and *The Teenager's Guide to Travel, Study, and Adventure Abroad* ($9.95 plus $1 book-rate postage or $2.50 first-class postage.)

The Information Center at the **Institute of International Education** (IIE, 809 UN Plaza, New York, NY 10017, tel. 212/984–5413) has reference books, foreign-university catalogs, study-abroad brochures, and other materials that may be consulted for free. The Information Center is open weekdays 10–4 and is closed on holidays.

Traveling with Children

Getting There The advisability of traveling with children in Yucatán, as in many foreign destinations, will depend to a great extent on the age and maturity of the child. Infants may be bothered by the heat, and finding pure water or fresh milk may be a problem. Since children are especially prone to diarrhea, special care must be taken with regard to food. If they enjoy travel in general, children will probably do well in Yucatán, where they can clamber over ruins and frolic on beaches.

All children, including infants, must have a valid passport for foreign travel. Family passports are no longer issued. On international flights, children under age 2 who do not occupy a seat pay 10% of the adult fare. Various discounts apply to children from ages 2 to 12, so check with your airline when making reservations. Regulations about infant travel on airplanes are in the process of changing. Until they do, however, if you want to be sure your infant is secure, you must bring your own infant car seat and buy a separate ticket. Check with the airline in advance to be sure your seat meets the required standard. If possible, reserve a seat behind one of the plane's bulkheads, where there's usually more legroom and enough space to fit a bassinet (which should be available from the airlines). The booklet *Child/Infant Safety Seats Acceptable for Use in Aircraft* is available from the Federal Aviation Administration (APA-200, 800 Independence Ave., SW, Washington, DC 20591, tel. 202/267–3479). If you opt to hold your baby on your lap, do so with the infant outside the seat belt rather than inside it so that he or she doesn't get crushed in case of a sudden stop. When reserving tickets, also ask about special children's meals or snacks. The February 1990 issue of *Family Travel Times* (next published in 1992) includes "TWYCH's Airline Guide," which contains a rundown of the children's services offered by 46 different airlines. (*See* Publications, below, for ordering information.)

Hotels Several hotel chains provide services that make it easier to travel with children. The **Westin Camino Real Hotel** (tel. 800/228–3000) in Cancún offers free summer activities for children and a comprehensive recreational and sports program for teenagers. At the **Intercontinental Cancún** (tel. 800/327–0200), one child under age 14 can stay free in his or her parents' room. Family suites, consisting of one room with a king-size bed, one room with twin beds, and a parlor (which contains a sofa bed), are also available and end up costing significantly less than do individual rooms. The **Cancún Sheraton Hotel** (tel. 800/334–8484) provides connecting "family rooms" at regular rates. **Club Med** (tel. 800/CLUB–MED) offers special programs for children and teenagers, including visits to Cancún's attractions.

Baby-sitting English-speaking baby-sitters are available through a number **Services** of Cancún's large hotels and resorts. Ask the concierge at your hotel or the local tourist office for further information.

Publications *Family Travel Times* is a newsletter published 10 times a year by **TWYCH** (Travel With Your Children, 80 8th Ave., New York, NY 10011, tel. 212/206–0688). A one-year subscription costs $35 and includes access to back issues. The organization also offers a free phone-in service with advice and information on specific destinations.

Great Vacations with Your Kids, by Dorothy Jordan and Marjorie Cohen, presents complete advice on planning your trip with children, from toddlers to teens. If unavailable from your local bookseller, it can be ordered directly from E. P. Dutton (tel. 800/331–4624).

Kids and Teens in Flight, a useful brochure about children flying alone, is available from the U.S. Department of Transportation. To order a free copy, call 202/366–2220.

Hints for Disabled Travelers

Disabled people, if they enjoy beaches and ruins from the vantage of a spectator, will appreciate the beauty of Yucatán as much as anyone. However, getting around can be difficult because few hotels, restaurants, or other attractions have special facilities or means of access.

The **Information Center for Individuals with Disabilities** (Fort Point Pl., 1st Floor, 27-43 Wormwood St., Boston, MA 02210, tel. 617/727–5540; TDD 617/727–5236) offers useful problem-solving assistance, including lists of travel agents who specialize in tours for the disabled.

Moss Rehabilitation Hospital Travel Information Service (1200 W. Tabor Rd., Philadelphia, PA 19141-3009, tel. 215/456–9600; TDD 215/456–9603) charges a small fee for information on tourist sights, transportation, and accommodations in destinations around the world.

Travel Industry and Disabled Exchange (TIDE, 5435 Donna Ave., Tarzana, CA 91356, tel. 818/368–5648) publishes a quarterly newsletter and a directory of travel agencies and tours that cater specifically to the disabled. The annual membership fee is $15.

Mobility International USA (Box 3551, Eugene, OR 97403, tel. and TDD 503/343–1284) is an internationally affiliated organization. For a $20 annual fee, it coordinates exchange programs for disabled people around the world and offers information on accommodations and organized study programs.

Hotels Many chain hotels are wheelchair-accessible, including the **Radisson Paraiso Cancún** (tel. 800/333–3333), the **Hyatt Cancún Caribe** (tel. 800/228–9000), and the **Hyatt Regency** (tel. 800/228–9000).

Publications *The Itinerary* (Box 2012, Bayonne, NJ 07002, tel. 201/858–3400) is a bimonthly travel magazine for the disabled. Call for a subscription ($10 for one year, $18 for two); it's not available in bookstores.

Access to the World: A Travel Guide for the Handicapped, by Louise Weiss, offers tips on travel and accessibility around the world. If it's not available at your local bookseller, you may order it directly from Henry Holt & Co. for $12.95 plus $2.50 shipping (tel. 800/247–3912; the order number is 0805 001417).

Twin Peaks Press (Box 129, Vancouver, WA 98666, tel. 206/694–2462 or 800/637–2256 for orders only) specializes in books for the disabled. *Travel for the Disabled* presents helpful hints as well as a comprehensive list of guidebooks and facilities geared to the disabled. *The Directory of Travel Agencies for the Disabled* lists more than 350 agencies throughout the world. Twin Peaks also publishes *Traveling Nurse's Network*, which provides registered nurses to accompany and assist disabled travelers.

Hints for Older Travelers

Active older travelers who enjoy outdoor attractions, especially water-related activities, will enjoy Yucatán. Being in good physical shape is a definite advantage. If proximity to medical services is a major concern, travelers of all ages should keep to the major resorts and cities.

The **American Association of Retired Persons** (AARP, 1909 K St. NW, Washington, DC 20049, tel. 202/662–4850 or 800/523–5800) has two programs for independent travelers: (1) the **Purchase Privilege Program,** which offers discounts on hotels, airfare, car and RV rentals, and sightseeing, and (2) the **AARP Motoring Plan,** provided by Amoco (tel. 800/334–3300), which furnishes emergency road-service aid and trip-routing information for an annual fee of $33.95 per person or couple.

AARP also arranges group tours through Mexico, one of which is an eight-day "Mayan Antiquities" land package, through **AARP Travel Experience** (Box 5850, Norcross, GA 30091, tel. 800/927–0111) from American Express. AARP members must be 50 years or older; annual dues are $5 per person or couple.

If AARP or other senior-citizen identification cards are honored by hotels for reduced rates, you must mention that you're a cardholder at the time you make your reservation, not when you check out. At participating restaurants, show your card to the maître d' before you're seated, because discounts may be limited to certain menus, days, or hours. When you rent a car, be sure to ask about special promotional rates that may offer greater savings than the AARP rate.

Elderhostel (75 Federal St., 3rd Floor, Boston, MA 02110, tel. 617/426–7788) is an innovative educational program for people aged 60 and older. Participants live in dorms on some 1,200 campuses around the world. Mornings are devoted to lectures and seminars; afternoons, to sightseeing and field trips. Fees for two- to three-week trips—including room, board, tuition, and round-trip transportation—range from $1,800 to $4,500.

Mature Outlook (6001 N. Clark St., Chicago, IL 60660, tel. 800/ 336–6330), a subsidiary of Sears Roebuck & Co., is a travel club for people over age 50 that provides hotel and motel discounts and publishes a bimonthly newsletter. Annual membership is $9.95; there are currently 800,000 members. Instant membership is available at Sears stores and participating Holiday Inns.

National Council of Senior Citizens (925 15th St., NW, Washington, DC 20005, tel. 202/347–8800) is a nonprofit advocacy group with some 5,000 local clubs across the United States. Annual membership is $12 per person or couple. Members receive a monthly newspaper with travel information and an ID card for reduced-rate hotels and car rentals.

Saga International Holidays (120 Boylston St., Boston, MA 02116, tel. 800/343–0273) specializes in group travel for people over age 60. A selection of variously priced tours allows you to choose the package that meets your needs.

Publications *The International Health Guide for Senior Citizen Travelers*, by W. Robert Lange, MD, is available for $4.95 plus $1 for shipping from Pilot Books (103 Cooper St., Babylon, NY 11702, tel. 516/422–2225), if unavailable at your local bookstore.

The Discount Guide for Travelers Over 55, by Caroline and Walter Weintz, lists helpful addresses, package tours, reduced-rate car rentals, and so forth in the United States and abroad. If it's not available at your local bookstore, send $7.95 plus $1.50 shipping and handling to NAL/Cash Sales (Bergenfield Order Dept., 120 Woodbine St., Bergenfield, NJ 07621, tel. 800/526–0275).

Further Reading

Most English-language books about Yucatán focus on the ancient Maya and the archaeological sites. Popularized scholarly descriptions of Mayan history, architecture, religion, astronomy, and culture include *The Maya*, by Michael D. Coe; *Maya*, by Charles Gallenkamp; *The Ancient Maya*, by Sylvanus G. Morley; *The Rise and Fall of Maya Civilization*, by J. Eric S. Thompson; and *World of the Maya*, by Victor Von Hagen. *The Maya World*, by Demetrio Sodi Morales, weaves information on the modern-day Mayan region into a discussion of architecture and history, but the book is sold only in Mexico. For a more contemporary overview of the ground-breaking work that has revolutionized our understanding of the Maya, see the handsome coffee-table book entitled *The Blood of Kings: Dynasty & Ritual in Maya Art*, by Linda Schele and Mary Ellen Miller. Also by Linda Schele, with David Freidel, is the newer *A Forest of Kings: The Untold Story of the Ancient Maya*. For a scholarly overview of the region's history, people, politics, and literature, try *Yucatán: A World Apart*, edited by E. H. Moseley and E. D. Terry.

Some older but still enlightening books include *Incidents of Travel in Central America, Chiapas, and Yucatán* (1841), which contains the vivid impressions of John Lloyd Stephens, one of the first white men to explore and chart the Mayan ruins; *The Caste War of Yucatán*, by Nelson Reed, an unusually detailed account of the massacre that enveloped the peninsula in the 1840s; and Robert Redfield's *The Folk Culture of Yucatán*, an anthropological classic. Frans Blom, archaeologist and explorer extraordinaire, wrote a colorful account of *The Conquest of Yucatán* in 1936. A translation of one of the earliest Spanish chronicles is to be found in *The Discovery of Yucatán*, by Francisco Hernández de Córdoba. Many of these older books are now out of print and available only in libraries.

One of the few recent pieces of fiction to focus on Yucatán is *Gringos*, by Charles Portis, which uses the peninsula as a backdrop for the antics of a motley group of North Americans. Mary Morris has written *Nothing to Declare*, her memoirs of a Mexican sojourn that encompassed parts of Yucatán and Central America. *Time Among the Maya: Travels in Belize, Guatemala, and Mexico*, by Ronald Wright, is another recent travelogue/ethnographic book. But it is Kate Simon's exquisitely written *Mexico: Places and Pleasures* (1962), with its timeless descriptions of Isla del Carmen, Campeche, Cozumel, and Mérida, that reigns supreme on the Mexico travel-writing shelf.

Arriving and Departing

From the United States by Plane

There are three types of flights: nonstop, with no changes or stops; direct, with no changes but one or more stops; and connecting, with two or more planes and one or more stops.

Airports and Airlines Airports in Cancún, Cozumel, and Mérida receive nonstop flights from the United States and Canada. Campeche, Chetumal, and Playa del Carmen have smaller airports served primarily by domestic carriers. Some of the ruins have airstrips that can handle small planes.

The number of airlines serving Mexico from the United States changes frequently with revisions of bilateral agreements. At press time, scheduled airlines with nonstop and/or direct service to Cancún, Cozumel, and Mérida included **Aeromexico** (tel. 800/237–6639), from Houston, Miami, and New York to Cancún, and from Cancún, Mexico City, Miami, and Villahermosa to Mérida; **American** (tel. 800/433–7300), from Dallas and Raleigh/Durham to Cancún and Cozumel; **Continental** (tel. 800/231–0856), from Houston to Cancún and Cozumel; **Mexicana** (tel. 800/531–7921), from Chicago, Dallas, Los Angeles, Miami, New York, and San Francisco to Cancún, and from Dallas and Miami to Cozumel; **Northwest** (tel. 800/447–4747), from Tampa to Cancún; **Pan Am** (tel. 800/221–1111), from Miami to Cancún; and **United** (tel. 800/538–2929), from Chicago and Washington, DC, to Cancún.

In addition, since 1986 more charter carriers, along with several smaller domestic Mexican airlines, have been providing service. Among them are **Aerocancún** (tel. 212/679–0360) and **LaTur** (tel. 212/599–2203, 800/24–LATUR from the northeastern United States, or 800/32–LATUR from elsewhere), serving Cancún by charter from 14 U.S. cities. **LACSA** (tel. 800/225–2272), the national airline of Costa Rica, now has nonstop charter service from New York to Cancún and continuing service to Guatemala, Honduras, and Costa Rica. **American** and **Transair** also charter from New York to Cancún. **Aviateca** (tel. 800/327–9832), a Guatemalan carrier, runs service from Houston to Mérida.

Flying Time   Flight times to Cancún are: from Los Angeles, 5 hours; from New York, 4 hours; from Chicago, 3½ hours; from Dallas, 2½ hours; from Houston, 2 hours; from Miami, 2 hours. Flights to Cozumel and Mérida are comparable in length.

Enjoying the Flight   If you're lucky enough to be able to sleep on a plane, it makes sense to fly at night. Unless you're flying from Europe, jet lag won't be a problem, since the time difference between most points in the United States and Yucatán is relatively small. Because the air on a plane is dry, it helps, while flying, to drink a lot of nonalcoholic beverages; drinking alcohol contributes to jet lag, as does eating heavy meals on board. Feet swell at high altitudes, so it's a good idea to remove your shoes at the beginning of your flight. Sleepers usually prefer window seats to curl up against; those who like to move about the cabin should ask for aisle seats. Bulkhead seats (located in the front row of each cabin) have more legroom, but seat trays are attached rather awkwardly to the arms of the seats rather than to the back of the seats ahead. Generally, these seats are reserved for the disabled, the elderly, or parents traveling with babies.

Discount Flights   The major airlines offer a range of tickets that can vary the price of any given seat by more than 300% depending on the date of purchase. As a rule, the further in advance you buy the ticket, the less expensive it is and the greater the penalty (up to 100%) for canceling. Check with the airlines for details.

The best buy is not necessarily an APEX (advance-purchase) ticket on one of the major airlines, because these tickets carry certain travel restrictions. If you can work around their drawbacks, however, APEX are among the best-value fares available.

Another good deal for travelers who are willing to put up with some restrictions and inconveniences is the substantially reduced airfares that are offered in exchange for air-courier services. A person who agrees to be a courier must accompany shipments between designated points. There are two sources of information on courier deals. For a telephone directory that lists courier companies by the cities to which they fly, send $5 and a self-addressed, stamped, business-size envelope to Pacific Data Sales Publishing (2554 Lincoln Blvd., Suite 275-I, Marina Del Rey, CA 90291). Alternatively, *A Simple Guide to Courier Travel* costs $14.95 (including postage and handling) and can be ordered from Box 2394, Lake Oswego, OR 97035; for more information call 800/344–9375.

Charter flights offer the lowest fares, but they often depart only on certain days and seldom on time. Though you may be able to arrive at one city and return from another, you may lose all or most of your money if you cancel your trip. Don't sign up for a charter flight unless you've checked with a travel agency about the reputation of the packager. It's particularly important to know the packager's policy concerning refunds should a flight be canceled; some travel agents recommend that travelers purchase trip-cancellation insurance if they plan to book charter flights. In addition to the Mexican charter airlines listed above, reputable charter operators include **Club de Vacaciones** (Huntington, NY, tel. 516/424–9600), **Odyssey Adventures** (Woodmere, NY, tel. 516/569–2812), and **Spanish Heritage** (Queens, NY, tel. 718/520–1300).

Another option is to join a travel club that offers special discounts to its members. Four such organizations are **Discount Travel International** (114 Forrest Ave., Narberth, PA 19072, tel. 215/668–7184), **Moment's Notice** (425 Madison Ave., New York, NY 10017, tel. 212/750–9111), **Travelers Advantage** (CUC Travel Service, 49 Music Sq. W, Nashville, TN 37203, tel. 800/548–1116), and **Worldwide Discount Travel Club** (1674 Meridian Ave., Miami Beach, FL 33139, tel. 305/534–2082). Their cut-rate tickets should be compared with APEX tickets on the major airlines.

Smoking On a domestic flight where smoking is permitted, a no-smoking seat can be reserved when you book your flight or during check-in. If the airline tells you that no seats are available in the no-smoking section, insist on one. U.S. Department of Transportation rules apply to all domestic carriers on international routes, and the airline must find seats for all nonsmokers, provided they meet check-in requirements. DOT regulations, however, do not apply to foreign carriers flying out of, or into, the United States.

From the United States by Ship

Cozumel and Playa del Carmen have become increasingly popular ports for Caribbean cruises. Cruise lines that depart from Miami include **Carnival** (tel. 800/327–9501), **Chandris** (tel. 305/576–9900), **Dolphin** (tel. 800/222–1003), **Norwegian** (tel. 800/327–7030), and **Royal Caribbean** (tel. 800/327–2055). From other Florida ports, including Fort Lauderdale, Port Everglades, Palm Beach, Tampa, and St. Petersburg: **Costa Cruises** (tel. 800/327–2537), **Crown** (tel. 800/841–7447), **Holland America** (tel. 800/426–0327), **Ocean Quest** (tel. 800/338–3483), and **Princess Cruises** (tel. 800/446–6690). From New Orleans: **Commodore** (tel. 800/327–5617). From New York: **Regency** (tel. 800/457–5566).

Two agencies specializing in cruises provide significant discounts on unsold berths. Call **World Wide Cruises** (tel. 305/720–9000 in FL or 800/882–9000 outside FL) or **Cruise Shoppers Hotline** (tel. 900/740–3400).

Staying in Cancún and Yucatán

Getting Around

By Plane **Aerocaribe** (tel. 800/531–7921 in the United States, 800/531–7923 in Canada) makes stops in Cancún, Cozumel, Mérida, and Veracruz. **Aerocozumel** (tel. 52/988–48103) provides service from Cancún and Mérida to Chetumal, Chichén Itzá, Ciudad del Carmen, Cozumel, Huatulco, Minatitlán, Playa del Carmen, Veracruz, Villahermosa, and Belize.

By Bus Bus travel in Yucatán, as throughout Mexico, is very inexpensive by North American standards, with rates averaging about $1 per hour. While there is not much difference in price between first- and second-class fares, there is a great difference in service. **ADO** (Autobuses del Oriente) is the principal first-class bus company serving the peninsula. First-class buses make fewer stops, travel faster, run more frequently, and are far more modern and comfortable. Travel by second-class bus is more adventurous, however: You are likely to travel standing up, and you may share space with entire families, livestock (including pigs and chickens), and fresh produce en route to market. The buses themselves may be rickety old jalopies.

By Car The road system in the Yucatán peninsula is extensive and generally in good repair. **Route 307** parallels most of the Caribbean Coast from Punta Sam, north of Cancún, to Tulum; there it turns inward to Chetumal and the Belize border. **Route 180** runs west from Cancún to Valladolid, Chichén Itzá, and Mérida, then turns southwest to Campeche, Isla del Carmen, and on to Villahermosa. From Mérida, there is also **Route 261** south to Campeche and Francisco Escárcega, where it joins Route 186 going east to Chetumal. These highways are two-lane roads. **Route 295** (from the north coast to Valladolid and Felipe Carrillo Puerto) and **Route 134** (which crosses the peninsula from Felipe Carrillo Puerto until it meets **Route 261** in central Yucatán) are also good two-lane roads.

Once off the main highways, however, motorists will find the roads in varying conditions. Some roads are unmarked, which makes it confusing to reach a given destination. Many are unpaved and full of potholes. If you must take one of the smaller roads, the best course is to allow plenty of daylight hours and never to travel at night. Always slow down when approaching towns and villages—which you are forced to do by the ubiquitous *topes* (speed bumps)—because you will find small children and animals in abundance.

Check rental cars thoroughly to make sure everything is in good working order before you leave the agency, because mechanics can be hard to find. If you want air-conditioning or automatic transmission in a rental car, you should reserve in advance. Always park your car in parking lots, or at least in a populated area. Never leave anything of value in an unattended car.

Mexican insurance is an absolute necessity. Do not rely on credit card companies' assurances that you do not have to purchase auto insurance in Mexico unless you are ready to fork over large sums and be reimbursed later. If you are involved in an accident, Mexican authorities will demand that damage be paid for on the spot, in cash.

Speed Limits Mileage and speed limits are given in kilometers. In small towns, observe the posted speed limits, which can be as low as 30 kph (18 mph).

Fuel PEMEX franchises all gas stations, so prices throughout Yucatán will be the same. Prices tend to be comparable to those in the United States; stations in Mexico, however, do not accept credit cards or dollars. Unleaded fuel is not widely available. When filling your tank, ask for a specific peso amount of gas rather than for a number of liters. Keep the tank full, because gas stations are not plentiful.

National Road Emergency Services The Mexican Tourism Ministry operates a fleet of some 250 pickup trucks, known as the *Angeles Verdes* or Green Angels, to render assistance to motorists on the major highways. The bilingual drivers provide mechanical help, first aid, radio-telephone communication, basic supplies and small parts, towing and tourist information. Services are free, and spare parts, fuel, and lubricants are provided at cost. Tips are always appreciated.

The Green Angels patrol fixed sections of the major highways twice daily from 8 AM to 8 PM. If your car breaks down, pull as far as possible off the road, lift the hood, hail a passing vehicle, and ask the driver to notify the patrol. Most bus and truck drivers will be quite helpful. The Green Angels' 24-hour nationwide hotline number is 250–4817.

If you witness an accident, do not stop to help, but instead locate the nearest official.

By Ferry Yucatán is served by a number of ferries and boats, ranging from the spiffy, usually efficient jetfoils (motorized catamarans) between Playa del Carmen and Cozumel to the more modest launches plying the waters from Puerto Juárez and Cancún to Isla Mujeres, and the tiny craft and catamarans heading out to the smaller offshore islands (Isla Contoy, Isla Holbox, Isla del Carmen, the Alacranes Reef).

Schedules are approximate and often vary with the weather and the number of passengers. Prices are quite reasonable.

Car ferries are also available from Punta Sam (north of Cancún) to Isla Mujeres and from Puerto Morelos to Cozumel. This service is slow but reliable.

Telephones

International phone calls can be made from many hotels, but excessive taxes and surcharges—on the order of 60%—usually apply. Cancún, Cozumel, and Mérida are putting up more and more "Ladatel" phone booths on streets and in hotel lobbies; these phones allow you to charge your calls on a credit card for considerably less. Throughout Mexico you dial 09 to place an international call; 02 for long-distance calls; 04 for local information; and 01 for international information. AT&T operators can be accessed in Cancún from a number of the larger international hotels.

Time Zone

The Yucatán Peninsula remains on central standard time year-round.

Mail

Postal Rates Postcards to the United States cost P$1,000; to Great Britain, P$1,200. Letters to the United States cost P$1,500; to Great Britain, P$1,700.

Receiving Mail Mail can be sent either to your hotel or to the post office. In the latter case, have it addressed to your name, "LISTA DE CORREOS," followed by the city, state, postal code, and country. A list of names for which mail has been received is posted and updated daily by the central post office in each location. American Express cardholders can have mail sent to them at the local American Express office. In Yucatán, these are **American Express Travel Service** (Avs. Tulum and Brisas, Suite A, Cancún, QR 77500); **Fiesta Cozumel** (Av. Rafael Melgar 27, Cozumel, QR 77600); **Turismo Bahamita** (Calle 41-A No. 3-E, Plaza Carmel, Cd. del Carmen, CAMP 24140); and **Viajes Programados** (Prolongacíon Calle 56, Edif. Belmar Depto. 5, Campeche, CAMP 24000).

Be forewarned, however, that mail service to and within Mexico is notoriously slow and can take anywhere from 10 days to three weeks. Never send anything of value to Mexico through the mails.

Tipping Because of the value-added tax on most goods and services throughout Mexico, it is not necessary to add a tip to your restaurant bill unless you feel the service was exceptional. Bellhops and porters should be given around P$2,000 per bag, or P$4,000 at deluxe hotels; hotel maids, P$2,000 per day. Tour guides warrant the equivalent of $2 for a half-day tour, $3 for a full day, and $20 to $25 per person for a week. Tour bus drivers should receive $1 per person per day. Car watchers and windshield wipers (usually young boys), as well as gas station attendants and theater ushers, should be satisfied with the equivalent of 50¢. Taxi drivers and shoeshiners do not expect tips.

Shopping

Throughout Yucatán, you'll find original Mexican handicrafts, including basketry, gold and silver filigree jewelry, leather goods, *huipiles* (embroidered cotton dresses), *hamacas* (hammocks), *huaraches* (leather sandals), and *jipis* (Panama hats). Prices will vary depending on where you purchase items. Shopping is convenient in such resort areas as Cancún and Cozumel, but often you'll be paying top peso for items that you can find in smaller towns for less money. As for bargaining, it is widely accepted in the markets, but you should understand that in many small towns the locals earn their livelihoods from the tourist trade. Start off by offering no more than half the asking price and then slowly come up, but never pay more than 70% of the original price. Bargaining is not accepted in most shops except when you are paying cash.

Sports and Outdoor Activities

Archaeology Major Mayan ruins at such sites as Cobá and Tulum (*see* Chapter 6, Mexico's Caribbean Coast), Chichén Itzá and Uxmal (*see* Chapter 8, Mérida and the State of Yucatán), and Campeche (*see* Chapter 7, Campeche) continue to attract professional and amateur archaeologists as well as historians interested in ancient culture.

Bird-watching The Yucatán peninsula is one of the finest areas for birding in Mexico. Habitats range from wildlife and bird sanctuaries to unmarked lagoons, estuaries, and mangrove swamps. Frigates, tanagers, warblers, and macaws inhabit Isla Contoy and the Laguna Colombia on Cozumel; more than 350 bird species, including sparrow hawks and woodpeckers, are to be found in the Sian Ka'an biosphere reserve on the Boca Paila peninsula south of Tulum. Along the north and west coasts of Yucatán—at Río Lagartos, Laguna Rosada, and Celestún—flamingos, herons, ibis, cormorants, pelicans, and peregrine falcons thrive.

Fishing Sportfishing is popular in Cozumel and throughout the Caribbean Coast. The rich waters of the Caribbean and the Gulf of Mexico support hundreds of species of tropical fish, making the entire Yucatán coastline and the outlying islands a paradise for deep-sea fishing, sportfishing, fly-fishing, flatfishing, and bonefishing. Particularly between the months of April and July, the waters off Cancún, Cozumel, and Isla Mujeres teem with sailfish, marlin, red snapper, tuna, barracuda, and wahoo, among other fish. Billfishing is so rich around Cozumel that a tournament is held here each year.

Farther south, along Boca Paila peninsula, banana fish, bonefish, mojarra, shad, permit, and sea bass provide great sport for flatfishing and fly-fishing, while oysters, shrimp, and conch lie on the bottom of the Gulf of Mexico near Campeche and Isla del Carmen. At Progreso, on the north coast, sportfishing for grouper, dogfish, and pompano is quite popular.

Hunting Hunting, although increasingly frowned upon as a result of Mexico's heightened ecological awareness, is good along the northwestern side of the peninsula and around Mérida and Campeche. Game includes waterfowl, deer, quail, and wild boar.

Water Sports All manner of water sports—jetskiing, Hobie Catting, sailboarding, waterskiing, sailing, and parasailing—are practiced along the Caribbean Coast, which has numerous marinas and well-equipped water-sports centers.

Scuba Diving and Snorkeling Divers and snorkelers come to Cozumel and Akumal and other parts of Mexico's Caribbean Coast for the clear turquoise waters, the colorful and assorted tropical fish, and the exquisite coral formations along the Belize reef system. Currents allow for drift diving, and both reefs and offshore wrecks lend themselves to dives, many of which are safe enough for neophytes. The peninsula's cenotes, or natural sinkholes, provide an unusual dive experience. Individual chapters will direct you to the dive sites that will best suit you.

Beaches

Cancún and the Yucatán area provide beach goers with a variety of options from which to choose. Cancún and Yucatán offer a stunning variety of beaches: There are white sand, rocky coves and promontories, curvaceous bays, and murky lagoons. Those who thrive on the resort atmosphere will probably enjoy Playa Chac Mool and Playa Tortugas on the windward side of Cancún, which is calmer if less beautiful than the leeward side. On the north end of Isla Mujeres, Playa Cocoteros and Playa Norte offer handsome sunset vistas. Beaches on the east coast of Cozumel—once frequented by buccaneers—are rocky, and the swimming is treacherous, but they are deserted and powdery.

On the relatively sheltered leeward side are the widest and best sand beaches.

The Caribbean Coast abounds with tiny, hidden beaches (at Xcaret, Paamul, Chemuyil, Xcacel, Punta Bete, south of Tulum, and along the Boca Paila peninsula), but there are also long stretches of white sand, usually filled with sunbathers, at Puerto Morelos, Playa del Carmen, and especially Akumal.

Travelers to Campeche and Progreso will find the waters of the Gulf of Mexico deep green, shallow, and tranquil. Such beaches as Payucán, Sabancuy, Isla del Carmen, and Yucalpetén are less visited by North Americans; facilities are minimal, but some prefer it that way.

Dining

The mystique of Yucatecán cooking has a lot to do with the generous doses of local spices and herbs, although generally the food tends not to be too spicy. Among the specialties are *cochinita píbil* and *pollo píbil* (succulent pork or chicken baked in banana leaves with a tangy sour-orange sauce); *poc chuc* (Yucatecán pork marinated in the same sour-orange sauce with pickled onions); *panuchos* (fried tortillas covered with turkey, pickled onions, and avocado, with fried beans on the side); *papadzules* (tortillas piled high with hard-boiled eggs and drenched in a sauce of pumpkin seed and fried tomato); and *codzitos* (rolled tortillas in pumpkin-seed sauce). *Achiote* (annatto), cilantro (coriander), and the fiery *chile habanero* are heavily favored condiments.

Yucatecáns are renowned for—among other things—their love of idiosyncratic beverages. *Iztabentún*, a liqueur made of fermented honey and anise, dates back to ancient Mayan times; like straight tequila, it's best drunk in small sips between bites of fresh lime. Local brews, such as the dark bock León Negra and the light Carta Clara and Montejo, are excellent but hard to find in peninsular restaurants. Yucatecán *horchata*, a favorite all over Mexico, is made from milled rice and water flavored with vanilla. Also try the *licuados*, either milk- or water-based, made from the tropical fruits of the region. For more Mexican specialties and translations, *see* the Menu Guide at the back of this book.

The rule of thumb in such areas as Cancún, Isla Mujeres, and Cozumel is to stay away from restaurants in the large chain hotels because prices there tend to be exorbitant. Also, when buying fish from beachside and roadside palapas, make sure the facilities are sanitary so you don't get food poisoning. Be especially careful with shellfish and anything to which mayonnaise may have been added.

Restaurants in Yucatán, including those in hotels, are for the most part very casual. The exceptions will be noted within reviews.

Lodging

If you plan to stay in Cancún or Cozumel, you'll have a variety of accommodations and package deals from which to choose, depending on desired amenities, price, location, season, and length of stay. There are luxurious and expensive internationally affiliated properties with numerous food and beverage outlets, the latest room amenities, boutiques, and sports facilities. These beach resorts also feature more modest hostelries—usually a short walk from the beaches—for budget-minded travelers. As you get into the less populated and less touristed areas of Yucatán, particularly the cities, accommodations tend to be simpler and more "typically Mexican." The hotels discussed in this book all meet a minimum standard of cleanliness, and most of them possess a certain rustic charm. Inexpensive bungalows, campsites, and places to hang a hammock along many of the beaches are other options.

Apartment and Villa Rentals Both **Villas International** (71 W. 23rd St., New York, NY 10010, tel. 212/929–7585) and **Hideaways Int'l** (Box 1270, Littleton, MA 01460, tel. 508/486–8955) have condominiums and villas to rent in Cancún and Akumal, to the south.

Home Exchange Exchanging homes is a surprisingly inexpensive way to enjoy a vacation abroad, especially if you plan a lengthy visit. The largest home-exchange company, **International Home Exchange Service** (Box 3975, San Francisco, CA 94119, tel. 415/435–3497), publishes three directories a year. The $45 membership entitles you to one listing and all three directories (there is an additional charge for postage). Photos of your property cost an additional $10, and listing a second home costs $10.

Loan-a-Home (2 Park La., Apt. 6E, Mount Vernon, NY 10552, tel. 914/664–7640), which publishes two directories (in December and June) and two supplements (in March and September) each year, is popular with professors on sabbaticals, businesspeople on temporary assignments, and retirees on extended vacations. There is no annual membership fee or charge for listing your home, but one directory and a supplement cost $35. All four books together cost $45.

Credit Cards

The following credit-card abbreviations are used throughout this book, particularly in the Dining and Lodging sections: AE, American Express; DC, Diners Club; MC, MasterCard; V, Visa.

Personal Security

When visiting Yucatán, even in such resort areas as Cancún and Cozumel, use common sense. Wear a money belt, make use of hotel safes when available, and carry your own baggage whenever possible. Don't bother reporting a crime to the police unless you speak excellent Spanish and have a great deal of patience.

Women traveling alone are likely to be subjected to catcalls, although this is less true of Yucatán than of other parts of Mexico. Avoid direct eye contact with men on the streets—it invites further acquaintance. Don't wear tight clothes if you don't want to call attention to yourself. If you speak Spanish and are being harassed, pretend you don't understand and ignore would-be suitors or say "no" to whatever they say. Don't enter street bars or cantinas alone.

2 Portraits of the Yucatán Peninsula

Maya Chronology and History of Yucatán

11,000 BC   Hunters and gatherers settle in Yucatán.

Preclassical Period: 1500 BC–AD 200

1500–900 BC   The emergence and expansion of early civilizations, including the powerful and sophisticated Olmec Gulf of Mexico in the present-day states of Veracruz and Tabasco. Primitive farming communities develop in Yucatán.

900–300 BC   The rise of the Olmecs, whose iconography and social institutions strongly influence the rapidly expanding Mayan population. The Maya adopt the Olmecs' concepts of tribal confederacies and small kingships as they move across the lowlands.

600 BC   Tikal and Edzná are settled.

300 BC–AD 200   The emergence of large population centers and city-states (Tikal, El Mirador, Kaminaljuyú, Izapa) in highlands and on Pacific Coast of Guatemala, Honduras, and El Salvador. New architectural elements include the corbeled arch and roofcomb.

400 BC–AD 100   Dzibilchaltún had an important center, in a sector west of Progreso–Mérida highway known as Komchen. By this time Becán and Uaxactún (as well as Dzibilchaltún) were settled.

300 BC–AD 900   Florescence of Edzná.

AD 200   Cancún is settled.

Classical Period: 200–900

A formative stage for lowland Mayan culture, marked by the emergence of the calendar and the written word. Architectural highlight of the period is stepped platforms topped by limestone and masonry superstructures (temple-pyramids with frontal stairways), arranged around plazas and decorated with stelae, bas-reliefs, and frescoes.

200–600   Economy and trade flourish. Mayan culture becomes increasingly secular and warlike.

Development of Petén architectural style (polychrome modeled-stucco decoration and uniform room size and construction) in the Petén lowlands and along Usamacinta River at Palenque, Bonampak, Yaxchilán, Piedras Niegras, Tikal, Uaxactún.

250–300   Fortification ditch and earthworks built at Becán.

300   San Gervasio is built on Cozumel.

300–600   Florescence of Kohunlich.

400–1100   Florescence of Cobá.

431–799   The Palenque dynasty is founded.

432   The first settlement is established at Chichén Itzá.

6th Century Major Mayan centers in Petén, Tabasco, southern Campeche, Belize, parts of Guatemala and western Honduras strongly influenced by Teotihuacán. Larger, more elaborate palaces, temples, ballcourts, roads, and fortifications evident.

500–700 Florescence of Becán, Xpuhil, Chicanná.

600–900 Northern Yucatán ceremonial centers become increasingly important as centers farther south reach and pass developmental climax; the influence of Teotihuacán wanes. Three new Mayan architectural styles develop: Puuc (exemplified by Chichén Itzá and Edzná and used at the "Route of the Convents" sites, including Uxmal, Kabah, Sayil, and Labná) is the dominant style; Chenes (in northern Campeche, between the Puuc hills and the Río Bec area) is characterized by ornamental facades with serpent masks; and Río Bec (at Río Bec and Becán) features small palaces with high towers exuberantly decorated with serpent masks.

600–900 Florescence of Jainá.

700–1000 First florescence of Tulum.

9th Century Putún (Chontal) Maya from Tabasco and southern Campeche occupy southern Petén and possibly Cozumel.

Postclassical Period: 900–1541

900–1050 Classical Mayan centers of Petén and southern lowlands are abandoned, probably through a combination of overpopulation, weather calamities, and misuse of land.

ca. 920 Itzá, a branch of Putún Maya, establish themselves at Champotón and then at Chichén Itzá.

987 Toltecs, a Nahua-speaking tribe from central Mexico, leave their capital at Tula for Yucatán, under the leadership of Quetzalcoatl or Kukulcán, the "feathered serpent."

987–1185 Toltec/Itzá rule at Chichén Itzá, a cosmopolitan city in which architecture and sculpture can be seen alongside forms more like those of Central Mexico.

987–1007 The Xiu settle near ruins of Uxmal.

1200–1250 Decline and overthrow of Chichén Itzá.

1200 The Itzá abandon Chichén Itzá for Lake Petén Itzá.

1224–1244 The Itzá return to the abandoned Chichén Itzá as squatters.

1224 The Cocomes, an Itzá dynasty that emerged as a dominant group in Mayapán, force Itzá out of Chichén Itzá and rule northern Yucatán until mid-15th century.

1250–1450 The League of Mayapán—including the key cities of Uxmal, Izamal, Chichén Itzá, Mayapán—is formed in northern Yucatán.

15th Century By this time most of the coastal cities had been founded and were developing.

1263–1283 Mayapán, under rule of Cocomes aided by Canul (Tabascan mercenaries), becomes most powerful city-state in Yucatán.

1441 Mayan cities under Xiu rulers sack Mayapán, ending centralized rule of peninsula. Yucatán henceforth is governed as 18 petty provinces, with constant internecine strife. The Itzá return to Lake Petén Itzá and establish their capital at Tayasal (modern-day Flores).

ca. 1443 Ah-Canul chieftainship is founded at Calkiní.

15th Century Cancún is abandoned.

1502 A Mayan canoe is spotted during Columbus's fourth voyage.

1511 Aguilar and Guerrero, Spanish sailors, are shipwrecked off Yucatán.

1517 Fernández de Córdoba discovers Isla Mujeres.

1517 Córdoba lands at Campeche, marking first Spanish landfall on mainland. He is defeated by the Maya at Champotón.

1518 Juan de Grijalva reaches Cozumel.

1519 Hernán Cortés lands at Cozumel.

1527, 1531, 1541 Unsuccessful Spanish attempts to conquer Yucatán.

1540 Montejo founds Campeche, the first Spanish settlement in Yucatán.

Colonial Period: 1541–1821

1542 Mayan chieftains surrender to Montejo at T'Ho; 500,000 Indians are killed during the conquest of Yucatán. Indians are forced into labor under the *encomienda* system, by which conquistadores are charged with their subjugation and Christianization. The Franciscans contribute to this process.

1542 Mérida is founded on the ruins of T'Ho.

1543 Valladolid is founded on the ruins of Zací.

1546 A Mayan group attacks Mérida, resulting in five-month-long rebellion.

1549 The Indian population of Yucatán numbers 235,000.

1562 Bishop Diego de Landa burns Mayan codices at Maní.

1600 Cozumel is abandoned after smallpox decimates population.

1639 The Indian population of Yucatán falls to 210,000.

1624 The Spanish captain sent to subdue the Maya at Tayasal has his heart torn out.

1686 Campeche's walls are built, ending the pirates' reign of terror.

1697 The last independent Mayan kingdom, at Tayasal, is destroyed.

1700 182,500 Indians account for 98% of Yucatán's population.

1712 The Tzeltal uprising in Chiapas.

1736 Indian population of Yucatán declines to 127,000.

1761 The Cocom uprising near Sotuta leads to death of 600 Maya.

1794 Indian population of Yucatán: 254,000.

1810 Port of Sisal opens, ending Campeche's ancient monopoly on peninsular trade and its economic prosperity.

Post-Colonial/Modern Period: 1821– Present

1823   Yucatán achieves statehood.

1840s   Tulum serves as outpost of Chan Santa Cruz Indians; Chan
        Santa Cruz is modern-day Felipe Carrillo Puerto.

1847   Mexico City, in the struggle to regain Texas, imposes heavy
        taxes and forced military service on Yucatán's resentful Creole
        population, which arms and recruits Maya to fight the capital.
        Following years of oppression, the Indians attack Valladolid,
        launching War of the Castes, which continues fitfully until
        1901.

1846–1850   The Indian population of Yucatán is nearly halved during Caste
            War.

1848   Indians occupy four-fifths of the peninsula but abandon their
        arms during corn-planting season.

ca. 1848   Twenty refugee families from the Caste War settle in Cozumel,
           which has been almost uninhabited for centuries. By 1890,
           Cozumel's population numbers 500.

1863   Campeche achieves statehood.

1869   The Chamula, a Tzotzil-speaking Mayan group in Chiapas, rise
        up against San Cristóbal de las Casas.

1872   The founding of Progreso.

1898   Mexican forces capture Chan Santa Cruz, the last stronghold of
        Maya rebels.

1898   The founding of Payo Obispo (present-day Chetumal).

1880–1914   Yucatán's monopoly on henequen, enhanced by plantation own-
            ers' exploitation of Mayan peasants, leads to its Golden Age as
            one of the wealthiest states in Mexico.

1890–1910   Waves of Middle Eastern immigrants arrive in Yucatán and be-
            come successful in commerce, restaurants, cattle ranching, and
            tourism.

1901   The Caste War virtually ends with Porfirio Díaz's defeat of
        most Maya.

1902   Díaz creates the Territory of Quintana Roo to isolate rebellious
        pockets of Indians and increase his hold on regional resources.

1915–1924   Felipe Carrillo Puerto, Socialist governor of Yucatán, insti-
            tutes major reforms in land distribution, labor, women's
            rights, and education during Mexican Revolution.

1934–1940   President Lázaro Cárdenas implements significant agrarian
            reforms in Yucatán.

1935   Chan Santa Cruz rebels in Quintana Roo relinquish Tulum and
        sign a peace treaty.

1930–1980   With collapse of the world henequen markets, Yucatán gradu-
            ally becomes one of the poorest states in Mexico.

1974   Quintana Roo achieves statehood; development of Cancún tour-
        ism begins.

The Mayan People

By Kate Simon

The Mayans, in Antonio de Herrera's account of the "Indies," published in 1615:

The whole country is divided into 18 districts, and in all of them were so many and such stately stone buildings that it was amazing and the greatest wonder is, that having no use of any metal, they were able to raise such structures, which seem to have been temples, for their houses were always of timber and thatched.

For the space of 20 years there was such plenty through the country, and the people multiplied so much, that old men said the whole province looked like one town, and then they applied themselves to build more temples. . . .

They flattened their heads and foreheads, their ears bored with rings in them. Their faces were generally good, and not very brown, but without beards, for they scorched them when young, that they might not grow. Their hair was long like women, and in tresses, with which they made a garland about the head, and a little tail hung behind. The prime men wore a rowler eight fingers broad round them instead of breeches, and going several times round the waist, so that one end of it hung before and the other behind, with fine featherwork, and had large square mantles knotted on their shoulders, and sandals or buskins made of deer's skins.

The abundance of questions and conjecture which mists a clear view of Mexican origins also hangs over the Mayans. A quick glimpse at any archaeological map of the peninsula will reveal a crowding of sites already discovered, and there are probably some yet to be stumbled on. Where did the hordes of people come from to build and serve these cities, to haul the stone and carve it so lavishly, to shape the varieties of pottery, to perfect a calendar and imagine a concept of zero, to devise a style of writing, to model magnificent pieces of sculpture?

Theories of early settlement divide, unevenly, into the two most common for all Indian life on the continent. One states that nomadic hordes wandered from the Orient through the Bering Straits, spread southward and, after centuries, stopped here and there to establish rudimentary agricultural settlements. The less popular theory holds that some of the cultures made their way across the Pacific at a much later date; proof offered is the presence and importance of jade (reduced to the status of "jadeite" by some opponents of the theory), the marked epicanthic fold of the Mayan eyelid, the common appearance of the Mongolian spot on spines of Mayan babies, and especially, resemblances in art forms.

In that case, say the Bering Straits men, why didn't they bring the tools of the Orient or, more important, the wheel?

The argument seesaws and is further frenzied by later complications. Pottery characteristics, decorative building elements, the hieroglyphs of the Olmecs, and the people of the early Oaxacan periods show up in early Mayan art. How did this come about? Why were the great Mayan cities abandoned? What was the relationship among them? Was there a "capital" among subject towns or were they city-states, balancing independence and interdependence? These unknowns are not the residue of neglect; the Mayans have been explored and studied for a long time by many scholars and from various points of view, but all the knowledge of this gifted civilization has not yet fallen into clear shape.

E vidence of a distinctly "Mayan" style begins to appear four or five centuries before the Christian era, with the construction of ceremonial buildings, refinements in pottery, and, quite likely, the development of the calendar. From AD 200 to 800 was the time of greatest flowering: the temple-palaces of Palenque in Chiapas, of Tikal in Guatemala, and Copan in Honduras were built; the pottery evolved in delicate shapes and color; mathematics, the calendar, and systems of recording (numerals and hieroglyphs) became more complex and efficient; the crescent arts produced the masterpieces of Palenque, Jaina, and Bonampak. Then, the vast centers were abandoned. The causes may have been crop failures of several years' running, exhaustion of the soil, catastrophic weather, plague, hit-and-run attacks by other peoples, or dire prophecies of the priests, which, as in the case of Moctezuma, made a climate of disaster and a bending toward it. Whatever the reason, it is believed that the peoples of these cities migrated northward and eastward to the Yucatán peninsula, where they built Uxmal and the centers that surround it (AD 800 to 1000). On the heels of these refugees came a tribe of invaders, possibly invited to help one of the warring cities against another, who called themselves the Itzás. Whatever *their* backgrounds, they brought with them the full complement of Toltec matters: the worship of Quetzalcoatl (here called Kukulcán), feathered-serpent columns, and the architectural concepts whose flowering was their city, Chichén Itzá. It was this period (the 12th and 13th centuries) that saw a coalition government of the three important centers, Uxmal, Chichén Itzá, and Mayapan, followed by a century or two of truce, and again a period of warfare during which intellectual and artistic achievement came to a standstill. By the 15th century the Mayan-Toltec vitality was an extinguished candle.

In spite of Mayan apologists, it was not altogether the sweet, reasonable society they like to picture. In essence it was rather like the other Mexican cultures, a structure of priest-nobles and warriors at the apex of a social pyramid

that broadened downward from merchants and artisans to
something very near slaves, a vast population bedeviled by
an elaborate pantheon of gods and subgods who could blow
hot or cold for their own arcane reasons. These gods, like
the others, had to be fed; the favored method was to throw
virgins into the sacred wells (cenotes), which are Yucatán's
only sources of fresh water and, consequently, the abode of
powerful and greedy spirits.

The Mayan may or may not have been as enthusiastic
for blood as the Aztec; he was a valiant and stubborn
fighter and would not be conquered by the Conquest.
In battle and in guerrilla warfare, Mayans killed more
Spaniards than did any other group. Some committed sui-
cide rather than submit, while others fled into remote areas
to hold out against the Spaniards for over 100 years after
the rest of the country was subjugated. Sporadic rebellions
against white rule went on into the beginning of the 20th
century. One of the most violent of these uprisings, which
brought the Indians short-term control of practically all of
the peninsula, occurred in 1847. It was inspired and aided
by the corruptions of Mexican politics of the time and by
conditions described by Stephens only a short while earlier:

In consideration of their drinking the water *of the hacienda
the workers are obliged to work for the master without pay
on Monday. When they marry and have families, and of
course need more water, in addition to their work on
Mondays they are obliged to clear, sow and gather 20
mecates of maize for the master, each* mecate *being 24
square yards. . . . The authority of the master or his dele-
gate over them is absolute. He settles all disputes between
the Indians themselves, and punishes for offences, acting
both as judge and executioner. . . . There is no obligation
upon him (the Indian) to remain at the hacienda unless he
is in debt to the master, but practically, this binds him hand
and foot. . . . A dishonest master may always bring them
in debt, and generally they are really so. If he is not able to
pay off his debt, and the Indian wants to leave, the master
must give him a paper to the effect that "Whatever señor
wishes to receive the Indian named—, can take him,
provided he pays me the debt he owes me." When he has obtained it, he goes round to the different haciendas until he
finds a proprietor who is willing to purchase the debt, with
a mortgage upon him until it is paid.*

Like most subject people the Mayan continued as stubborn-
ly as he could to hold on to his language and his customs. His
isolation from the rest of Mexico—early explorers called
the Yucatán an island—helped the peasant cling to his indigenous image as it helped the rich to achieve a rare cosmo-
politanism. Until slow chicle and mahogany trains were
drawn through swamps and jungle and, later, highways,
the only way to get to and from Mérida was by boat via the
port of Progreso. It was easier to go to Havana and on to

Europe for education or pleasure than to Mexico City. One still finds elderly physicians with degrees from Leipzig, and matrons whose old-fashioned china was bought in Limoges. Add to this a mild disdain for the Johnny-come-lately, imperfect peoples of the north, and the lack of impassioned nationalism becomes understandable. Yucatán is to Mexico what Sicily is to Italy, without the bitterness; what Brittany is to France, without the tight-lipped shrewdness.

Yucatán's Great Archaeology

By Kate Simon

Although they seem to lie very near one another, the going among Mayan sites can be rough. Some of the edifices are still shrouded in heavy jungle, others were too thoroughly destroyed by time and warfare to make much structural or aesthetic sense. For the visitor who comes equipped with a normal amount of time (five to seven days in Yucatán) and interest, the twin splendors of Uxmal and Chichén, both easily accessible, plus the less-known Kabah, Labná, and Sayil, should suffice for a good view of "Mayan" architecture and art. (Keep in mind that Uxmal and Kabah can be visited on your way from Campeche to Mérida—and possibly the others as well—particularly easy if you are driving.)

One doesn't necessarily have to be taken by the hand to Uxmal and Chichén. They have been described and photographed almost as much as the splendors of Egypt and their looks become familiar to most of the civilized world. Pamphlet in hand—available in town and at the sites—one can wander through the ruins on a do-it-yourself basis. Buses run to both cities frequently; the trip to Chichén takes about two hours, to Uxmal it is about an hour and a half. A taxi needn't be wildly expensive and the drivers are usually well informed or will put you in the hands of a local guide if you like. *His* fee will be little but he may suffer from a common form of Mayaphilia: he may insist that everything you look at is "pure" Mayan, whatever that may mean.

Like Uxmal, Kabah sits close to the road, but the wait for a bus to take you there from Uxmal or back may be hot and time-consuming. Guide services usually make Uxmal-Kabah one trip and Sayil-Labná another. For those with prodigious stamina, Uxmal, Kabah, and Sayil can be arranged as a long one-day trip.

Kabah is a bitter structure, with the inelegant proportions of a squat fortress. It sits on a height of terraces and platforms as befits a fortress but its most imposing building has been given a singularly nonbelligerent name, the Palace of the Rolled Mat (Codz-Pop). This refers to the "nose" of the stylized masks of the rain god, Chac, a characteristic of local ornamentation valued by adherents of the trans-Pacific theory of Mayan origin as proof that the migrants brought with them a memory of the elephant's trunk. Opponents consider it phallic, or an ornamental step device which facilitated scrambling up and down the building.

Tour cars or jeeps continue on to Sayil; check at Uxmal or Kabah to find out if the road is ready for your car. The

Palacio at Sayil (the guides like to expound on it salaciously as a fertility center) is, next to Palenque, the most dramatically placed of the structures now visible. High and alone, long, horizontal planes surrounded by a silent, motionless sea of green, it echoes the isolated Greek temple at Segesta in Sicily. The three-layered building bears sections of Mayan frieze, including the mask motif, and a preponderance of small columns as architectural and ornamental elements. Tight clusters of columns like pipers of Pan (Puuc style) flank the doorways, then change to sets of thicker, peculiarly shaped columns; one of each pair is straight, the other softly indented—rather like a waist—suggesting a primitive female figure. Other than these details, there is not much on or in the Palacio to surprise or enchant: it is the total effect—the ride through the brush, the stillness, the sudden sight of the isolated, regal building. There are ruined buildings of which one says, "I would love to have seen it before it fell apart," but not of Sayil. Like the Greek temples, it must have been covered with much more ornament and brilliant color and, like the Greek temples now, has achieved a new beauty in decay.

One of the best places from which to get a distant view of the building in its setting is at the "observatory," a few minutes away by car. From here one walks a short distance to suggestions of other buildings, and on to a grove in which lies a huge figure of a priapic god who may have fallen from a set of columns nearby. In another direction from the Palacio, a short ride and short walk again, there is a cave on which is clearly carved a figure of a woman in a froglike squatting position, and just below her, on a ledge farther back in the curve of the wall, the figure of what might be another woman, or more possibly, a baby; it has no breasts, its shape is rounder and less clearly defined than the other figure—more evidence of fertility rites, the guide eagerly points out.

The road to Labná should be usable in dry weather. Labná, again judging from jungle-choked mounds, must have been a very large city, and to judge from what is left, an ornately beautiful one. It has some of the clustered, banded columns of Sayil, the elaborated rain-god masks of the whole area, the open work, and the geometric ornaments of stone mosaic which adorn Uxmal. The famous arch of Labná, of itself strikingly large and tall, offers a clear demonstration of how near the Mayans were to the keystone arch, and also how much they could do without it—as they did without the wheel and without metal until late in their history.

With more time and the proper passion for Mayan you might investigate (always checking the condition of roads) the Cave of Balancanche, less than three miles from Chichén, which revealed, some years ago, a good number of pottery objects still to be dated. Chacmultun gives evi-

dences of once having been a large center and its frescoes
are not altogether gone. It is reached via Muna and Ticul, a
town which embroiders *ipiles* and whose inhabitants are
purportedly the descendants of the Xius, kings of Uxmal.

Or try either the ruins of Dzibalchen or Xtampak (savoring
the pleasure of rolling these names out when you get home).

Much less demanding is Dzibilchultun, off the
Progreso road, now being excavated and poten-
tially an enormous, important site. At the present writing it shows a few structures, including remains of
an ancient church, one tall pyramid, and a platform holding
a plump column. The rest is a small museum, the first stir-
rings of a university, and a few distinguished statuettes
that were found in the Temple of the Seven Dolls (now in the
museum). One wonders how long it will take Tulane University and the National Geographic Society to rebuild the
large city, which was, it is said, in continuous use from 1000
BC until the arrival of the Spaniards. It is not a particularly
rewarding site at present except for the young picnickers
who play their portable phonographs and swim at the edge
of the cenote. Or go by bus to Progreso, an unprepossessing
port town whose beaches are steadily coming out of a long
slump. At the end of a road shortly before one reaches
Progreso, there are two beaches equipped with cabins and
snack bars and numerous of the local young: Chelen and
Yucapeten. From Progreso one turns left for the white
sands of Sisal, and right to Chixulub, whose fine sand holds
interesting shells and a respected seafood restaurant.
Should you be in Mérida in mid-August—a daring time—
find out the precise dates of the Chixulub fiesta, which includes regional dancing, lots of seafood, and often a bullfight. If you have the energy, take a walk along the avenue
which parallels the beachfront for a glimpse of some of the
wildest domestic architecture extant, and some very good
modern. On your return, get to the bus station early. For
one thing, this obviates waiting through the filling and departure of two buses before you get a seat, but more important, the bus station is the pulse of the town and to sit on one
of its benches is to be the spectator of an eloquent pageant.
A bus from Mérida delivers a covey of old ladies in white,
their thin hair pulled back tightly into the clublike knot
which has been the fashion for centuries; a few wear shoes.
Two younger women glowing in white rayon heavy with
bright embroidery and lace, hung with gold chains and earrings, with stiff new sandals on their feet, step down sol-
emnly, like young priestesses. The general factotum of the
bus—not yet of the aristocracy of drivers—helps an old
man lift down a cake of ice wrapped in cloth and rope which,
somehow, survived the hour's trip of many stops. A sack of
dried kernels of corn to be soaked and made into tortilla
mash is the next bundle down, and the assistant arranges it
as a great deep hat on the head of a Mayan woman who is

also carrying a large, ugly doll dressed in a man's hat and a cloth whose embroidered banner names it Saint Michael.

At the entrance to the station, a timeless tableau goes on: A young man, red-eyed, weaving, his gestures watery, is trying to placate a girl of 15, an unkempt, savage little beauty, who answers him in snarls and grunts. He had taken her to the beach for the night, rather than the hotel room he had promised, and drank up the fare money which was to take them back to Mérida. They approach the factotum-collector of the bus, who assures them in a reasonable manner that he cannot take them to Mérida without fares. They start to walk down the dusty road, separate and morose.

An insistent drunk who has been gently urged off two buses now boards yours. The man of all work of the bus, resigned to his company, helps him curl up under some seats and at each stop, when the bewildered head rises to look around blindly, pats him back to sleep in a mixture of Spanish and Mayan. When his charge is asleep and all the fares collected, the young man fixes a doll, adjusts a slipping bundle, and dandles one of a pair of babies while the mother attends to the second.

The return from this second-class bus ride might be just the time to leave Yucatán, carrying the savor of its pretty, generous people whose sophisticated lineage shows in their profiles, in their open, trusting manner, their easy smiling, and complete lack of xenophobia. You interest them, they assume they interest you, and they make it clear that the encounter is a mutual pleasure.

3 Cancún

Introduction

Cancún is Mexico's most popular destination, and the second most popular tourist spot in the Caribbean, after Puerto Rico. Hailed by the travel industry for having become an overnight success after its creation in 1974, the resort now draws nearly 2 million foreign visitors a year who come for the cleaned, groomed beaches; affordable prices; luxury hotels; and American-style cuisine and nightlife, all topped with a hint of Mexican flavor. It is true, however, that culturally Cancún is only vaguely Mexican. Even the president of the Mexican Hotel Association described the resort as being "more like an American destination with a foreign name." So travelers who are more interested in the traditional backpacking, adventure, nature, and archaeology deride it loudly. If they go to Cancún at all, it is only because Cancún has the international airport closest to the rest of the Yucatán peninsula.

Cancún is well-chosen for those looking for an easy vacation with sun, very little language barrier (many people in the tourist industry speak English), water sports, and creature comforts. The sun shines an average of 240 days a year (rainy season is May–September), reputedly more than at almost any other Caribbean spot; temperatures linger at about 80°F (27°C); and the white porous limestone sand stays cool throughout the year.

What also sets this 22½-kilometer (14 mile) barrier island apart from its Caribbean neighbors is that the tourist is sheltered from the less pleasant local realities—namely, the unsightly pockets of poverty where drug abuse, alcoholism, and delinquency are rampant. It is enclave tourism at its cleverest and most notorious. Yet Cancún is close enough to the Mayan ruins to make it more than just a one-dimension beach destination, and the snorkeling and scuba diving at the surrounding reefs and other islands—notably Isla Mujeres and Cozumel—easily rival those of the Bahamas, the Caymans, or Bonaire.

Regarding beach resorts, Cancún is among the more attractive and modern, with architecture that was deliberately designed as a cross between the traditional Mediterranean and what has been termed "neo-Mayan." Typical Mediterranean structures—low, solid, rectangular, with flat, red-tile roofs and white stucco walls covered with exuberantly pink bougainvillea—acquire *palapas* (pre-Hispanic thatched roofs) and such ornamental devices as colonnettes, latticework, and beveled cornices.

Cancún has gone through the life cycle typical of any tourist destination. At its inception, the resort inevitably drew the jet set; lately, it has attracted increasing numbers of less affluent tourists, primarily package-tour takers and college students, particularly during spring break when hordes of flawless, tanned young bodies people the beaches and restaurants and just about everywhere are roisterous pool parties. Though they arrive in great numbers, these vacationers tend to stick to package plans that include meals and other costs, leaving little precious hard currency behind them.

As for the island's history, not much was written about it before the astonishing epiphany almost 20 years ago. It's marshy nature kept Cancún from being of much use to the ancient

Maya, although they settled it during the preclassical era, in about AD 200, and remained until about the 14th or 15th century. The island does not even appear on the early navigators' maps. In the mid-19th century minor Mayan ruins were sighted; however, they were not studied by archaeologists until the 1950s and mid-1970s. In 1970 then-President Luis Echeverría first visited the site that had been chosen to retrieve Quintana Roo from obscurity and abject poverty. Unfortunately, Cancún's environment has paid the price for the island's success. Lagoons and mangrove swamps may be polluted beyond repair, and conch and lobster have disappeared. But in the eyes of the world, Cancún has prospered and, though its once-heralded virginity is forever tarnished, the destination performs its vocation in the manner of a true star.

Essential Information

Important Addresses and Numbers

Tourist Information
The federal tourist office, **SECTUR** (Av. Cobá and Calle Nader, S.M. 5, tel. 988/43238 or 988/43438), is open weekdays 8–3:30. The **Cancún tourist office** (tel. 988/4803) shares a space with SECTUR, and runs a booth near the market (Av. Tulum and Calle Tulipanes. The **state tourist office** (Av. Tulum 26, S.M. 5, tel. 988/48073), located next to Multibanco Comermex, is open daily 9–9. From any of these offices you can pick up a copy of *Cancún Tips*, a free pocket-size guide to hotels, restaurants, shopping, and recreation, that usually contains a discount card for use at various establishments. Although it's loaded with advertising, the booklet, published twice a year in English and Spanish editions, has useful maps. The magazine staff also runs an information center at Plaza Caracol (tel. 988/44609 or 988/41458) that is open daily 10–10, and one at the convention center (tel. 988/30447) that's open from 9 to 1 and 4 to 8 except Wednesday afternoons and Sundays. Several similar publications, including *Cancún Scene*, *Cancún Inside*, and *Passport Cancún*, are also available.

Consulates
U. S. Consulate (Av. Nader 40, S.M. 2A, Edificio Marruecos 31, tel. 988/42411 or 988/46399) is open daily 9–2 and 3–6.

Canadian Consulate (Plaza México Local 312, upper floor, tel. 988/43716; in Mérida, tel. 91/992–30173) is open daily 11 AM–1 PM.

Emergencies
Police (tel. 988/42342 or 988/41913); **Red Cross** (Av. Xcaret and Labná, S.M. 21, tel. 988/41616); **Highway Patrol** (tel. 988/41107).

Medical Clinics
Central Quirúrgica Bonampak (Calle Tierra 5, S.M. 4, tel. 988/45530 or 988/46523), **Clinica Cancún** (Pta. Tanchacte 1, S.M. 24, tel. 988/41702 or 988/44703), **Hospital Central de Cirurgías** (Claves 9, S.M. 22, tel. 988/41092), and **Seguro Social Hospital** (Av. Tulum and Cobá, tel. 988/41120) provide emergency medical care.

Late-night Pharmacies
Farmacia Turística (Plaza Caracol, tel. 988/31894) and **Farmacia Extra Extra** (Plaza Caracol, tel. 988/32827) deliver to hotels 9 AM–10 PM. **Farmacia Paris** (Av. Yaxchilán in the Marrufo Bldg., tel. 988/40164) also fills prescriptions.

Banks Generally, banks in Cancún are open weekdays 9–1:30. To exchange or wire money try one of the locations of **Banamex** (Av. Tulum, tel. 988/43759; Av. Chichén Itzá, tel. 988/46275; and El Parián/convention center, tel. 988/31128). Also try **Bancomer** (Av. Tulum, tel. 988/43508, or Plaza Kabah, tel. 988/49234).

English-language **Librería Don Quijote** (Av. Tulum 27, tel. 988/41294) and **La**
Bookstores **Surtidora** (Av. Tulum 17, tel. 988/41103) sell a variety of English- and Spanish-language books.

Travel Agencies Cancún-based agencies include **Ceiba Tours** (Av. Nader 146,
and Tour Operators tel. 988/41962 or 988/42062), **Intermar Caribe** (Calle Cereza 37 at Av. Bonampak, S.M. 2A, tel. 988/44266), **Turismo Aviomar** (Calle Venado 30, S.M. 20, tel. 988/46742), and **Viajes Bojórquez** (Calle Tulipanes 101-G, tel. 988/45892).

Arriving and Departing by Plane

Airport **Cancún International Airport** is 16 kilometers (9 miles) south-
and Airlines west of the heart of Cancún City, 10 kilometers (6 miles) from the southernmost point of the hotel zone. **Aeromexico** (tel. 800/ 237–6639) flies nonstop from Houston and New York. **American** (tel. 800/433–7300) has nonstop service from its hub in Dallas and from Miami. **Continental** (tel. 800/231–0856) offers daily service from Houston and New York. **Mexicana**'s (tel. 800/531– 7921) nonstops depart from Chicago, Dallas, Denver, Los Angeles, Miami, New York, San Antonio, San Francisco, and Tampa. **Northwest** (tel. 800/225–2525) flies direct from Tampa. **Pan Am** (tel. 800/221–1111) flies from Miami. **United** (tel. 800/ 241–6522) flies to Cancún from Chicago and Washington. **AeroCancún** (tel. 212/679–8360) and **LaTur** (tel. 800/32– LATUR)—New York–based Mexican charter companies—run charters from Los Angeles, New York, and Orlando.

Between the Airport Amber-colored vans or collective taxis called *combis* provide
and Hotels transportation from the airport to hotels for about $2 per person, depending on the exact destination. Private taxis to downtown or the hotel zone run about $14; from downtown or the hotel zone to the airport, they charge $8 and up.

For those traveling to Isla Mujeres, collective taxis will drive you to the ferries at Puerto Juárez and Punta Sam for under $10.

Arriving and Departing by Car or Bus

By Car Cancún is at the end of Route 180, which goes from Matamoros on the Texas border to Campeche, Mérida, and Valladolid. The road trip from Texas to Cancún can take up to three days. Cancún can also be reached from the south via Route 307, which passes through Chetumal and Belize. Gas stations on these roads are few in number, so try to keep your tank filled.

By Bus The bus terminal (Av. Tulum and Av. Uxmal, tel. 988/41378 or 988/43948) downtown serves first-class buses making the trip from Mexico City and first- and second-class buses arriving in Cancún from Puerto Morelos, Playa del Carmen, Tulum, Chetumal, Cobá, Valladolid, Chichén Itzá, and Mérida. Public buses (Route 8) make the trip out to Puerto Juárez and Punta Sam for the ferries to Isla Mujeres.

Getting Around

Motorized transport of some sort is necessary, since the island is somewhat spread out. Public bus service is good and taxis are relatively inexpensive.

When you first visit Cancún City (downtown), you may be confused by the layout. There are four principal avenues: Tulum and Yaxchilán, which run north–south; and Uxmal and Cobá, running east–west. Streets bounded by those avenues and running perpendicular to them are actually horseshoe-shaped, so you will find two parallel streets named *Tulipanes*, for instance. However, street numbers or even street names are not of much use in Cancún; the proximity to landmarks, such as specific hotels, is the preferred way of giving directions.

By Bus Public buses run between the hotel zone and downtown from 6 AM to midnight; the cost is P$1,000. There are bus stops, but drivers can also be flagged down along Paseo Kukulcán. Avoid public buses before 10 AM and after 6–8 PM, because these are rush hours for the local workers and the crowds make this a prime time for pickpocketers.

By Car and Moped Renting a car for your stay in Cancún is probably an unnecessary expense, entailing tips for valet parking, as well as gasoline and rather costly rental rates (on a par with those in any major resort area around the world). However, if you plan to do some exploring, using Cancún as a base, the roads are excellent within a 100-kilometer (62-mile) radius.

Car Rentals Rental cars are available at the airport or from any of a dozen agencies in town, and most are standard-shift subcompacts and jeeps; air-conditioned cars with automatic transmissions should be reserved in advance. Rental agencies include **Avis** (tel. 988/42328 or 988/42147 at the airport, 988/30828 at Hotel Viva, or 988/30803 at Galería Mayfair); **Budget** (tel. 988/40730 or 988/40204, with offices at the airport and at the Galería Mayfair and Plaza Caracol malls); **Econo-Rent** (tel. 988/42147 at the airport, 988/41826 or 988/41435 at Calle Tulipanes 16); or **National** (tel. 988/49908 on Av. Chichén Itzá, between Avs. Uxmal and Tulum). The **Car Rental Association** (tel. 988/40616) can help you arrange a rental as well.

Moped Rentals Mopeds and scooters are also available throughout the island. While fun, they are risky, and there is no insurance available for the driver or the vehicle. The accident rate is high, especially downtown, which is considered too congested for novice moped users.

By Taxi Taxis to the ferries at Punta Sam or Puerto Juárez cost $5–$16 or more; between the hotel zone and downtown, $6 and up; and within the hotel zone, $2–$4, depending on the distance, your negotiating skills, and whether you pick up the taxi in front of the hotel or go onto the avenue to hail a green city taxi (the latter will be cheaper). Taxis may be called in advance (tel. 988/30237). Also, large, late-model air-conditioned cars with English-speaking chauffeurs may be hired through hotel travel desks.

By Ship Boats leave Puerto Juárez and Punta Sam (both north of Cancún City) for Isla Mujeres every couple of hours.

Telephones

Local telephone prefixes have recently changed to "988." Ladatel (the Mexican long-distance phone service) phones, which enable you to pay for calls by credit card, are now located in many hotels and on the streets (including Avenida Tulum downtown, opposite the San Francisco de Asis supermarket). There is also a long-distance phone booth at Avenida Sunyaxchén 51. Direct-dial international calls can be made through AT&T operators from most of the hotels on Paseo Kukulcán, but the hotels also charge $3–$5 per call extra for this service. Bypassing the Mexican phone system is worthwhile, however, even if it means calling collect, because of the 60% tax on overseas calls.

Mail

The **post office** (Av. Yaxchilán at S.M. 28, tel. 988/41418) is open weekdays 8–5, Saturday 9–1. Mail can be received here if marked "Lista de Correos, Cancún, QR 77500, México." Bear in mind, however, that postal service to and from Mexico is extremely slow and may take two weeks or more. If you have an American Express card, you can have mail sent to you at the **American Express Cancún Office** (c/o Hotel América, Suite A, Av. Tulum, Cancún, QR 77500, tel. 988/41999); the office is open weekdays 10–1 and 3–5.

Guided Tours

There are no guided tours of Cancún per se, because other than several tiny Mayan ruins, there is virtually no sightseeing on the island. However, you may wish to take a tour to the surrounding islands, the beaches along the Cancún–Tulum corridor (Akumal is the best known), or the Mayan ruins on the peninsula.

Cruises A lobster-dinner cruise on board the 62-foot vessel *Columbus* (tel. 988/31488 or 988/31021) includes a full lobster or steak dinner, open bar, and dancing for $46; the boat departs the Royal Mayan Yacht Club Monday–Saturday, and sails from 4:30 to 7:30. A "Pirate's Night" cruise on *El Tropical* (tel. 988/31021 or 988/31488) goes to Treasure Island on Isla Mujeres and departs the Playa Langosta Tropical Dock Monday–Saturday at 5:30 PM; the $39 price includes a beach cookout, drinks, music, and entertainment. Reservations are necessary. **Mexico's Beach Fiesta** (tel. 988/46656 or 988/46742), on board a triple-decker boat that sails from Playa Linda pier, features live music, a buffet dinner with open bar, and a comedy show. Children are not allowed on these cruises because alcohol is served. **Asterix Tours** (tel. 988/45328) has a cruise to Nichupté Lagoon that includes lunch, an open bar, and two hours' snorkeling (with gear) around the coral reefs at Punta Nizuc. Departure is at 10 AM from Villa Cerdeña Marina, and there is a 50% discount for children. **Nautibus** (tel. 988/31004 or 988/33216), or the "floating submarine," offers a 1–1½-hour lagoon and Caribbean-reef cruise that departs the Hotel San Marino dock daily at 10, noon, 2, and 4; the $22 price includes music and drinks.

Air Tours A $45 seaplane ride over the lagoons and Caribbean reefs departs from **Pelican Pier** (Paseo Kukulcán, Km 5.5, tel. 988/30315 or 988/31935), across from the Casa Maya. A 15-minute helicopter ride can be arranged by contacting **Heliservicio Campeche** (Paseo Kukulcán, Km 9, tel. 988/31366 or 988/31820, ext. 86), at the Cancún Clipper Club, for $35 per person (minimum two people). Private tours to Tulum, Xel-Há, and Isla Mujeres can also be arranged but tend to run around $500 for one hour.

Special-Interest **Aeroquetzal** (Plaza del Sol, Av. Yaxchilán 31-9, tel. 988/44969 or 988/44119), a small Guatemalan carrier, flies between Cancún and Guatemala City, continuing on to Flores and the ruins at Tikal, for $270 round-trip.

Intermar Caribe (tel. 988/44266) offers tours (Monday–Saturday 8–8) on horseback through the jungle to unexcavated ruins. The price includes beer, soft drinks, and a cockfight.

Exploring

The island of Cancún, which is shaped roughly like the numeral 7, is divided into two zones, with the hotel zone constituting the much larger of the two and occupying both legs of the 7. Picture the horizontal leg as extending east from the mainland into the Caribbean; Punta Cancún is where the vertical leg takes over, going north–south. Hotel development began at the north end (close to the mainland), headed east toward Punta Cancún, and is slowly moving south to Punta Nizuc, where the tip of the seven almost joins up again with the mainland. The other zone— Cancún City or downtown Cancún, known as *el centro*—is actually 4 kilometers (2½ miles) west of the hotel zone on the mainland. The 7 is separated from the mainland by a system of four lagoons: Nichupté, the largest (about 29 sq. km/18 sq. mi), containing both fresh and salt water; Bojórquez, at the juncture of the two legs of the 7; del Amor; and Río Inglés. North of the horizontal leg lies Bahía de Mujeres, the 9-kilometer- (5½-mile-) wide bay that separates Cancún from Isla Mujeres. Regularly placed kilometer markers on the roadside help indicate where you are; they go from Km 1 on the mainland, near downtown, to Km 20 at Punta Nizuc.

Paseo Kukulcán is the main drag in the hotel zone, and because most of the 7 is less than a kilometer wide, both the Caribbean and the lagoons can be seen from either side of it. The hotel zone consists entirely of hotels, restaurants and shopping complexes, marinas, and time-share condominiums; there are no residential areas as such. It's not the sort of place you can get to know by walking. Paseo Kukulcán does not even have sidewalks but is punctuated by driveways with steep inclines turning into the hotels, most of which are set at least 100 yards from the road. The lagoon side of the boulevard consists of scrubby stretches of land, many of them covered with construction cranes, alternating with marinas, shopping centers, and restaurants. What is scenic about Cancún is the pleasurable contrast between the vivid turquoise-and-violet sea and the blinding alabaster-white sands.

Numbers in the margin correspond to points of interest on the Cancún map.

Cancún's scenery includes a pleasant contrast between the vivid turquoise-and-blue sea and the blinding white-alabaster white sand. Otherwise there is little else for the sightseer to focus on except for a few intriguing sites tucked away among

the modern hotels. Heading north from Punta Nizuc and keeping your eye on the seaside, as many as eight hotels are situated within the space of 1 kilometer: one right after the next, with
❶ barely any distance between them. The small **Ruinas del Rey** are located on the lagoon side at Km 17, roughly opposite El Pueblito and Playa de Oro (formerly the Holiday Inn Crowne Plaza) hotels; look for the small wood sign. First mentioned in a 16th-century travelogue and then, in 1842 when they were sighted by American explorer John Lloyd Stephens and his draftsman, Frederick Catherwood, the ruins were finally explored by archaeologists in 1910, though excavations did not begin until 1954. In 1975 archaeologists, along with the Mexican government, began the restoration of El Rey and San Miguelito (*see* below).

Although El Rey is not particularly impressive, it may be worth a look, if only to say you've seen an archaeological ruin. It is noted primarily for its unusual architecture: two main plazas bounded by two streets. Most of the other Mayan cities, which were not in any sense planned but had developed over centuries, contained one plaza with a number of ceremonial satellites and few streets. The pyramid, topped by a platform, houses stucco paintings inside its vault. Skeletons found buried both at the apex and at the base indicate that the site may have been a royal burial ground. Originally named Kin Ich Ahau Bonil, Maya for "King of the Solar Countenance," the 2nd–3rd-century BC site was linked to astronomical practices in the ancient Mayan culture. *Km 17, lagoon side. Admission free. Open daily 8–5.*

About half a kilometer away from El Rey—between Km 16 and 17—but on the east side of Kukulcán, is another Mayan site:
❷ **San Miguelito,** a very small stone building (about the size of a shack) with a number of columns about 4 feet high. There is no signage so if you take a taxi, make sure the driver knows how to reach the site.

❸ Another ruin, **Yamil Lu'um** (meaning hilly land), stands on the highest point on Cancún and is situated at Km 12, to the left of the Sheraton. A small sign at the hotel will direct you to the dirt path leading to the site. Although it's composed of two structures—one probably a temple, the other probably a lighthouse—this is the smallest of Cancún's ruins. Discovered in 1842 by John Lloyd Stephens, the remains date from the late 13th or early 14th century.

Just after Km 12, near the Melia Turquesa, Sheraton, and Radisson hotels, you'll come in sight of Laguna Bojórquez on your left; buildings span nearly the entire length of the spit of land that encloses the lagoon. On the far side of that spit, along the road that forks to the right (between Km 6 and Km 7), is
❹ **Pok-Ta-Pok** golf course, whose Mayan name means ballgame. Situated on the 12th hole is yet another Mayan ruin, consisting of two platforms and vestiges of other buildings.

Approaching the northern tip of the vertical leg of the 7—
❺ Punta Cancún—you'll pass **Playa Chac Mool** at Km 10, one of the few public beaches on Cancún, with restaurants and changing areas. Leaving the beach, you'll round the corner to the bay side (Bahía de Mujeres). Calmer waters prevail here, as opposed to the sea side, where you can also swim, and which has the more beautiful beaches. On the ocean side of the tip of

Cancún

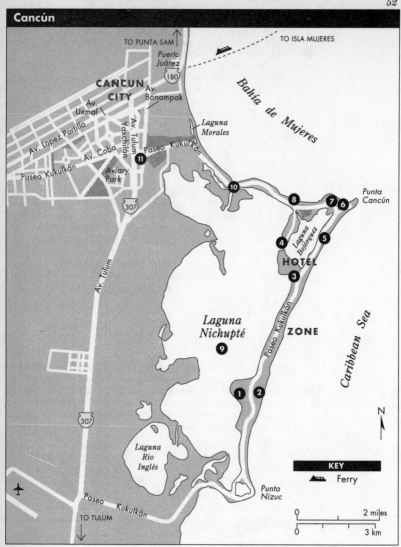

TO PUNTA SAM

Puerto
Juárez
180

TO ISLA MUJERES

**CANCÚN
CITY**

Av.
Bonampak

Av.
Uxmal

Av. López Portillo

Av. Tulum
Yaxchilán

Paseo Kukulkán

*Laguna
Morales*

Bahía de Mujeres

Av. Cobá

Aviary
Park

11

307

10

8

7 6

Punta
Cancún

4

5

*Laguna
Bojorquez*

HOTEL

3

Paseo Kukulkán

Caribbean Sea

Av. Tulum

*Laguna
Nichupté*

9

ZONE

307

1 2

*Laguna
Río
Inglés*

N

KEY

Ferry

Punta
Nizuc

0   2 miles

0   3 km

Paseo Kukulkán

TO TULUM

Bullring, **11**
Convention Center, **6**
Laguna Nichupté, **9**
Playa Chac Mool, **5**
Playa Linda, **10**
Playa Tortugas, **8**
Pok-Ta-Pok, **4**
Ruinas del Rey, **1**

San Miguelito, **2**
Shopping Malls, **7**
Yamil Lu'um, **3**

Punta Cancún, look for the fourth Mayan ruin, a tiny shrine that is fairly insignificant except that it's been cleverly incorporated into the architecture of the **Hotel Camino Real.**

⑥ After the beach, you'll come upon a roundabout at Km 9, where the **convention center** (tel. 988/30199)—part of El Parián shopping complex—is located and where you can see the *ballet folklórico* (*see* The Arts and Nightlife, below).

⑦ Between El Parián and the Stouffer Presidente—Cancún's first hotel—is a ½-mile-long string of **shopping malls,** including Plaza Caracol, La Mansión–Costa Blanca, Plaza Lagunas, Plaza Terramar, and Galería Mayfair.

⑧ Right beyond the Stouffer Presidente, at Km 7, is **Playa Tortugas,** the other beach where those staying at the beachless downtown hotels are welcome. To the south, on your left, you'll **⑨** reach **Laguna Nichupté,** the center for most of the water-sports activities. Also in the lagoon are swampy areas that host mangrove trees and more than 200 species of bird life. Ask your hotel to arrange for a boat and guide.

⑩ Continue along Paseo Kukulcán past the numerous hotels. Just before you cross the causeway onto the mainland, at the Hotel Calinda, you'll come to **Playa Linda,** from which ferries depart for Isla Mujeres. The less expensive public ferries leave for the island from Puerto Juárez, about 9 kilometers or 6 miles farther west.

As you enter downtown Cancún, Paseo Kukulcán turns into Avenida Cobá at the spot where it meets **Avenida Tulum,** the main thoroughfare and the location of many restaurants and shops (*see* Shopping, below). Life-size reproductions of ancient Mexican art, including the Aztec calendar stone, giant Olmec head, the Atlantids of Tula, and the Maya Chac Mool (reclining rain god), line the grassy strip dividing Tulum's northbound and southbound lanes. Visitors looking for shopping bargains, however, generally find better prices if they stick to the parallel Avenida Yaxchilán.

⑪ The Cancún **bullring,** a block south of the Pemex station, hosts year-round bullfights and wrestling matches. *Paseo Kukulcán at Av. Bonampak, tel. 988/70681 or 988/70679. Bullfight admission: $27, Wed. 3:30 PM. Wrestling admission: $14, Sat. 9:30 PM.*

Shopping

Resort wear and handicrafts are the most popular purchases in Cancún, but the prices rank among the highest in the country and the selection is quite predictable, so if you are traveling elsewhere in Mexico you'd do best to wait. Still, you can find a respectable variety of Mexican handicrafts ranging from blown glass and hand-woven textiles to leather to jewelry made from local coral and tortoiseshell. (Because it comes from endangered species, tortoiseshell products cannot be brought into the United States and several other countries.)

Caveat emptor applies as much to Cancún as it does to the "bargain" electronics stores on Fifth Avenue in New York City or in Hong Kong. Throughout Mexico you will often get better prices by paying with cash (pesos or dollars) or traveler's checks. This is because Mexican merchants are averse to the commissions charged by credit card companies, especially American Express, and frequently tack that commission—6% or more—onto your bill. If you can do without the plastic, you may even get the 15% sales tax lopped off.

Bargaining is expected in Cancún, but mostly in the market. Suggest half the asking price and slowly come up, but do not pay more than 70% of the quoted price. Shopping around is a good idea, too, because the crafts market is very competitive. But closely examine the merchandise you are purchasing: Some "authentic" items—particularly jewelry—may actually be shoddy imitations.

In Cancún, shopping hours are generally weekdays 10–1 and 4–7, although more and more stores are staying open throughout the day rather than closing for siesta between 1 and 4 PM. Many shops keep Saturday morning hours, and some are now open on Sunday until 1 PM. Shops in the malls tend to be open weekdays from 10 AM to 8–10 PM.

Shopping Districts, Streets, Malls

Shopping can be roughly categorized by location: In the malls and in-house boutiques in the hotel zone, prices are generally—but not always—higher than in the shops and markets downtown. However, tourists shopping downtown are often conned into paying outrageous prices for what is essentially junk.

Downtown The wide variety of shops downtown along Avenida Tulum (between Avenidas Cobá and Uxmal) and Avenida Cobá (between Avenidas Bonampak and Tulum) includes the **Plaza México** (Av. Tulum 200, tel. 988/43506), a cluster of 50 handicrafts shops. Next door, visit **Pama** (Av. Tulum and Calle Lluvia, tel. 988/41839), a department store offering clothing, beachwear, sports gear, toiletries, liquor, and *latería* (crafts made of tin). Also on Tulum is the oldest and largest of the crafts markets, **Ki Huic** (Av. Tulum, between Bancomer and Banco Atlantico, no phone), which is open daily from 9 AM to 10 PM and houses about 100 vendors. Nearby is **Margarita's** (Av. Tulum 10, tel. 988/42359), one of the better silver shops.

Hotel Zone Fully air-conditioned malls (known as *centros comerciales*), as streamlined and well kept as any in the United States or Canada, sell everything from fashion clothing, beachwear, and sportswear to jewelry, household items, video games, and leather goods.

Flamingo Plaza (Km 11, across from the Hotel Flamingo, tel. 988/32855 or 988/32945), the latest addition, includes a toy store, full-service gym, bank, exchange house, travel agency, real estate office, and several silver shops.

El Parián (Km 9, opposite Cancún Clipper Club, tel. 988/30203) is part of the convention center complex and one of the older malls in Cancún. Housed inside are an information center, folk art shops (including Victor's, reputed to be the best such shop in town), a liquor store, a restaurant, and a pizzeria. While at the convention center, venture into the three buildings housing the crafts market (*mercado artesanal*), where bargaining is a must.

Just across from the convention center is the **Plaza Caracol I & II** (tel. 988/32805 or 988/32450), the largest and most contemporary mall in Cancún, with nearly 300 shops and boutiques, including two pharmacies, art galleries, and folk art and jewelry shops, as well as cafés and restaurants. Fashion boutiques include Benetton, Fiorucci, Gucci, and Ralph Lauren; in all these stores, prices are half those in their U.S. counterparts. Aca Joe, a chain store excelling in trendy beachwear, and Explora, one of the more interesting shops selling ecology-minded T-shirts and towels, are also housed here.

Plaza Nautilus (Km 3.5, lagoon side, tel. 988/31903), the mall closest to downtown and a favorite of American shoppers, has a bookstore, liquor store, art gallery, perfumery, folk art shop, and Super Deli, as well as about 65 other shops.

Other malls include the pink stucco **La Mansíon–Costa Blanca** (just south of Plaza Caracol, tel. 988/41272), which specializes in designer clothing and has several restaurants, a bank, and a liquor store. **Plaza Lagunas** (tel. 988/30955), located next to Plaza Caracol, is dedicated primarily to sportswear shops, such as Ellesse and Ocean Pacific. **Plaza Terramar** (tel. 988/31588), opposite the Hotel Fiesta Americana, sells beachwear, souvenirs, and folk art, and has a restaurant and a pharmacy.

Specialty Shops

Galleries **Orbe** (tel. 988/31333), in the Plaza Caracol mall, specializes in sculptures and paintings by contemporary Mexican artists; **La Galería** (no phone), in the Costa Blanca mall, is both the showroom and studio of Gilberto Silva; **Las Palmeras** (tel. 988/31415), also at Costa Blanca, and **Akakena** (tel. 988/30539), by the convention center, display replicas of Mayan art, temple rubbings, and contemporary painting and sculpture. Temporary exhibits are also displayed and sold in the **Galerie du Mexique** (tel. 988/30448) in Paseo Kukulcán at Avenida Bonampak, downtown. The **Galería Sergio Bustamante** (Hyatt Cancún Caribe, tel. 988/30044), in the Hyatt Cancún Caribe, focusing on the works of this popular contemporary Mexican artist, also features pieces for sale.

Grocery Stores Major supermarkets include **Comercial Mexicano** (Av. López Portillo at Libramiento Kabah, tel. 988/71202 or 988/71303); **San Francisco de Asís** (Av. Tulum, S.M. 5, at Av. Xel-Há, tel. 988/42812); **Super Deli** (Av. Tulum at Xcaret, tel. 988/41122; open 24 hours); and **Comercial Mexicana de la Glorieta** (Av. Tulum, S.M. 2, where it crosses Av. Uxmal, tel. 988/71303).

Sports and Fitness

Golf The main course is at **Pok-Ta-Pok** (Paseo Kukulcán between Km 6 and Km 7, tel. 988/30871), a private club with fine views of both sea and lagoon, whose 18 holes were designed by Robert Trent Jones, Sr. The club also has a practice green, swimming pool, tennis courts, and restaurant. The greens fees are $27; electric cart, $20; clubs, $12; pull cart, $7; caddies, $7; and golf clinics, $23 per hour. Playing hours are 6 AM–4 PM, but you'll see the most action 11–2, when the pros are most likely to be around. There are also a 9-hole golf course at the **Oasis Hotel** (Paseo Kukulcán, Km 20, tel. 50225) and a small 5-hole "executive course" at the **Hotel Melia Cancún** (Paseo Kukulcán, Km 12, tel. 988/51160).

Health Clubs Most of the deluxe hotels have their own health clubs. There are, however, two gyms in Cancún: Both **Gold's Gym** (Plaza Flamingo, tel. 988/32933 or 988/32966) and **Michel's Gym** (Av. Sayil 66, S.M. 4, tel. 988/42394 or 988/42550) feature modern equipment and exercise facilities.

Jogging Although to some people the idea of jogging in the intense heat of Cancún sounds like a form of masochism, fanatics should know that there is a 14-kilometer (9-mile) track extending along half the island, running parallel to Paseo Kukulcán from the Punta Cancún area into Cancún City.

Water Sports Water sports—particularly snorkeling, scuba diving, and deep-sea fishing—are popular pastimes in Cancún, because some 500 species of tropical fish, including sailfish, bluefin, marlin, barracuda, and red snapper, live in the adjacent waters. Sports centers and marinas (which provide gear and charters) are scattered around the island, both at hotels and on the lagoon side, where most of the water-related activities take place. Other popular activities include parasailing, sailboarding, waterskiing, sailing, and jetskiing.

Snorkeling gear can be rented for $7–$8 per day. Sailboards are available for $25 an hour; classes go for about $20 an hour. Parasailing costs $30 for 8 minutes; waterskiing, $55–$60; jetskiing, $25–$30. Hobie Cats rent for about $15 per hour, without instruction.

Fishing Deep-sea fishing boats and other gear may be chartered from outfitters for about $180 for four hours, $270 for six hours, and $360 for eight hours. Charters generally include a captain, a first mate, gear, bait, and beverages. **Pez Vela** (tel. 988/30992), **Avioturismo** (tel. 988/30315), and **Barracuda** (tel. 988/44551) are just a few of the companies that operate large fishing fleets.

The newest and most ambitious marina, **San Buenaventura**, situated on the mainland between Bahía de Mujeres and Laguna Nichupté, is scheduled to be open by 1992 and will be located in downtown Cancún, near the bullring. Other marinas include **Aqua Tours Dive Center and Marina** (tel. 988/30400 or 988/31137), **Aqua-quin** (tel. 988/30100), **Club Lagoon** (tel. 988/31111), **Mauna Loa** (tel. 988/30072), and **Playa Blanca** (tel. 988/30606).

Sailboarding Although some people sailboard on the ocean side in the summer, activity is limited primarily to the bay between Cancún and Isla Mujeres. If you visit the island in July, don't miss the National Windsurfing Tournament (tel. 988/43212), in which athletes test their mettle. The **International Windsurfer Sailing School** (tel. 988/42023), located at Playa Tortugas, rents equipment and gives lessons.

Snorkeling and Scuba Diving Snorkeling is best at Punta Nizuc, Punta Cancún, and Playa Tortugas, although you should be especially careful of the strong currents at the latter. Some charter-fishing companies offer a two-tank scuba dive for about $50. **Barracuda** (tel. 988/44551), for example, runs two-hour snorkeling tours of the Belize Barrier Reef, a 40-minute boat ride from the Marina Punta del Este, opposite the Hyatt Cancún Caribe. As the name implies, **Scuba Cancún** (tel. 988/31011) specializes in diving trips and offers NAUI, CMAS, and PADI instruction. **Aqua Tours**

Dive Center and Marina (tel. 988/30400 or 988/31137) offers scuba tours and a resort course.

Beaches

Cancún Island is one long, continuous beach, although about 7 kilometers (4 miles) of beachfront were eroded by Hurricane Gilbert in 1988. Some stretches lost as much as 40 meters (131 feet) to the storm. However, if you've never been here, you won't know the difference.

By law the entire coast of Mexico is federal property and open to the public; in practice, however, hotel security guards keep peddlers off the beaches, and hotel guests are easily identified by the color of the towels they place on their beach lounge chairs. Most properties have lifeguards on duty, but drownings do occur. Overall, the beaches on the windward stretch of the island—those closest to the city, facing the Bahía de Mujeres—are best for swimming; farther out, the undertow can be tricky. Keep away from the water when red danger flags fly by the sea; yellow flags indicate that you should proceed with caution; green or blue means waters are calm. In any case, you should always avoid swimming off lonely stretches of beach. One last word, which should be obvious to devoted beach goers but bears remembering under a tropical sun: Avoid prolonged exposure during peak sunlight hours (noon–4) and always use sunscreen or sunblock.

Two popular areas, **Playa Tortugas** (Km 7) and **Chac Mool** (Km 10), have restaurants and changing areas, making them especially appealing for vacationers who are staying at the beachless downtown hotels. Be careful of strong waves at Chac Mool, where it's tempting to walk far out into the delightfully shallow water.

Dining

By Judith Glynn

At last count, there were more than 1,200 restaurants in Cancún, but—according to one profiting restaurateur—only about 100 are worth their salt, so to speak. Finding the right restaurant in Cancún is not easy. The downtown restaurants that line the noisy Paseo Kukulcán often have tables spilling onto pedestrian-laden sidewalks; gas fumes and gawking tourists tend to detract from the romantic outdoor-café ambience.

One key to good dining in Cancún is to find the haunts where locals go for good Yucatán-style food prepared by the experts. Seafood prepared with fresh lime juice and authentic Mexican specialties highlight many menus, but the experience is furthered by added touches, such as waiters artistically preparing meals at tableside; exotic flaming cocktails; and good, attentive service. A cheap and filling trend in Cancún's dining scene is the sumptuous buffet breakfasts offered by an increasing number of restaurants on the island. These buffets run about $5, and when eaten late in the morning can actually last you until dinner time (usually between 7 and 10 PM). Another hint: Many Very Expensive and Expensive restaurants feature floor shows during peak months (mid-December–late March). Usually there are two seatings nightly, each including entertainment and dinner; reservations are advised, since the shows draw crowds.

Generally speaking, dress is casual here, but many restaurants will not admit diners with bare feet, short shorts, or no shirts. The "casual but neat" code implies that a restaurant is a bit upscale and that slightly fancier attire is acceptable.

When reviewing Cancún's restaurants, we looked for places where your money will best be spent and your meal most enjoyed. It's important to note that although hotels make strong efforts to keep guests on the premises, you'll be paying exorbitant prices for what may well be an average meal. Therefore, only the truly exceptional hotel restaurants are listed, allowing for more comprehensive coverage of independently operated cafés. Unless otherwise stated, restaurants serve lunch and dinner daily.

Highly recommended restaurants are indicated by a star ★.

Category	Cost*
Very Expensive	over $35
Expensive	$25–$34
Moderate	$15–$24
Inexpensive	under $15

per person, excluding drinks, service, and the 15% sales tax

Very Expensive **Blue Bayou.** Six levels of snug dining areas, decorated in wood, rattan, bamboo, and flourishing greens, create the atmosphere for a memorable evening. Sounds from the cascading waterfall and waiters dressed in white pants and blue blazers further accent the sophisticated tone, set off by jazz that drifts in from the adjoining bar. Blackened meat, fish, and lobster—Cajun and Creole style—are featured on the menu, which is nicely balanced by a number of Mexican specialties. *Hyatt Cancún Caribe, Paseo Kukulcán, Hotel Zone, tel. 988/30044. Reservations advised. Dress: casual but neat. AE, MC, V. No lunch.*

★ **Bogart's.** Several theme rooms, complete with Persian rugs, swirling fans, velvet-cushioned banquettes, cloth-covered ceilings, fountains, and pools of shimmering water, remind diners of Casablanca or Marrakesh, Morocco. With captains sporting turbans and waiters with fezzes and white suits, the point is hard to miss. The menu features Lobster Three Wishes, a special in which lobster is presented three ways: Thermidor (cubed and mixed with a cream sauce and sprinkled with grated cheese), Newburg, and grilled. After dinner stop by the lounge for live piano music. *Paseo Kukulcán, Hotel Krystal, Hotel Zone, tel. 988/31133. Reservations required; seatings at 7 and 9:30. Dress: casual but neat. AE, MC, V. No lunch.*

Maxime. Although the management has changed again, the French chef and 19th-century French-country decor, with its ornate furnishings, remain. As part of the undertaking, it is hoped that the new proprietors will do something to get rid of the musty smell in the inside dining area. The outside terrace, with lush greenery and a fountain, makes for a relaxing lunch spot when it's open, during May, June, and July. Also during high season, tune into the sounds of piano and classical guitar. Year-round, the upstairs bar, with a billiard table, offers an alternative to sunbathing. *Calle Pez Volador 8, Hotel Zone, tel. 988/30438. Reservations suggested during high season. Dress: casual but neat. AE, MC, V.*

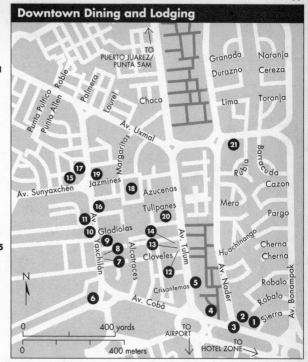

Downtown Dining and Lodging

Expensive **Casa Rolandi.** Authentic northern Italian and Swiss dishes are skillfully prepared by the Italian owner-chef, who grew up near the Swiss border. Homemade lasagna, baked in the large stucco ovens, and an ample salad bar make for a filling dinner. Understated pale-gray decor adds to the subdued ambience. *Plaza Caracol, Hotel Zone, tel. 988/31817. Reservations suggested during high season. Dress: casual. MC, V.*

Chac Mool. One of the few beachfront restaurants in the Hotel Zone, this establishment takes full advantage of the setting. Though the patio-style decor tends to be a bit unfriendly and not overly comfortable, the piped-in classical music, complemented by the sound of the surf, attracts the repeat clientele. Homemade rolls shaped as treble clefs emphasize the musical theme, while a sculpture of Chac Mool, the Mayan god of rain and plenty, decorates the front lawn. *Paseo Kukulcán, next to the Aristos Hotel, Hotel Zone, tel. 988/31107. Reservations suggested. Dress: casual but neat. MC, V. No lunch.*

du Mexique. The combination of an upstairs art gallery and a restaurant that serves Mexican fare with a nouvelle twist presents a creative alternative for diners who are looking for something new. The decor features dark-wood floors, a vaulted white stucco ceiling, and sleek contemporary design. *Av. Cobá 44, Downtown, tel. 988/41077. Reservations suggested. Dress: casual but neat. AE, MC, V. No lunch.*

★ **El Mexicano.** One of Cancún's largest restaurants seats 320 for a folkloric dinner show in a beautifully decorated, shrimp-colored, expansive room resembling the patio of a hacienda. De-

Dining

Augustus Caesar, **12**
Blue Bayou, **19**
Bogart's, **17**
Captain's Cove, **3, 26**
Carlos 'n Charlies, **6**
Casa Rolandi, **13**
Chac Mool, **18**
Gypsy's, **20**
Hacienda El
Mortero, **17**
Jalapeños, **8**
Karl's Keller, **13**
Maxime, **5**
El Mexicano, **12**
Savios, **13**
Splash, **7**

Lodging

Albergue CREA, **1**
Aston Solaris, **29**
Cancún Playa, **27**
Cancún Viva, **10**
Conrad Cancún, **30**
Fiesta Americana
Cancún, **11**
Fiesta Americana
Condesa, **23**
Fiesta Americana
Coral Beach
Cancún, **14**
Hyatt Cancún Caribe
Villas & Resort, **19**
Hyatt Regency
Cancún, **16**
Marriot
Casamagna, **21**
Meliá Cancún, **22**
Oasis, **24**
Omni Cancún, **25**
Plaza Las Glorias, **2**
Royal Solaris, **31**
Stouffer Presidente, **9**
Suites Brisas, **28**
Villas Tacul, **4**
Westin Camino
Real, **15**

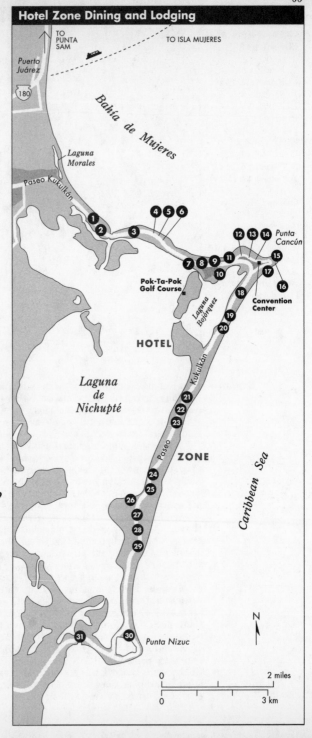

Hotel Zone Dining and Lodging

tails such as elaborately hand-carved chairs created by Indians from central Mexico and numerous regional Mexican dishes convey a feeling of authenticity. Try the *empanxonostle* (steamed lobster, shrimp, fish, and herbs); it promises to be as extravagant as El Mexicano's surroundings. When the final show ends, you're invited to dance until midnight. *La Mansión Costa Blanca Shopping Center, Hotel Zone, tel. 988/32220. Reservations required; show begins at 7:30. Dress: casual but neat. AE, MC, V.*

Hacienda El Mortero. Pampering waiters, strolling mariachi, lush hanging plants, fig trees, and candlelight make this reproduction plantation home a very popular spot to dine. The menu offers a selection of country cooking, and the steaks and ribs are first-class. *Paseo Kukulcán, Hotel Krystal, Hotel Zone, tel. 988/31133 or 800/231–9860. Reservations required for 7 and 9:30 seatings. Dress: casual but neat. AE, MC, V. No lunch.*

La Habichuela. This charmer—once an elegant home—is perfect for hand-holding romantics or anyone looking for a relaxed, private atmosphere. The candlelighted garden, with white, wrought-iron chairs, crushed stones, and thick, tropical greenery, exudes peacefulness, while a statue of Pakal, the Mayan god of astronomy and culture, surveys all. Try the *cocobichuela*—lobster and shrimp in a light Indian sauce served on a bed of rice inside a coconut—a specialty of the house. *Margaritas 25, Downtown, tel. 988/43158. Reservations suggested. Dress: casual but neat. MC, V.*

Savio's. Sea-green and peach decor, a white circular staircase, floor-to-ceiling windows, and a sleek design with lots of greenery make this restaurant a fresh, lively spot for lunch. For dinner, candlelight and guitar and flute music create a romantic setting. Filling out the menu are homemade pastas and seafood. *Plaza Caracol, Hotel Zone, tel. 988/32085. Reservations accepted. Dress: casual for lunch; casual but neat for dinner. AE, MC, V. Closed New Year's Day.*

Moderate **Augustus Caesar.** In spite of the shopping-center location and the constant stream of shoppers passing by, this restaurant produces classic Italian specialties with an emphasis on seafood in a sophisticated, impressive setting. The gray, pink, and black color scheme, enhanced by white stucco columns, tile floors, and soft jazz, creates a surprisingly lovely ambience at night. *La Mansión Costa Blanca Shopping Center, Hotel Zone, tel. 988/33384. Reservations suggested. Dress: casual. AE, MC, V.*

Bucanero. Quiet dining in a candlelighted marine atmosphere is the drawing card for this seafood restaurant, and the seafood—especially lobster specialties—is tops. For starters, try the lobster bisque or black bean soup, and round the meal out with the seafood combination, which includes lobster in garlic sauce, shrimp and squid brochette, and a fish fillet. Piano music played throughout the evening and waiters dressed as pirates add character to the place. *Av. Nader, Downtown, tel. 988/ 42280. Reservations accepted. Dress: casual but neat. MC, V. No lunch.*

Café Amsterdam. The Dutch wife–British husband team brings lots of flavor to this combination bakery, salad bar, and bistro. Visitors and locals find Amsterdam a bright and cheery lunch spot that serves a hearty meal at a low fixed price. Candles and flowers are brought out in the evenings for an intimate bistro effect. This café opens at 7AM, so it is also a good meeting place for breakfast. *Av. Yaxchilán 70, Downtown, tel. 988/44098. No reservations. Dress: casual. AE, MC, V. Closed Mon.*

Captain's Cove. Both waterfront locations feature popular breakfast buffets served under palapa roofs amid tropical decor and furnishings, such as rattan chairs and palm trees. The restaurant near the Casa Maya Hotel overlooks the Caribbean Sea toward Isla Mujeres; the other is situated beside the Nichupté Lagoon. Both present lunch and dinner menus filled with seafood dishes and charbroiled steaks. Parents appreciate the children's menu, featuring hamburgers and brownies. *Lagoonside, across from the Royal Mayan Hotel, tel. 988/50016; beachside, next to Casa Maya Hotel, tel. 988/30669. No reservations. Dress: casual. MC, V.*

★ **Carlos 'n Charlie's.** A lively atmosphere, a terrific view overlooking the lagoon, and good food make this restaurant suitable for just about everyone. You'll never run out of bric-a-brac to look at: The walls are catchalls with tons of photos; sombreros, bird cages, and wooden birds and animals hang from the ceilings. For dinner you may be tempted by the barbecued ribs sizzling on the open grill, or you may wish to try one of the steak or seafood specials. After your meal, dance off the calories under the stars at the Pier Dance Club. *Paseo Kukulcán, Km 5.5, Downtown, tel. 988/30846. No reservations. Dress: casual. AE, MC, V.*

Carrillo's. This restaurant, with a large, sweeping veranda and Mediterranean-style decor, features lobster specials including lobster brochette, thermidor, and Mexican style. Other house favorites include broiled red snapper smothered with ham, cheese, bacon, shrimp, and a red sauce, and one of the four ceviches. Carrillo's also provides lots of entertainment and festivities, beginning with happy hour from 6 to 8, and the musical trio that plays nightly. *Claveles 12, Downtown, tel. 988/41227. No reservations. Dress: casual. MC, V.*

El Pescador. It's first-come-first-served, with long lines, especially during high season. But people still flood into the open-air floors of this rustic Mexican-style restaurant with nautical touches. Heavy hitters on the menu include red snapper broiled with garlic and freshly-caught-lobster specials. For dessert consider sharing the cake filled with ice cream and covered with peaches and strawberry marmalade. *Tulipanes 28, Downtown, tel. 988/42673. No reservations. Dress: casual. MC, V. Closed Mon.*

★ **Gypsy's.** An added attraction at this all-time favorite restaurant is that it sits upon stilts and overlooks an illuminated lagoon where crocodiles and fish can be seen. The decor hints at Spain, and the two dinner shows (7:30 and 9:30) with flamenco dancers convey the message loud and clear. Don't pass up the paella prepared by a Spanish chef from León. *Paseo Kukulcán, Km 10.5, Hotel Zone, tel. 988/32015. Reservations suggested. Dress: casual. AE, MC, V. No lunch.*

Karl's Keller. The Bavarian atmosphere here offers a refreshing change of pace from the many seafood and Mexican restaurants on the island, and for breakfast this place really serves up a hearty meal. The German owner, who made the tables inside, also whips up a mean sauerbraten as well as other Old World specialties. Don't leave without trying the sausage. *Plaza Caracol, Hotel Zone, tel. 988/31104. No reservations. Dress: casual. MC, V.*

La Fonda Del Angel. This unpretentious restaurant in a Mexican colonial–style setting has walls that are painted pink, lemon, and aqua; wood beams and wrought-iron details add a bit more pizzazz. The menu, which includes a variety of Mexican dishes, features the special Fillet Angel (beef covered with melted cheese and mushroom sauce). During high season, the outside patio offers a quiet alternative. Live music is played nightly. *Av. Cobá 85, Downtown, tel. 988/43393. Reservations suggested. Dress: casual. AE, MC, V.*

La Parrilla. If you're looking for the place where local Mexicans—young and old—hang out, you've found it in this always jammed and busy downtown spot. Everything from the food to the bougainvillea and palapa roof is authentic. Popular dishes include the grilled beef with garlic sauce and the *tacos al pastor* (tacos with pork, pineapple, coriander, onion, and salsa). *Av. Yaxchilán 51, Downtown, tel. 988/45398. No reservations. Dress: casual. MC, V. No lunch; closed Christmas.*

Mi Ranchito. Don't come looking for privacy at this lively spot situated along a busy sidewalk, but come here for fun and you're guaranteed to find it. Serapes, piñatas, and straw sombreros hang from the ceiling, and a Mexican party every Saturday night provides a festive atmosphere. Meals are prepared by Mayan chefs who cook up a banana flambé crepe covered with flaming peaches and tequila tableside while dancing waiters balance trays of 20 drinks on their heads. *Av. Tulum 15, Downtown, tel. 988/47814. No reservations. Dress: casual. MC, V.*

Perico's. Find the antique car perched atop the palapa roof and you've found this zany, eclectic restaurant and bar. Saddles top bar stools, skeletons peek around corners, masks adorn the walls, and waiters in firemen's uniforms serve flaming desserts. The Mexican menu, including Pancho Villa (grilled beef with Mexican side dishes), is reliable, but the real reason to come here is the party atmosphere that begins nightly at 7 when the mariachi and marimba bands play. *Av. Yaxchilán 71, Downtown, tel. 988/43152. No reservations. Dress: casual. MC, V.*

Pizza Rolandi. Bright red-and-yellow decor, plants, wood beams, ceiling fans, and visible wood ovens have turned this otherwise simple sidewalk pizza place into a quick-dining treat. Ten homemade pasta dishes and 16 different pizzas—some with chicken or fish—make up a large part of the huge wooden menu that's slid across the floor from table to table. *Av. Cobá 12, Downtown, tel. 988/44047. No reservations. Dress: casual. MC, V.*

★ **Rosa Mexicano.** One of Cancún's prettiest Mexican colonial–style restaurants presents waiters dressed as *charros* (Mexican cowboys), pottery and embroidered wall hangings, floor tiles with floral designs, and a cozy, softly lighted atmosphere. For extra romance, make a reservation for the candlelighted patio. If you're in the mood for meat, try the *tibone especial* (T-bone steak with red-wine sauce); seafood lovers should try the *camarones al ajillo* (shrimp sautéed in olive oil and garlic, with chili peppers). *Calle Claveles 4, Downtown, tel. 988/46313. Reservations advised. Dress: casual. MC, V. No lunch.*

Splash. Good-quality art-deco furnishings set amid a purple-and-aqua color scheme and neon lights add to the sleek design of this restaurant. During high season, go upstairs to the large bar and terrace, where in the distance you can see the water. Downstairs offers a more intimate dining experience. You can't go wrong with any of the homemade pastas or the grilled bora-

bora fish with mango slices. *Paseo Kukulcán, Hotel Zone, no phone. No reservations. Dress: casual. MC, V. No lunch.*

Inexpensive **El Tacolete.** Only tacos are served here, and the standard order includes three. Mix and match fillings, but don't overlook the filet mignon taco. Bowls of sliced limes and salsa come with your order, in keeping with the very casual tone of this brightly tiled and comfortable place. *Av. Cobá, Downtown, no phone. No reservations. Dress: casual. MC, V.*

★ **Jalapeños.** Popular, inexpensive breakfast buffets, zany happy hours, and dancing under the stars to reggae music have made this place soar. Seven TV screens broadcast major sports events, while bartenders whip up tropical fruit drinks and margaritas to go along with jalapeños stuffed with shrimp or red snapper wrapped in a banana leaf and smothered with jalapeño sauce. *Paseo Kukulcán, Km 7, Hotel Zone, tel. 988/ 32896. No reservations. Dress: casual but neat. MC, V.*

Yamamoto. Formerly the Ashima restaurant until Hurricane Gilbert reduced it to a smaller, renamed version, this is still the place where locals and many Japanese visitors come for traditional Japanese dishes and the *Sushi Especial*, a combo of shellfish and local and imported fish. The unpretentious setting (with limited seating) inside and the outside patio, complete with Japanese lanterns shining on the potted palms, offer a subdued, relaxed atmosphere. *Av. Uxmal 31, Downtown, tel. 988/45533. No reservations. Dress: casual. AE, MC, V. Closed New Year's Day.*

Lodging

The most important buildings in Cancún are its hotels, which presently number more than 100 (the number of new hotels is increasing by 5–10 per year). Choosing from this variety can be bewildering, because most hotel brochures sound—and look—alike. Many properties were built in the mid-1970s by international hotel chains known for their streamlined, standardized versions of hospitality, and some were substantially renovated following the damage wrought by Hurricane Gilbert in 1988. Hotels here tend to favor "neo-Mayan" architecture (palapa roofs, massive pyramidal stone structures, and stucco walls interspersed with red tile roofs and quasi-Mediterranean Moorish arches), colonial furniture, and pastel hues. As for the amenities—particularly in luxury hotels—expect minibars, satellite TV, and marble baths (which can be treacherous when wet).

Hotels that are affiliated with international chains tend to be large in terms of both the number of rooms (averaging more than 200) and the size of individual rooms (averaging about 538 square feet). Properties in the hotel zone offer rooms with both sea and lagoon views unless otherwise noted. The lagoon views are generally less expensive, but some properties do not differentiate in price, and in those cases you should ask for a sea view.

If proximity to downtown is a priority, then staying at one of the hotel zone properties at the island's northern end (around Punta Cancún) is advantageous; many of the malls are within walking distance, and taxis to downtown and to the ferries at Puerto Juárez cost less than from hotels farther south. If, however, you seek something more secluded, there is less development at the southern end, toward Punta Nizuc and the airport.

All hotels have air-conditioning and private bathrooms unless otherwise noted. In addition, all properties in the Very Expensive and Expensive categories have water-sports facilities and parking unless otherwise noted. All Cancún hotels are within the 77500 postal code. Rates quoted refer to the peak winter season, mid-November–March. For more information, but *not* for reservations, contact the **Cancún Hotel Association** (Box 1339, Cancún, QR 77500, tel. 988/42853 or 988/45895, fax 988/47115).

Highly recommended hotels are indicated by a star ★.

Category	Cost*
Very Expensive	over $160
Expensive	$90–$160
Moderate	$35–$89
Inexpensive	under $35

All prices are for a standard double room, excluding the 15% tax.

Hotel Zone

Hotel Zone properties are located on the Hotel Zone Cancún Dining and Lodging map.

Very Expensive **Conrad Cancún.** One of Cancún's newest luxury properties (opened spring 1991), this hotel stands at the southern end of the island on Punta Nizuc, which makes it one of the few hotels with direct access to both a 1,600-foot beach and Laguna Nichupté, which it shares with Club Med. Consisting of four low-rise buildings in traditional Mexican style, the hotel successfully combines sleek contemporary angularity with elegant decor. Understated beige guest rooms are enhanced by handsome rustic furnishings. Concierge towers and suites are available. *Paseo Kukulcán, Km 20 (Box 1808), tel. 988/50086, 988/50537, or 800/HILTONS; fax 988/50074. 391 rooms. Facilities: 3 restaurants, 2 bars, 5 pools, a fitness center, 2 lighted tennis courts, 6 whirlpools, water-sports center and marina, travel agency, in-room safes, hair dryers. AE, DC, MC, V.*

Fiesta Americana Cancún. From the outside, this hotel (the chain's first of five ventures in Cancún) is difficult to distinguish from its younger sister, the Fiesta Americana Condesa: Both sport a studied Italianate look, replete with unusual windows, varied roof shapes, and many colors. The main difference is that this one has about half the number of rooms and is closer to downtown. All rooms are spacious; brightly furnished with rattan, white wood, and smoky glass; and decorated with white, cobalt-blue, and coral hues. Ask for a room with a balcony. The pool area boasts the obligatory waterfalls, and the lobby flaunts the inevitable palm trees. Suites are available. *Paseo Kukulcán Km 9.5 (Box 696), tel. 988/31400 or 800/FIESTA–1; fax 988/32502. 281 rooms. Facilities: 4 restaurants, 3 bars, pool. AE, DC, MC, V.*

Fiesta Americana Condesa. Floridian decor abounds in this sprawling but unpretentious hotel. The Mediterranean-style facade features flat tile roofs, balconies, rounded arches, and ocher walls. Inside, the theme continues—particularly in the spacious lobby bar set under an enormous palapa, with Tiffany-style stained-glass awnings, tall palms, and ceiling fans. Three seven-story towers overlook a tranquil inner courtyard with hanging plants and falling water. The rooms, highlighted by dusty-pink stucco walls and gray-blue carpets, offer the same tranquility. Balconies are shared by three standard rooms; costlier rooms have their own balconies. Of this chain's five Cancún properties, the Condesa is the southernmost, and it has meeting facilities, an amenity that attracts conventioneers. Suites are available. *Paseo Kukulcán (Box 5478), tel. 988/51000 or 800/FIESTA–1; fax 988/51800. 500 rooms. Facilities: 4 restaurants, 3 bars, health club, 3 indoor tennis courts, game room, jogging path, beauty parlor, boutiques, in-room safes. AE, DC, MC, V.*

Fiesta Americana Coral Beach Cancún. Opened in late 1990, this all-suite hotel lies just in front of the convention center and shopping malls at a roundabout opposite the Hyatt Regency. Unlike the other Fiesta properties, the Coral Beach consists of one enormous, multiwing structure, and the room rates tend to be slightly higher than other Fiesta properties. Inside, black-and-white tiled floors, floor-to-ceiling marble columns, potted palms, and curlicued iron grillwork perk up the lobby in art-nouveau fashion. All rooms are ample in size, with oceanfront balconies, marble floors, rounded doorways, and stained-glass windows; slate-blue, lavender, and beige tones create a soothing, pleasant mood. As for outdoor activities, choose between the 1,000-foot beach and the 660-foot pool. This is Cancún's largest convention hotel; expect the clientele to match. *Paseo Kukulcán (Box 14), tel. 988/32900 or 800/FIESTA–1; fax 988/32502. 602 suites. Facilities: 4 restaurants, 8 bars, pool, health club, 3 indoor tennis courts, shopping arcade. AE, DC, MC, V.*

Hyatt Cancún Caribe Villas & Resort. Intimate yet endowed with modern conveniences, this small semicircular property—one of the first hotels in Cancún—was recently rebuilt. An eclectic, primarily contemporary room decor now predominates: white walls and ceilings, red tile floors, curtains and upholstery in bright prints, and slightly garish furniture. Regency Club rooms feel more tranquil, with beige walls, marble floors, and colonial furniture. Beach-level rooms have gardens, and all rooms in the main tower have ocean views. *Paseo Kukulcán (Box 353), tel. 988/30044 or 800/228–9000; fax 988/31514. 198 rooms, including 62 beachfront villas; rooms for disabled people available. Facilities: 2 restaurants, café, 2 bars, 3 lighted tennis courts, 2 pools, marina, Jacuzzis, putting green, jogging path, car rental, travel agency, boutique, beauty salon. AE, DC, MC, V.*

Hyatt Regency Cancún. A cylindrical 14-story tower with the Hyatt trademark—a striking central atrium filled with tropical greenery and topped by a skylit dome—affords a 360° view of the sea and the lagoon. Plants spill over the inner core of the cylinder, at the base of which is a bar. Pink and purple tones prevail in the rooms, which also feature glossy gray-marble floors and warm hardwood furniture. This hotel, much larger and livelier than its sister property, boasts an enormous two-level pool with a waterfall. The Punta Cancún location is convenient to the convention center and several shopping malls. Suites are available. *Paseo Kukulcán (Box 1201), tel. 988/*

30966, 988/31566, or 800/228–9000; fax 988/31438. 300 rooms; rooms for disabled people available. Facilities: 3 restaurants, 4 bars, shops, car rental, travel agency, game room, pool, fitness center. AE, DC, MC, V.

Marriott Casamagna. One of Cancún's newest luxury properties, the Marriott is a palatial six-story hotel designed with graceful Moorish domes and arches and a handsome pool area that surrounds two restaurants and features Doric columns and an abundance of palm trees. The rooms, decorated in contemporary Mexican style, have tile floors and ceiling fans and follow a soft rose, mauve, and earth-tone color scheme. Suites are available. *Paseo Kukulcán (Retorno Chac L-41), tel. 988/5200 or 800/228–9290; fax 988/51731. 488 rooms, including 38 suites. Facilities: 4 restaurants, 2 bars, whirlpool, in-room safes, 2 lighted tennis courts, health club, shops, car rental, beauty salon, parking. AE, DC, MC, V.*

★ **Meliá Cancún.** The stunning new Meliá Cancún dares to differ from its neighbors: Forgoing the ubiquitous "neo-Mayan" decor and colonial furnishings, this one is boldly modern, with an impressive sheer black marble wall and a waterfall at the entrance. The spacious, airy atrium, filled with lush tropical flora, is dappled with sunlight flooding in from corner windows and from the steel-and-glass pyramid skylight overhead. Public spaces, displaying loving attention to detail, exude elegance. Ivory, dusty-pink, and light-blue hues softly brighten rooms (all with private balconies); white-lacquered furniture and wall-to-wall carpeting create a neat and relaxed ambience. The long two-level pool is deliciously unobstructed; service is unusually courteous and fast. Suites are available. *Paseo Kukulcán, Km 12, tel. 988/51160 or 800/336–3542; fax 988/51085. 447 rooms. Facilities: 4 restaurants, 5 bars, 5 pools, in-room safes, shopping arcade, beauty salon, car rental, travel agency, 5-hole golf course, health center, 3 tennis courts. AE, DC, MC, V.*

Omni Cancún. This enormous pink-and-orange hotel includes 11 stories topped off by a sloping red-and-orange tile roof. The small lobby, with a waterfall, conveys the same modern but comfortable feel as the guest rooms, which feature white marble floors, pale pink stucco walls, and pink marble baths. Some rooms have balconies. Ranking as a primary attraction is the two-level pool, divided by a bar. Suites are available. *Paseo Kukulcán L-48 (Box 127), tel. 988/50226 or 800/THE–OMNI; fax 988/50059. 327 rooms, including 9 villas. Facilities: 3 restaurants, 2 bars, hair dryers, gym, pool, 2 tennis courts, marina, shops. AE, DC, MC, V.*

★ **Villas Tacul.** This low-key villa complex, on its own stretch of beach, is endowed with a charming rustic decor, including red-tile floors and authentic Mexican colonial–style furniture, wagon-wheel chandeliers, and mirrors. The Mexican motif continues in the palapa restaurant, with its large clay bowls and piñatas; in the pool area, clusters of palm trees flourish. An individual housekeeper keeps each villa (all have from two to five bedrooms) spotless and serves private breakfasts. *Paseo Kukulcán, Km 5.5 (924 Farmington Ave., West Hartford, CT 06107), tel. in the U.S. 203/523–1609 or 800/842–0193; outside the U.S. 988/30000 or 988/30080; fax 988/30349. 23 villas. Facilities: restaurant, bar, pool, 2 tennis courts. AE, MC, V. Prepayment must be made by check; credit cards are accepted for incidentals only.*

Westin Camino Real. This classic hotel, situated at the tip of

Punta Cancún, won the AAA Four-Diamond award in 1990 for luxury accommodations and "above-average" management, staff, housekeeping, and maintenance. The property consists of two separate buildings: the older one, with four stories, features the sloping facade common to Camino Real resorts; the new tower has 18 floors and 69 Royal Beach Club rooms, each with its own balcony. Whichever building you choose, all rooms promise luxury and space. A small Mayan ruin was incorporated into the older structure. *Punta Cancún (Box 14), tel. 988/30100 or 800/228–3000; fax 988/31730. 381 rooms. Facilities: 4 restaurants, 2 bars, disco, pool, 2 beaches, shopping arcade. AE, DC, MC, V.*

Expensive **Aston Solaris.** The lobby's low domed ceilings and ceiling fans make the space at this three-building, eight-story village-style property more intimate. The prevailing Moorish theme continues in the white stucco facade and red roof, arched doorways, wicker chairs, potted plants, and beige tile floors. Thirty-five of the units are time-share apartment suites, with large living rooms, kitchenettes, and bathtubs (as opposed to the shower stalls in the smallish standard rooms). Studio rooms, which also have kitchenettes, offer twice the space of superior rooms. *Paseo Kukulcán, Km 20, tel. 988/50225 or 800/92–ASTON; fax 988/50975. 184 rooms. Facilities: 3 restaurants, 2 bars, small grocery store, pool, tennis court, car rental, travel agency. AE, DC, MC, V.*

★ **Cancún Playa.** This hotel boasts an airy lobby, strikingly decorated in white and turquoise and with plenty of marble and cozy sunken sofas. Smartly modern, the property has white facades and royal blue canvas-topped lean-tos at the pool area, which is nicely divided by lawns. The rooms are equally spiffy, with lovely pine furniture, and corner suites are equipped with private hot tubs and large terraces. The property—built by Spanish investors and now owned by Madrid-based Oasis International Hotels—caters to Spanish tour groups. Suites are available. *Paseo Kukulcán, Lote 60, tel. 988/51111, 988/51115, or 800/44–OASIS; fax 713/965–9943 or 988/51151. 410 rooms. Facilities: 3 restaurants, 3 bars, 2 pools, gym, 2 lighted tennis courts, car rental, travel agency, shopping arcade. AE, MC, V.*

Oasis. The modern tone of this hotel—one of the largest in Mexico—is enhanced by the twin waterfalls and black-gray marble floors in the lobbies. A seemingly endless arrangement of pools allows for unobstructed swimming, while a great lawn, wood walkways (easy on bare feet in the hot sun), and Japanese-style wood bridges provide pedestrian access. Inside, beige rooms with light blue drapes, dusty-blue bedspreads, and dark wood furniture provide a subdued but stylish ambience. Though not yet completed, the Oasis complex will eventually comprise four four-story buildings grouped around a taller trapezoid structure. *Paseo Kukulcán, Lote 42, tel. 988/50867 or 800/44–OASIS; fax 988/50131. Facilities: 6 restaurants, 5 bars, pool, 2 tennis courts, 9-hole golf course. AE, DC, MC, V.*

Royal Solaris. Located at the extreme southern end of the island near the tiny Mayan ruin called El Rey, this eight-story pyramid-shaped hotel's outstanding feature is its neo–art deco lobby, decorated tastefully with dark wood beams, potted palms, and lavender stucco walls and royal blue tropical bar furniture. The pink-and-yellow rooms have been furnished with light pine furniture, ceramic tile floors, and pink print bedspreads and sitting chairs but lack such amenities as in-room safes and minibars. Overall, the units tend to be poorly lit and don't quite meet the standards of other Cancún properties in this category; but since the former Ramada Renaissance was recently taken over by the Solaris group and converted into an all-inclusive resort, improvements are expected. *Paseo Kukulcán, Km 23, tel. 988/50100 or 800/368–9779; fax 988/50354. 280 rooms; 1 room for disabled people. Facilities: 2 restaurants, 2 bars, pool, Jacuzzi, shop, car rental, travel agency. AE, MC, V.*

Stouffer Presidente. Located 200 yards from Plaza Caracol, this hotel—the first to open in Cancún, but extensively remodeled in 1988—boasts a quiet beach and an extravagant Mayan-style pyramid atop the waterfall by the pool. Winner of the AAA Four-Diamond award in 1990, the property prides itself on its superior service. Well-appointed, larger-than-average-size rooms offer either one king-size or two queen-size beds, and are decorated in blue, cream, and pink pastels with lightwood furnishings and tile floors. *Blvd. Cancún 7, tel. 988/30202, 988/30218, or 800/HOTELS–1; fax 988/32602 or 988/32515. 294 rooms, including 15 suites; rooms for disabled people and no-smoking rooms available. Facilities: 3 restaurants, 2 bars, in-room safes, nightclub, fitness center, 2 pools, 5 Jacuzzis, lighted tennis court, travel agency, car rental, beauty parlor, shops. AE, MC, V.*

Suites Brisas. This no-frills, no-nonsense four-story hotel, squeezed in among the more expensive properties at the southern end of the Hotel Zone, is basically unimpressive, although renovations were under way at press time. With parking spaces in front, and simple, uninspired architecture, the property's facade resembles nothing so much as a motel. Functional rooms with kitchenettes are large but simply furnished, with white walls and pale blue, white, and beige fabrics. *Paseo Kukulcán, Km 19.5 (Box 1731), tel. 988/50499; fax 988/50060. 205 suites. Facilities: restaurant, bar, deli, pool, lighted tennis court. AE, DC, MC, V.*

Moderate **Cancún Viva.** This pink stucco 10-story building—part of a Mexican chain—is not one of the most attractive in town, but it makes a reliable standby and is in a good location, on the north beach near many malls. The rooms have marble floors; some have private balconies, ocean views, and kitchenettes. The property also features a small garden, a beach, and Mexican-theme restaurants. *Paseo Kukulcán, Km 8 (Box 673), tel. 988/30108 or 988/30019. 210 rooms. Facilities: 3 restaurants, bar, pool, 2 lighted tennis courts, shops. AE, DC, MC, V.*

Plaza Las Glorias. This three-story hotel has been around since 1973, but thanks to renovations the age doesn't show. The convenient location (close to Plaza Nautilus) and storefront facade convey a distinctly citified feel. White stucco rooms feature private balconies, tile floors, and wood furnishings. *Paseo Kukulcán, Km 3.5 (Box 227), tel. 988/30811 or 800/342–AMIGO. 110 rooms. Facilities: 2 restaurants, bars, pool. AE, DC, MC, V.*

Inexpensive **Albergue CREA.** This modern, government-run youth hostel on the beach has glass walls, cable TV, a pool, and dormitory beds (separate rooms for men and women). A cafeteria and lounge on the ground floor lend themselves to the sort of congenial mingling one expects of a youth hostel. *Paseo Kukulcán, Km 3, tel.*

988/31337. 100 rooms (350 beds) with shared baths. Facilities: cafeteria, basketball, volleyball, Ping-Pong. No credit cards.

Downtown

Downtown properties are located on the Downtown Cancún Dining and Lodging map.

Moderate **Antillano.** This old but prettily appointed property features wood furnishings, a cozy little lobby bar, and a tiny pool. Extras such as tiled bathroom sinks and air-conditioned hallways (in addition to air-conditioned rooms) make this hotel stand out a bit from the others in its league. *Av. Tulum at Calle Claveles, tel. 988/41532 or 988/41132. 48 rooms. Facilities: disco, pool, travel agency, shop. AE, DC, MC, V.*

Caribe Internacional. Located on one of the less-trafficked cross streets downtown, this relatively modern hotel can be somewhat noisy. The gray concrete exterior is matched by big stucco walls and ceilings, and the rooms—though on the small side and sparsely furnished—are pleasant enough with brightly colored walls. The small pool in a garden at the back adds a bit to this otherwise average property. *Sunyaxchén 36 at Av. Yaxchilán, tel. 988/43999 or 800/223–6510; fax 988/41993. 80 rooms. Facilities: restaurant, cafeteria, pool, shop, travel agency, parking. MC, V.*

Margarita Cancún. This five-story property—situated just across from the Caribe Internacional—is Mission-style white adobe with red-tile trim; inside, the rooms feature marble furnishings, from the bathroom walls to the tiled floors, and a vivid turquoise-and-gray color scheme that seems a bit strident for the '90s. Ask for a room with a view of the pool. *Av. Yaxchilán, S.M. 22, tel. 988/49333 or 800/223–9815. 100 rooms. Facilities: restaurant, snack bar, lounge, pool, shops, car rental, travel agency, parking. AE, DC, MC, V.*

★ **Plaza del Sol.** Popular with students, Europeans, and Canadians, this three-story colonial-style hotel is situated on a relatively quiet side street downtown. Inside are a pleasant lobby bar and nondescript-but-functional, small-but-carpeted rooms with large bathrooms. Ask for a view of the pool. *Av. Yaxchilán 31, tel. 988/43888 or 800/221–6509. 87 rooms. Facilities: 2 bars, restaurant, pool, car rental, free shuttle to beach, travel agency, parking. AE, DC, MC, V.*

Inexpensive **Hacienda Amigotel.** Part of a local Yucatán hotel chain, this property features a colonial-style lobby, an inner courtyard with a small pool, and a palapa-covered restaurant/bar. The rooms were originally decorated in a faintly colonial manner but have long since faded into what can best be termed "Mexican generic." Those with a pool view are slightly larger. *Av. Sunyaxchén, Lote 39-40, S.M. 24, tel. 988/43672 or 800/458–6888; fax 988/41208. 36 rooms. Facilities: cafeteria, bar, pool, travel agency. AE, MC, V.*

★ **María Lourdes.** The María Lourdes has a fairly large lobby and nice touches throughout, such as the colonial-style restaurant with rust-and-white stucco walls. Another appealing detail is the garden surrounding a small pool in the back. The rooms are bright with sparse, functional decor. *Av. Yaxchilán 80, tel. 988/44744; fax 988/41242. 51 rooms. Facilities: restaurant, pool, game room. AE, DC, MC, V.*

Plaza Carrillo. One of the first hotels to be built in Cancún City, this one is conveniently located in the heart of the downtown area next to the Plaza Carrillo shopping arcade and the Lobster House Restaurant, which are under the same ownership. The rooms are simply furnished but clean and well maintained (compared to other hotels in this category) and are equipped with small refrigerators. *Calle Claveles 12, tel. 988/41227 or 988/44833. 43 rooms. Facilities: restaurant, pool, travel agency. MC, V.*

Posada Lucy. This place isn't much to look at, but its location, on a quiet side street, is good. The cheerful blue-and-white rooms in the main building are small, with no views, but some include kitchenettes; there are another 12 rooms in an adjacent building behind Restaurant Pericos. The restaurant is the highlight here, with its oversize, gaily painted colonial decor. *Gladiolas 25, S.M. 22, tel. 988/44165. 25 rooms. Facilities: restaurant (closed Apr.–mid-May.). AE, MC, V.*

The Arts and Nightlife

The Arts

Film
Local movie theaters showing American and Mexican films include **Espectáculos del Caribe** (Av. Tulum 44, tel. 988/40449) and **Cines Cancún 1 and 2** (Av. Cobá 112, tel. 988/41646).

Performances
The **ballet folklórico** dinner show at the convention center consists of stylized performances of regional Mexican dances including the hat dance and *la bamba*. By comparison with the far superior Ballet Nacional Folklórico of Mexico City, this troupe suffers, but if it's all you'll get to see of the brilliant Mexican dance traditions, which blend pre-Hispanic and Iberian motifs, then go for it. Admission includes the buffet—a sampling of regional Mexican cooking—the show, and one drink. *Paseo Kukulcán, Km 8.5, tel. 988/30527 or 988/30921. Admission: about $38. Performances Mon.–Sat.; dinner 7 PM, show 8:30 PM.*

Cancún's **Jazz Festival** (tel. 800/542–8953), which premiered in the last week of May 1991 and featured top musicians, including Wynton Marsalis and Chick Corea, is expected to become an annual event. Cosponsored by the newly formed Cancún Office of Special Events and the Cancún Hotel Association, it's likely that the 1992 festival will be included in tour packages available from the United States.

Nightlife

Mexican **fiestas**, including dinner and folkloric dance performances, are staged at several of the large chain hotels.

A Mexican *charreada*, or rodeo show, is performed Monday–Saturday at 7 PM at El Corral de JF (Km 6, Prolongación Av. López Portillo). In addition to the show you get dinner and domestic drinks.

Discos
Cancún wouldn't be Cancún without its glittering discos and hotel-lobby bars. Generally discos start jumping about 10:30. **Dady'O** (Paseo Kukulcán, Km 9.5, tel. 988/33184) is presently a very "in" place. **Aquarius** (Westin Camino Real, tel. 988/30100) opens around 9 PM and prides itself on its subdued elegance and its ocean view. **Christine** (Hotel Krystal, tel. 988/31133) is among the most spectacular and popular joints in town. **La Boom** (Paseo Kukulcán, Km 3.5, tel. 988/31458; closed Sun.) in-

cludes a video bar with a light show and is not always crowded, although it can squeeze in 1,200 people. **Mine Company** (Club Verano Beat, tel. 988/30722) was the first disco in Cancún and has long been a favorite with the locals. Visit the **Hard Rock Café** (Plaza Lagunas, Paseo Kukulcán, tel. 988/32024) for nostalgic rock music.

Music **Cat's Reggae Bar** (Av. Yaxchilán 12, tel. 988/40407) plays island music starting at 9 PM. You can also hear live reggae at **Tequila Boom** (Paseo Kukulcán, Km 3.5, tel. 988/31458 or 988/31152) nightly from 8. **Batacha** (Hotel Miramar Misión, tel. 988/31755) is a piano bar with a small dance floor. **La Palapa** (Club Lagoon Hotel, tel. 988/31111), offering dancing on a pier over the lagoon, inspires romance. **Reflejos** (Hyatt Regency, tel. 988/30966) has a chic lounge with a small dance floor. Other popular places include **Jarro Café** (Plaza Laguna, tel. 988/32024), and **Bananas Beach** (Paseo Kukulcán, tel.988/32084).

4 Isla Mujeres

Introduction

A flat sandbank of an island about 9 kilometers (6 miles) long by 1 kilometer (⅗ mile) wide, Isla Mujeres offers an array of sandy beaches and rocky promontories; offshore coral reefs lure snorkelers and divers. Because of the strong currents, the waters display some of the most vivid blues in the Caribbean. The island has only one town and a population of about 13,500 devoted principally to fishing and tourism.

Isla Mujeres was discovered in 1517 by Hernández de Córdoba, a Spanish captain who had sailed with three ships from Cuba in search of slaves for the Cuban mines. He and his crew named it Isla Mujeres—the Isle of Women—probably for the female stone figurines they found at the temple on the island's southern tip. Córdoba returned to Cuba with tales of the gold he had found on the island; later, Isla Mujeres became the site of a fishing village and a pirate hideaway.

In the days before Cancún, Isla Mujeres was called the poor man's Cozumel. In the old days, before American tourism got into full swing, it was primarily a destination for Mexicans; during the '60s it became a sanctuary for the hippies who soaked up the sun and the laid-back pace but who put little money into the economy. Since the late '70s, however, Isla Mujeres has felt a ripple effect from Cancún's tourism: Boatloads of day-trippers stop by, prices have risen, and proprietors of what hotels, restaurants, and shops there are are seeing more activity than ever. The island is adapting to the influx of tourists and flourishing in the warm glow of the foreign currencies that they are bringing in. These tourists are not just North Americans coming over from Cancún but, increasingly, Europeans who stop by en route to the Mayan ruins on the mainland.

Isleños (islanders) are hospitable and friendly toward the outsiders on whom their livelihoods depend, but because recent development and growing popularity have put Isla Mujeres in the spotlight, they also have concerns about the long-term future. After Hurricane Gilbert devastated the island in 1988, a big part of the relief funds and supplies that had been sent from abroad somehow got "mislaid." The chicanery prompted 27 local women to band together as Mujeres por Isla Mujeres (Women for Isla Mujeres). The association raised money, bought pink paint at a discount from Sherwin-Williams, and soon spruced up many of the buildings. Someone gave them a truck, which they now use to take their children around, and a reforestation project is under way. (The palms in Quintana Roo and Yucatán have been decimated by the yellowing palm disease.)

Other changes are in the wings for Isla Mujeres. There is talk of a charter service to Florida, Mérida, Chichén Itzá, and Tikal, Guatemala; and the municipal dock is being rebuilt in hopes that it can receive cruise ships from Cancún. An international hotel chain is stirring up rumors of expansion. And time-share condos are cropping up all over. The primary challenge ahead for Isla Mujeres will be to maintain its low-profile image.

Essential Information

Important Addresses and Numbers

Tourist Information The **tourist office** (Calle Hidalgo, by the basketball court, tel. 988/20316), located on the *zócalo* (the square), 2 blocks from the ferry, is open weekdays 9–2 and 6–8. There, or at your hotel, you can pick up a copy of the monthly *Islander* magazine, which has most of the tourist information you'll need for your stay.

Emergencies **Medical Service** (tel. 988/20195); **Health Center** (tel. 988/20117); **Police** (tel. 988/20082).

Late-night Pharmacies **Farmacia Isla Mujeres** (Av. Juárez, next to the Caribbean Tropic Boutique, no phone) and **Farmacia Lily** (Avs. Madero and Hidalgo, no phone) are open Monday–Saturday 9 AM–8 PM.

Banks Banks are open weekdays 9–1:30 and exchange money from 10 to noon. They include **Banco del Atlántico** (Calle Juárez 5, tel. 988/20104 or 988/20005), **Banco Serfín** (Calle Juárez 3, tel. 988/20051 or 988/20083).

Arriving and Departing by Boat

Passenger ferries (tel. 988/20065) leave from the main dock for Puerto Juárez, on the mainland, theoretically at 6:30, 8:30, 9:30, 11:30, 1:30, 2:30, 3:30, and 5:30; the schedule varies depending on the season. The one-way fare is less than a dollar, and the trip takes about half an hour. A more convenient and more expensive service, the **Shuttle** (tel. 988/46433, in Cancún), runs directly from the Playa Linda dock in Cancún's hotel zone and costs $12 round-trip. The brand-new 91-foot *Caribbean Queen* (tel. 988/20253 or 988/20254), an air-conditioned ship with a bar, makes one or two 30-minute crossings daily; the fare is under $3 per person. Again, schedules vary, so you should call ahead or check the boat schedule posted at the pier. From Punta Sam, 5 kilometers (3 miles) north of Punta Juárez, big **municipal ferries** carry passengers and vehicles regularly from about 6 AM to 9 PM throughout the year, and until 11 PM in the summer. Ships leave for the 45-minute trip promptly according to times posted at the pier. The fare is under $1.50 per person. Private *lanchas* (motorboats) can be hired for about $18 (the price is the same whether you have one passenger or five); they make the crossing to Punta Sam in 15 minutes. When you leave the ferry, expect to be approached by young boys who will want to carry your baggage for a fee.

Getting Around

For orientation purposes, think of Isla Mujeres as an elongated fish: The southern tip is the head and the northern prong the tail; the peninsula enclosing a lagoon on the western or leeward side is one fin. The town itself is only 7 blocks long and 5 blocks wide. Along the lee side of the island runs Avenida Rueda Medina, the main paved road. Though much of Isla Mujeres is undeveloped, there are some smaller unpaved roads outside of town.

By Bus **Municipal buses** run at half-hour intervals daily between 6 AM and 9 PM from the Posada del Mar Hotel on Avenida Rueda Medina out to Colonia Salinas on the windward side. There is also service from the dock to Playa Lancheros or El Garrafón on the leeward side. As you might expect, however, the service is slow, because the buses make frequent stops.

By Car There is little reason for tourists to bring cars to Isla Mujeres, because there are plenty of other forms of transportation that cost far less than renting and transporting your own private vehicle. Moreover, the roads are not in great shape, and in many areas they are poorly lighted.

By Taxi If your time is limited you can hire a taxi (Av. Rueda Medina, tel. 988/20066) for a private island tour at about $6 an hour. Fares run $1–$2 from the ferry or downtown to the hotels on the north end, at Playa Cocoteros. Taxis line up right by the ferry dock between 5 AM and 2 PM.

By Moped The island is full of moped rental shops. **Motorent Kankin** (Calle Abasolo 15, tel. 988/20071) rents two-seater, three-speed Hondas for about $4 per hour or $15 per day; an $18 deposit is required. **Pepe's Motorenta** (Calle Hidalgo 19, tel. 988/20019) offers two-seater Honda Aero-C50s, Aero-C90s, and fully automatic Aeros, starting at $3 per hour, for a minimum of two hours. Although a deposit is required, Pepe's accepts American Express and Visa. It is open daily 8–5. **Ciro's Motorent** (Calle Guerrero N 11 at Calle Matamoros, tel. 988/20351) also has two-seater Aero-Honda 90-50 mopeds.

Moped and bicycle (*see* below) riders should watch for the many speed bumps on the island's roads. Everyone should be particularly cautious at night, because some areas are poorly lighted and mopeds and motorcylces may not have headlights.

By Bicycle Bicycles are available for hardy cyclists, but don't underestimate the hot sun and the rugged condition of the island roads. **Rent Me Sport Bike** (Calles Juárez and Morelos, 1 block from the main pier), offers five-speed cycles starting at $3 for four hours; you can leave your driver's license in lieu of a deposit, and it's open daily 8–7.

Mail The **post office** (tel. 988/20085), open weekdays 9–9 and Saturday 9–1, is located on Calle Guerrero, half a block from the market.

Telephones Long-distance phone service is available in the lobby of the **Hotel María José** (Calle Madero 21) or at **Club de Yates** (Calle Guerrero 8).

Guided Tours

Tour Operators Local agencies include **Club de Yates de Isla Mujeres** (Av. Rueda Medina, s/n, tel. 988/20173 or 988/202491), open daily 9–noon; and **La Isleña** (Calles Morelos and Juárez, tel. 988/20036), half a block from the pier, open daily 7–6. **Intermar Caribe** (Madero 2, tel. 988/20444), with headquarters in Cancún, is the only full-service travel agency, and is open daily, except Sunday.

Boat Tours **Cooperativa Lanchera** (waterfront, near the dock, no phone) offers four-hour launch trips to the Virgin, the lighthouse, the turtles at Playa Lancheros, the coral reefs at Los Mancheros, and El Garrafón, for $30. **Cooperativa Isla Mujeres** (Av. Rueda Medina, tel. 988/20274), next to Mexico Divers, rents out boats at $120 for a minimum of four hours and six people, and $15 per person for an island tour with lunch (minimum six people). A trip to **Isla Contoy** (45 minutes to the north), with a minimum of

10 people, costs $30 per person and includes a light breakfast, snorkeling, lunch, and drinks; it departs at 8 AM and returns at 4 or 5 (*see* Excursion to Isla Contoy, below).

Exploring

Numbers in the margin correspond to points of interest on the Isla Mujeres map.

We start our itinerary in the island's only town—also called Isla Mujeres—whose main street parallels the waterfront on the west side. It is little more than a village, sandwiched between sand and sea to the north, south, and east; there are no high rises to impede the view. Many of the island's activities
❶ take place around the small cluster of **piers,** on Avenida Rueda Medina between Calle Abasolo and Avenida Bravo, because
❷ ferries arrive and depart from here. The **main square** (*la placita*)—bounded by Calle Morelos, Avenida Bravo, and Calles Guerrero and Hidalgo—is unfettered by the kinds of monuments encumbering other Mexican plazas. Typical scenes here include basketball games on the permanent courts, children playing in the playground, locals gathered to chat in front of the Government Palace, and women selling fruit snacks. On holidays and weekends the square gets set up for dances, concerts, and fiestas.

❸ Follow any of the north–south streets out to **Playa Cocoteros,** one of the finest beaches on the island, where you can wade far out in the placid waters. Hurricane Gilbert's only good deed, according to isleños, was to widen this and other leeward-side beaches by blowing sand over from Cancún. Along the way sit congenial palapa bars for drinks and snacks, and stands where you can rent snorkel gear, jet-skis, floats, sailboards, and sometimes parasails. If you walk the full length of Cocos (as it's affectionately called) to the northern end (Punta Norte), you'll come
❹ to a small wood-plank bridge leading to what was once **Costa Azul**—formerly the Del Prado Hotel—on its own private islet. Presently, the ownership of the property is under negotiation. At low tide you can even wade across this narrow bit of water, and to the west side of the property you'll see some hotels, some beach chairs and palapas, a rocky point (the beach was washed away by the hurricane of 1988), and sand, sand, sand.

Time Out Try to get to Cocos in the late afternoon, just before sunset, and stop in for a beer at **Rutilio's y Chimbo's,** twin palapa restaurant-bars right on the beach, where locals come to drink beer, play dice, and chat. You can sit on the high stools and watch sailboarders or children playing beachball until the mesmerizing pink sun sets. Spending some time at a local hangout will give you an opportunity to mingle with the isleños. And here's what's marvelous about Isla Mujeres: The locals will talk to gringos! Totally unselfconscious, the islanders will bum cigarettes, ask where you're from, and behave in general in a far less jaded fashion than their neighbors on Cancún.

To explore the rest of the island, you'll need to take a moped or taxi south along the Avenida Rueda Medina, which leads out of town. The first landmark you'll pass after the piers is the
❺ **Mexican naval base,** which is closed to the public. From the road, however, you can see (but don't photograph) the modest

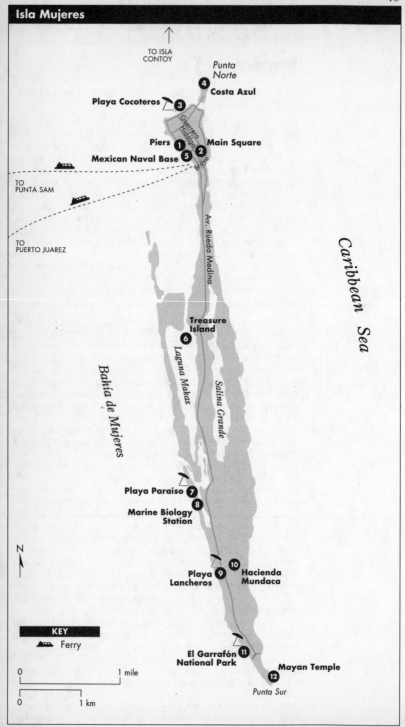

Isla Mujeres

TO ISLA CONTOY

Punta Norte

4 Costa Azul

3 Playa Cocoteros

Guerrero

Hidalgo

Piers 1 **2** Main Square

Mexican Naval Base 5

Bravo

TO PUNTA SAM

TO PUERTO JUAREZ

Caribbean Sea

Av. Rueda Medina

Treasure Island

6

Laguna Makax

Salina Grande

Bahía de Mujeres

Playa Paraíso 7

8

Marine Biology Station

N

10

Playa Lancheros 9 **Hacienda Mundaca**

KEY

Ferry

0   1 mile

0   1 km

El Garrafón National Park

11

Mayan Temple

12

Punta Sur

flag-raising and -lowering ceremonies at sunrise and sunset. Continuing southward, the *salinas* (salt marshes) will be on your left, and on your right you'll see the **Laguna Makax,** where pirates are said to have anchored their ships as they lay in wait for the hapless vessels plying Spanish Main (the geographical area in which Spanish treasure ships trafficked).

6 Follow the road until you come to an unmarked turnoff that leads to a bridge across the lagoon and out to **Treasure Island,** where there's **Pirates Cove,** a small theme park visited mostly by Cancún day-trippers. Though no one actually staying on Isla Mujeres seems to go here, families who do visit enjoy the model shipwreck, open-air theater, shops, restaurant, and some caged birds and animals.

7 Head back to the main road and travel south for about 4 kilometers (2½ miles); take the right turnoff at the sign to **Playa Paraíso.** The lovely beach is fronted by Hacienda Gomar, a good restaurant featuring a buffet lunch and marimba music. Also in the area you'll find boutiques and a beach bar with small palapas.

8 Walk about a ½ kilometer south, either along the beach or on the soon-to-be-paved dirt road, until you come to the sign that says "Pesca." This signals the entrance to the government-run **marine biology station,** which is devoted primarily to the study and preservation of the sea turtle, the lobster, and coral reefs. Technically the station is not open to the public, but during working hours visitors can examine various species and talk to the biologists about their work. The budget is small, but because the turtle population in the Mexican Caribbean continues to dwindle toward extinction, these dedicated ecologists have taken it upon themselves to care for young hatchlings until they are big enough to let out to sea. The efforts from 1990's summer project were so successful that biologists reported the hatching of 38,000 ridley turtles.

9 Just south of Paraíso lies **Playa Lancheros,** where you can eat lunch in the modest restaurant or shop for handicrafts, souvenirs, and T-shirts at the small stands. Also housed here, in a sea pen, are some pet sea turtles and harmless nurse sharks (*tiburón gato*). For a tip, a local man will hold one of the creatures while you hop on its back and have your picture taken. (While this makes a great shot for a photo album, local activists lobby hard against such activities because turtles are endangered and the conditions in which both species live are less than natural.) On the ocean side live the carnivorous *tintorera* (female sharks), which have seven rows of teeth and weigh as much as 500 kilograms (1,100 pounds). There is a small entrance fee to the beach, and you can buy refreshments and souvenirs. Live music is played on certain afternoons.

10 Off the main road, across from the entrance to Playa Lancheros, a tiny footpath cut through the brush leads to the remains of the **Hacienda Mundaca,** built by Fermín Mundaca de Marechaja, a 19th-century slave-trader-cum-pirate (he was more inclined to the former than to the latter). When the British navy began cracking down on slavers, he settled on the island and built an ambitious estate with resplendent tropical gardens. The story goes that he constructed it to woo a certain island woman who, in the end, chose another man. Poor Fermín died in sorrow in Mérida, but his tombstone was laid (although local lore has it that he was not actually buried here) in the cemetery on Isla Mujeres.

What little remained of the hacienda—something was left even after the 1988 hurricane—has mysteriously vanished, except for a sorry excuse of a guardhouse, an arch, a pediment, and a well. Locals say that the government tore down the mansion, or at least neglected its upkeep. (Purportedly, the government will soon rebuild the site in the cause of tourism.) If you push your way through the jungle—the mosquitoes are fierce—you'll eventually come to the ruined stone archway and triangular pediment, carved with the following inscription: *Huerta de la Hacienda de Vista Alegre MDCCCLXXVI* (Orchard of the Happy View Hacienda, 1876). Fermín's tombstone—which he is said to have carved himself though now it is nowhere in sight—reads, *As You Are, I Once Was; As I Am, So Shall You Be.*

⓫ The next major site along the main road is **El Garrafón National Park,** the much-hyped, overvisited snorkeling mecca for thousands of day-trippers from Cancún. Although still beautiful, Garrafón—which lies at the bottom of a bluff—was once almost magical in its beauty. Now, as a result of the hands and feet of eager divers, Hurricane Gilbert, and global warming, the coral reef here is virtually dead. There has been talk of closing the park to give the coral time to grow back (coral grows at the rate of 1 centimeter every 10 years), but too many locals make their living off it for this solution to be feasible. However, fish are still swarming about, and the waters throw off lovely shades of blue-green, though the coral formations have been bleached of their brilliance. The crowds, which are biggest between 11 and 2, make snorkeling even less enjoyable, and because of the undertow, swimming can be dangerous. Still, Garrafón is a nice spot for a picnic (there are food stands and souvenir shops galore), and there are palapas, lockers, equipment rental, and a small aquarium. *No phone. Admission: P$2,500. Open daily 9–5.*

Continuing around the southern tip of Isla Mujeres, about 1 kilometer (⅗ mile) from Garrafón, you'll come to the sad vestiges ⓬ of the **Mayan temple,** dedicated to Ixchel, the goddess of fertility. Though the significant part of the ruins were destroyed by Hurricane Gilbert, the adjacent **lighthouse** still stands, and the keeper sometimes allows visitors to go up. Just past that point, on the windward side, is one of the island's most scenic patches of coastline, from which you can also make out the skyline (and lights, if it's dark) of Cancún. From here, follow the road into town. It's about a two-hour walk; from Lancheros, however, you can catch a bus or taxi back.

Shopping

Shopping on Isla Mujeres used to be limited to basic resort wear, suntan lotions, and groceries. More and more Mexican crafts boutiques are opening here, but the prices are higher than on the mainland. Most shops accept major credit cards, but you'll probably pay more than if you use cash. Shopping hours are generally daily 10–1 and 4–7, although many stores now stay open through siesta.

Local Crafts **La Loma** (Calle Guerrero 6, tel. 988/20446) has a selection of exquisite crafts from all over Mexico and Guatemala, including amber, silver, black jade, leather jewelry, and masks, pottery, and textile bags. Although the shop is not inexpensive, La Loma offers the biggest and best collection on the island. Owner Judith Fernández does the buying herself and is a good source of information about the island.

Tienda Paulita (Calles Morelos and Hidalgo, tel. 988/20014) features a standard selection of folk art and handmade clothing in a fairly large space.

Rachat & Rome (Av. Rueda Medina, tel. 988/20250), housed in the pink building by the dock, sells gold, silver, and gemstones.

Casa del Arte Mexica (Calle Hidalgo 6, no phone) has a good choice of clay reproductions, silver and black coral jewelry, batiks, rubbings, wood carvings, leather, and hammocks.

Grocery Stores There are two fair-size groceries: **Super Betino** (Calle Morelos 3) and **Super Mirtita** (Calle Juárez and Av. Bravo). Food, including fresh fruit, can also be purchased in the municipal market on Calle Guerrero Norte.

Sports and Fitness

Water Sports

Fishing Billfish are a popular catch in spring and early summer; the rest of the year, you can fish for barracuda and tuna, as well as for shad, sailfish, grouper, and red snapper.

Bahía Dive Shop (Av. Rueda Medina, across from the pier, tel. 988/20131) charges $250 for a day of deep-sea fishing, $220 a day for cast fishing (tarpon, snook, and bonefish), and $25 an hour for offshore fishing (barracuda, snapper, and smaller fish).

Snorkeling and The best time to snorkel is during summer months between 8
Scuba Diving AM and 3 PM, when the water is warm and calm. Not only will more fish be attracted by the mild temperature, but the placid conditions also increase visibility. Divers should take care, however, because there has been a rise in the incidence of respiratory and gastrointestinal problems—probably caused by pollution—among those who enter the offshore waters.

The famous coral reefs at **El Garrafón** (*see* Exploring, above) have suffered tremendously from negligent tourists, Hurricane Gilbert, and the global warming that has been bleaching the coral. Though still a beautiful site, there is little to see besides rocks, seaweed, and tiny fish called *fieles*. Garrafón should be avoided during the hours between 11 and 2, when the tourists from Cancún throng the area. Good snorkeling can still be found, however, at the **Lighthouse** (*Farito*) at the northern tip of the peninsula on the leeward side. Underneath is a partially buried but still visible statue of the Virgin. One of the island's most alluring diving attractions is the **Cave of the Sleeping Sharks,** east of the northern tip. Opinion differs, though, as to how advisable it really is to share space with these creatures and how asleep they actually are.

At the extreme southern end of the island on the leeward side lies **Los Manchones.** At 30–40 feet deep and 3,300 feet off the southwestern coast, this coral reef makes a good dive site. **Los Cuevones,** to the southwest near La Bandera, reaches a depth of 65 feet. Another site, complete with two shipwrecked galleons, is on the windward side of the islet north of Mujeres. Dive shops will be able to direct you.

Bahía Dive Shop (Av. Rueda Medina, across from the pier, tel. 988/20131), also called Buzos del Caribe, rents snorkeling and scuba equipment and runs two-hour boat and dive trips to the reefs and the Cave of the Sleeping Sharks. Snorkel gear goes for $15 per hour; tanks, $40–$55 for 45 minutes. **Mexico Divers** (Av. Rueda Medina, 1 block from the ferry, tel. 988/20131), also called Buzos de México, is owned by Cooperativa Isla Mujeres and runs three-hour snorkeling tours for $10; trips for certified divers start at $25 per tank. Dive master Carlos Gutiérrez also gives a resort course for $80 and open-water PADI certification for $350.

Beaches

For any water sport, beaches on the north and west sides are the calmest. For more detailed descriptions of the following beaches, *see* Exploring, above. **Playa Cocoteros,** along with Punta Norte at the northern tip of the island, is tranquil and has powdery sand. Locals come here to drink beer and watch the sunset, but you can also rent sailboards or meander into a palapa-covered restaurant. Both the eastern end, by the Costa Azul, and the western end, at Nautibeach, have superb views and fine white sand. **El Garrafón,** on the southern side, has a coral reef 6 feet from shore, but it's been badly eroded by tourists and environmental conditions. On the western side of Mujeres are **Playa Paraíso** and **Playa Lancheros.**

Dining

Dining on Isla Mujeres offers what you would expect on a small island: lots of seafood—lobster, shrimp, conch, and fish. But foods, including shish kebab, pizza, and tacos, are featured as well. Items that you will see on various menus include *carne asada* (broiled beef with vegetables), *mole poblano* (a spicy sauce of chile, chocolate, sesame, and almonds), *pollo píbil* (chicken in a tangy sour orange sauce), and *poc chuc* (pork marinated in sour orange sauce with pickled onions). For other dishes, see the menu glossary in the appendix.

Generally, restaurants on the island are informal (shirts and shoes required), most have outdoor facilities or at least palapas, and the only dress requirement is that swimsuits and feet should be covered. Because life here usually involves getting up with the sun, dinner is eaten earlier than in the rest of Mexico. Unless otherwise stated, restaurants are open daily for lunch and dinner.

Highly recommended restaurants are indicated by a star ★.

Category	Cost*
Expensive	over $15
Moderate	$10–$15
Inexpensive	under $10

per person, excluding drinks, service, and sales tax (15%)

Expensive   ★   **Chez Magaly.** A very elegant restaurant on the grounds of the Nautibeach Condo-hotel, this mostly French restaurant is tastefully furnished with wood floors, plants, leather chairs, Chinese blinds, and handsome place settings. Seafood grills, lobster quiche, jambalaya (Caribbean paella), and tequila-flambéed mangos are among the specialties. To complement the meal, choose from an extensive wine list. *Av. Rueda Medina, Playa Norte, tel. 988/20259. Reservations advised. MC, V. Closed 2 weeks in June.*

Moderate   **Bucanero.** In addition to a good meal, you'll get a good view from this airy, traditional-style building situated on the main tourist street across from Pizza Rolandi. For breakfast, the *huevos motuleños* (fried eggs served on a corn tortilla heaped with beans, ham, cheese, peas, marinated red onions, all drenched in tomato sauce) are excellent and cheap; lunch and dinner specialties include avocado stuffed with shrimp, a seafood combination platter (lobster, fish fillet, shrimp, and snails), shrimp stuffed with fried cheese and egg, chicken brochettes, and *mar y cielo* (fish fillet and chicken breast with french fries and onions). Wood details and tropical plants enhance the peppy Caribbean ambience you'll find here. *Av. Hidalgo 11, tel. 988/20236. No reservations. AE, MC, V.*

Café Cito. This hole-in-the-wall with six tables serves a hearty European breakfast of crepes and waffles, but you should also come for the dinners or for cappuccino and dessert. German tourists flock to this place. *Calles Guerrero and Matamoros, no phone. No reservations. No credit cards. Closed Mon. and at lunch.*

Cocos Fríos. The rustic sidewalk tables here make a good place for people-watching, and the menu offers a variety of cuisines. Choose from such specialties as beef shish kebab, carne asada, cheese fondue, chicken with french fries, or fried fish. *Calle Hidalgo 4, no phone. No reservations. No credit cards.*

★   **La Peña.** This charming, informal restaurant situated on the edge of town offers a glorious view of the sea from the open-air terrace. From the gaily decorated palapa hang crepe-paper and papier-mâché animals, in keeping with the restaurant's Mexican cuisine. The menu features lobster tacos, mole poblano, pollo píbil, local fish, and assorted pizzas. During high season, salsa and reggae fill the premises, and dancing is encouraged on the open-air terrace. *Calle Guerrero 5, tel. 988/20321. No reservations. AE, V.*

El Limbo. This restaurant—housed in the Hotel Rocamar, which has been carved into the side of a cliff—offers a sensational view even though it's actually on the basement level. A post–Hurricane Gilbert renovation has made the restaurant more handsome, though the decor remains typical for the island: seashells and tortoiseshells adorn the walls, while simple, functional, and unpretentious furnishings fill the dining area. Included on the menu are pollo píbil, pork chops, and steak, as well as many seafood specials. You have the choice of fish or shellfish *a la italiano* (with tomato, onion, white wine, and rice), *a la veracruzana* (cooked in green oil from Lebanon, and garnished with olives and raisins), or *al ajo* (sautéed in garlic and served with rice or french fries and salad). *Av. Bravo and Calle Guerrero, at Hotel Rocamar, tel. 988/20101. No reservations. MC, V.*

Pizza Rolandi. Red tables, yellow director's chairs, green walls and window trim, and dark wood beams set the cozy tone at this very "in" chain restaurant. Select from a broad variety of Italian food: lobster pizzas, calzones, and pastas. The grilled shrimp is recommended, as are the salads. *Calle Hidalgo (between Calles Madero and Abasolo), tel. 988/20430. No reservations. MC, V.*

Inexpensive **Lonchería El Poc Chuc.** This tiny restaurant is named for the famous Yucatán dish of pork marinated in sour orange, which is a house specialty. This no-frills Mexican eatery has a decent breakfast, too. *Calle Juárez (between Calles Madero and Morelos), no phone. No reservations. No credit cards.*

Lodging

The approximately 25 hotels (about 600 rooms) on Isla Mujeres generally fall into one of two categories: The older, more modest places are situated right in town, and the newer, more expensive properties tend to have beachfront locations around Punta Norte and, increasingly, on the peninsula near the lagoon. Most hotels have ceiling fans and air-conditioning. Luxurious, self-contained time-share condominiums are another option, which you can learn more about from the tourist office (tel. 988/20316). All hotels share the 77400 postal code.

Highly recommended hotels are indicated by a star ★.

Category	Cost*
Very Expensive	over $85
Expensive	$50–$85
Moderate	$25–$50
Inexpensive	under $25

All prices are for a standard double room, excluding the 15% tax.

Very Expensive **Condominio Playa Norte Nautibeach.** A stunning new property
★ (it opened in November 1990), this condominium hotel boasts one of the best beaches on Isla Mujeres—right at the tip of Playa Cocoteros. The grounds resemble a villa setting, with well-kept lawns and bougainvillea adding splashes of color everywhere. The intimate, self-contained appeal of this property is enhanced by the small pool and palapa-covered poolside bar; Chez Magaly, a French restaurant; and the Calypso Bar next door. The lovely pink stucco exterior blends well with the grounds, and the suites, decorated in colonial style, are comfortable. All the rooms face the sea and have either terraces or balconies, dining rooms, and kitchenettes; the property promises satellite TV shortly. Although Nautibeach is considered top-notch, it is advised that you confirm reservations immediately before your visit because complaints have been regis-

tered against the management for juggling hotel guests against time-share owners. *Playa Norte, tel. 988/20259 or 988/ 20436; fax 988/20487. 20 2-bedroom units. Facilities: restaurant, bar, pool, beach. MC, V.*

Costa Azul. This seven-story hotel, once the most luxurious on the island, has gone downhill since it was dropped by the Stouffer Presidente chain. However, at press time the former Del Prado Hotel had just changed hands, and the new management has promised to turn it into an all-inclusive property by late summer '91. Future plans include a major renovation of all guest rooms and the addition of a tower. Other facilities scheduled for completion are a disco, game room, and international restaurant. Views should be gorgeous since this property sits on its own private beach, an extension of Playa Cocoteros, which is a five-minute walk from town. *Islote del Yunque/ Punta Norte, no phone at press time. 93 rooms. Facilities: disco, game room, restaurants, bar, pool, gift shop. AE, DC, MC, V.*

Expensive **Cristalmar.** Although the location of this condo-hotel (a five-minute drive from town) is inconvenient for those without their own transportation, the property—situated on a peninsula by the lagoon—boasts a stunning sea view. Other pluses include the spacious suites, from which you can choose one-, two-, or three-bedroom units, and the spanking modernity of the property overall. All rooms open to the courtyard, which has a pool and a palapa bar. Local artwork adorns the walls of this property and dark brown wicker furnishings and glass-top tables decorate the rooms. *Paraiso Laguna Mar, Lot 16, tel. 988/20007 or 800/622–3838. 37 suites. Facilities: small pool, beach, sauna, bar, kitchenettes. MC, V.*

★ **Na-Balam.** One of Isla Mujeres's newest hotels, this intimate, lovely, and informal place boasts a terrific location right on Playa Cocoteros. All rooms include dining areas, patios facing the beach, and refrigerators and are decorated with colonial-style furniture and old photographs of Mexico. The three rooms with balconies cost slightly more, but they're worth it. *Calle Zazil Ha 118, tel. 988/20446 or 988/20279; fax 988/20011. 12 suites. Facilities: cafeteria, beach. AE, MC, V.*

Moderate **Belmar.** Right in the heart of town, above Pizza Rolandi, sits this modern hotel; it shares an attractive inner courtyard with the restaurant. Standard rooms have tiled baths and odd white wood and glass furniture. One enormous suite features a private Jacuzzi, a patio with chairs, a tiled kitchenette, and a sitting area. Rooms with air-conditioning cost slightly more but are definitely more comfortable. *Calle Hidalgo (between Calles Madero and Abasolo), tel. 988/20430. 13 rooms. AE, MC, V.*

★ **Cabañas María del Mar.** This old beachfront property has been renovated and expanded, and it shows, though the standard rooms tend to be small and the decor is slightly garish. But the hotel's prime location—on Playa Cocoteros, next to Na-Balam—makes up for what is lacking aesthetically. When renting a cabaña, you have a choice: air-conditioning or ceiling fan, sea view or no view (prices vary accordingly). Deluxe rooms in the newest building, with its Moorish arcades, have pine furniture, tile floors and sinks, and custom-made ceramic lampshades. All deluxe rooms have sea views and light-blue-and-lavender color schemes. *Carlos Lazos 1, tel. 988/20213, 988/ 20179, or 800/826–6842; fax 305/531–7616 or 988/20173. 36* units. *Facilities: pool, moped rental, restaurant/bar, travel agency, car and boat service. MC, V.*

Mesón del Bucanero. A 1990 expansion of this hotel, which opened only the year before, has upgraded the colonial-style furnishings and added several suites with large bathtubs, small sitting areas, and small balconies. Standard rooms are basic in design, simply furnished, and very bright. *Calle Hidalgo 11, tel. 988/20126 or 988/20210. 14 rooms. Facilities: restaurant. AE, DC, MC, V.*

Perla del Caribe. The former three-story Roca del Caribe, on the eastern edge of town, offers rooms with balconies that look out to either the sea or the city and are priced accordingly. Though comfortable enough, with simple, functional furnishings, the Perla does seem to lack character. Live music is performed in the restaurant/bar most evenings. *Av. Madero 2 at Calle Guerrero, tel. 988/20444; fax 988/20011. 87 rooms. Facilities: restaurant/bar, pool, beach, travel agency, laundry, fishing boat. AE, MC, V.*

★ **Posada del Mar.** An older hotel situated in town, but just across the way from Playa Cocos, this property—which features a two-story wing, private bungalows, and a tropical garden with a lovely garden pool/bar and recently rebuilt restaurant—provides a pleasant atmosphere. Rooms, though simply furnished with outdated vintage-70s decors have small balconies overlooking the waterfront boulevard and are well maintained and clean. The pool bar has become a local hangout. *Av. Rueda Medina 15, tel. 988/20300, 988/20044, or 800/451–8891; fax 988/20266. 42 rooms. Facilities: restaurant, bar, pool. AE, MC, V.*

Inexpensive **Poc-Na.** The island's youth hostel, located at the eastern end of town, rents bunks or hammocks (which cost less), but it requires a deposit that's almost twice the cost of the accommodations. One bonus is its proximity to the beach. *Calle Matamoros 15, tel. 988/20090 or 988/20059. Facilities: dining room. No credit cards.*

Private Bungalows Several pretty, small bungalows near Garrafón are rented for the long term by the owner, Tino. Inquire at Mexico Divers (tel. 988/20131), at the main pier in town.

The Arts and Nightlife

The Arts

In addition to the many festivals and other cultural events (*see* Festivals and Seasonal Events in the Before You Go section of Chapter 1, Essential Information) on Isla Mujeres, you can engage in artistic activities year-round at the **Casa de la Cultura,** near the youth hostel. The organization offers classes in aerobics, music, drawing, and dance and has a small public library and book exchange. *Calle Guerrero, tel. 988/20307. Open Mon.–Sat. 9–1 and 4–8.*

For English-language films visit **Cine Blanquita** (Calle Morelos, between Calles Guerrero and Hidalgo, no phone).

Nightlife

Most restaurant bars feature a happy hour from 5 to 7; the palapa bars on the north beach are an excellent place to watch the sunset. **Restaurante La Peña** (Calle Guerrero 5, tel. 988/20321) has music and dancing on its open-air terrace overlooking the sea. Locals swear by the down-home ambience at **Calypso** (corner of Av. Rueda Medina and López Mateos, no phone). **Buho's** (Calle Carlos Lazo 1, tel. 988/20213), owned by Cabañas María del Mar, has just opened a disco on the beach. Go watch music videos at the video bar at **Tequila** (Calle Hidalgo 19, tel. 988/20019). Live tropical dance music is also played in the zócalo on Saturday nights beginning at 11.

Excursion to Isla Contoy

Isla Contoy (Isle of Birds) is a national wildlife park and bird sanctuary and a perfect getaway, even from Isla Mujeres. Birders, snorkelers, and fishing aficionados come here to enjoy the setting and the numerous varieties of animal life.

Important Addresses and Numbers

Government Office SEDUE (tel. 983/22887), the national ecology and urban-development ministry, can provide information about the island.

Getting There Only 6 kilometers (4 miles) long and less than a kilometer (about ⅗ mile) wide, Contoy is 24 kilometers (15 miles) from Isla Mujeres and 6 kilometers (4 miles) from the coast of Yucatán. The island can also be reached by boat from Cancún.

Guided Tours At least two of Isla Mujeres's boating cooperatives sell day
From Isla Mujeres tours to Contoy for about $30. Ricardo Gaitán Puerto's **Sociedad Cooperativa "Isla Mujeres"** (at the pier, tel. 988/20274) and **La Isleña** (½ block from the pier, at the corner of Calles Morelos and Juárez, tel. 988/20036) launch boats daily at 8 AM; they return at 4 or 5. Included in the package are a light breakfast; snorkeling (and gear) at Isla Che reef, which is 10–12 feet deep; trolling for barracuda; a tour of the leeward side, to Bird Beach and Puerto Viejo Lagoon; a stop at the park station to see the museum; and lunch and drinks. The tour requires a minimum of 6–10 people and accepts a maximum of 25; overnight excursions can be arranged.

From Cancún The **Thunderboat** (tel. 988/30062 or 988/30884) departs from Playa Linda dock Monday, Wednesday, and Friday at 9 AM and returns 5. The package includes swimming, snorkeling, a visit to the island museum, and an open-bar lunch.

Exploring Isla Contoy

Only 45 minutes north of Isla Mujeres, the sanctuary—a place of sand dunes, mangroves, and coconuts—remains beautiful and unspoiled. People come for the birds, the small museum, and the healthy waters on the leeward side. Seventy species of bird life—including gulls, pelicans, petrels, cormorants, cranes, ducks, flamingos, herons, frigates, sea swallows, doves, quail, spoonbills, and hawks—fly this way in late fall, some of them to breed and make their nests. Although the number of species is diminishing, Contoy is still a pleasure for rapt birders.

Snorkelers, divers, fishing hobbyists, and picnickers come here to glimpse the nearly deserted island's beautifully colored earth-tone coral and dazzling fish. The waters surrounding the island abound with mackerel, barracuda, flying fish, trumpetfish, and shrimp; in December, lobsters pass through in great numbers as their southerly migration route takes them past.

Black rocks and coral reefs fringe the island's east coast, which drops off abruptly 15 feet into the sea; at the west are sand, shrubs, and coconut palms. At the north and the south you find nothing but trees and small pools of water. The sand dunes inland on the east coast rise as high as 70 feet above sea level. Other than the birds and the dozen or so park rangers who make their home on Contoy, the only denizens are iguanas, lizards, turtles, hermit crabs, and boa constrictors.

Visit the outdoor museum, which displays about 50 photographs depicting the island, with captions in English, French, and Spanish. An observation tower offers a superb view of the surroundings. Wildlife lovers can even spend the night camping (bring a sleeping bag and insect repellent), but should contact SEDUE (*see* above) for information first.

5   Cozumel

Introduction

Cozumel provides a balance between Cancún and Isla Mujeres:
Though attuned to North American tourism, the island has
managed to keep development to a minimum. Its expansive
beaches, superb coral reefs, and copious wildlife—in the sea,
on the land, and in the air—attract a more active crowd than
does Cancún. Cozumel is not for jet-setters, but it is not inexpensive, either; the same young people who come for the excite-
ment of its diving and snorkeling also like to buy souvenirs.
Nonetheless, the island atmosphere is typically Mexican—relaxed and unpretentious—and the 60,000 islanders are genuinely friendly.

A 490-square-kilometer (189-square-mile) island 19 kilometers
(12 miles) to the east of Yucatán, Cozumel is mostly flat, its interior covered by parched scrub, dense jungle, and marshy lagoons. White sandy beaches with calm waters line the island's
leeward (western) side, which is fringed by a spectacular reef
system, while the powerful surf and rocky strands on the windward (eastern) side, facing the Caribbean, are broken up here
and there by calm bays and hidden coves. Most of Cozumel is
undeveloped, with a good deal of the land and the shores set
aside as national parks; crumbling Mayan ruins provide what
limited sightseeing there is aside from the island's glorious natural attractions. San Miguel is the only established town.

Before Cozumel was rediscovered by explorer Jacques Cousteau in the early 1960s, it was just another backwater, where
locals hunted alligators and iguanas and worked on coconut
plantations to produce copra (dried kernels from which coconut
oil is extracted). Zapote trees were cultivated for chicle, once
prized as the source of chewing gum, and Cozumeleños sub-
sisted largely on the fruits of the sea, including lobster, conch,
sea turtles, and fish, which remain staples of the economy.

Although the island was first inhabited by distant cousins of
the Maya, it was the Maya who transformed it into a key center
of trade and navigation as well as the destination for pilgrimages honoring Ixchel, the goddess of fertility, childbirth, and
the moon. The Maya called it *Ah-Cuzamil-Peten*, the Island of
Swallows.

In 1518, Spanish explorer Juan de Grijalva arrived on Cozumel
in search of slaves. His tales of gold and other treasures inspired the most famous Spanish explorer to come to Mexico—
Hernán Cortés—to visit the island the following year and,
shortly thereafter, to settle two missionaries there to convert
the Indians. Although the Spaniards never succeeded in colo-
nizing Cozumel disease eventually wiped out much of the native
population that had not already been massacred. By 1600 the
island was abandoned.

During the 17th and 18th centuries Cozumel became a hideout
for famous pirates and buccaneers, including Jean Laffite and
Henry Morgan, who found the catacombs and tunnels dug by
the Indians useful for burying their treasure. These corsairs
also laid siege to numerous cargo ships, many of which still lie
at the bottom of the surrounding waters. In the 19th century
Cozumel was primarily a fishing village and supply port for
shipping routes to Central America. At the start of this century, the island began to capitalize on the chewing-gum industry;

forays into the jungle in search of chicle led to interest in the archaeological remains. Many of the ruins still stand, but Cozumel's importance as a seaport and a chicle-producing region diminished with the advent of the airplane and the invention of synthetic chewing gum. In the 1950s the island eked out an existence as a health resort for wealthy Yucatecáns, and with the arrival of Cousteau—who had learned of the magnificent diving opportunities—Cozumel began its climb out of oblivion.

Cozumel's prolific wildlife has made this an island for exploring: Brilliantly feathered tropical birds, lizards, armadillos, coati, deer, and small foxes populate the undergrowth and the swamps, and you can even rescue turtle eggs as part of a nationwide campaign. Sportfishing and bonefishing are other popular pursuits, as are glass-bottom-boat trips to the reefs or lagoons. If you're planning to stay on Cozumel for three or more days, you may want to consider excursions to the mainland beaches around Akumal and to the ruined, walled city of Tulum. You can ferry over to Cancún for a day or fly to Chichén Itzá to spend the night, then come back to explore more of Cozumel's unique habitat.

Essential Information

Important Addresses and Numbers

Tourist Information
The **state tourism office** (tel. 987/21915 or 987/20218) is located upstairs in the Plaza del Sol, on the east end of the *zócalo* (the square), and is open weekdays 9–2. The office also has an information booth on the main pier, which is open daily 8–8. The following free booklets are provided by these offices: "What to Do/Where to Go," "Cozumel Today," and the "Blue Guide." Although they tend to be heavily advertiser-driven, they are helpful all the same. The "Brown Map" is the best available on the island and can be purchased in local shops. A good source of information on lodgings (as well as of general information) is the **Cozumel Island Hotel Association** (Calle 11 S at Av. Rafael Melgar, tel. 987/21097; fax 987/21599 or 987/20016), open weekdays 8–2 and 4–7. But *avoid* the "tourist information" booth on the main square: The young boy there is actually trying to sell time-share tours.

Emergencies
Police (Anexo del Palacio Municipal, tel. 987/20092); **Red Cross** (Av. Rosada Salas at Av. 20a S, tel. 987/21058); **Ambulance** (tel. 987/20639); **Port Captain** (tel. 987/20169); **Recompression Chamber** (Calle 5 S 21-B, between Av. Rafael Melgar and Av. 5a S, tel. 987/22387).

Medical Clinics
The **clinic** (Av. Circunvalación, tel. 987/20912) and the **hospital** (Av. 30a at Calle 11 S, tel. 987/20140) provide 24-hour emergency care.

Late-night Pharmacies
Farmacia Joaquín (zócalo, tel. 987/20125) is open Monday–Saturday 8 AM–10 PM and Sunday 9–1 and 5–9.

Banks
Banks are open weekdays 9–1:30, but foreign currency can be exchanged only between 10:30 and 12:30. Banks include **Banpaís** (across from the main pier, tel. 987/20318); **Bancomer** (Av. 5a at the zócalo, tel. 987/20550); **Banco del Atlántico** (Av.

5a S at Calle 1, tel. 987/20142 or 987/20182); and **Banco Serfin** (Calle 1 S between Avs. 5a and 10a, tel. 987/20030).

Money Exchange If you need to exchange money after banking hours, go to **Promotora Cambiaria del Centro** (Av. 5a S at Calle 1), which provides service Monday–Saturday 8–8 for a 1.15% commission.

English-language **Zodiaco** (zócalo, tel. 987/20031) carries a limited selection of
Bookstores guidebooks and English-language publications and is open weekdays 9–9, Saturday 9–2 and 5:30–9, and Sunday 9–1 and 6–9. **Dante** (Plaza Villamar, no phone), located on the second floor of the plaza, sells a good selection of dictionaries, travel books, maps, and books on archaeology and ethnography.

Travel Agencies Agencies with branches in Cozumel include **Intermar Caribe**
and Tour Operators (Calle 2 N 101-B between Avs. 5a and 10a, tel. 987/21535 or 987/21098; fax 987/20895), **Fiesta Cozumel** (Av. 11 and Av. 30, tel. 987/20725), **American Express** (Av. Rafael Melgar 27, tel. 987/20974 or 987/20831), and **Turismo Aviomar** (Av. 5a N 8 between Calles 2 and 4, tel. 987/20477 or 987/20588).

Arriving and Departing by Plane

Airport The **Cozumel Airport** is 3 kilometers (2 miles) north of town.
and Airlines **American** (tel. 800/433–7300) flies nonstop from Dallas/Fort Worth, Miami, and Raleigh/Durham. **Continental** (tel. 800/231–0856) provides nonstop service from Houston. **Mexicana** (tel. 800/531–7921) flies nonstop from Dallas/Fort Worth, Los Angeles, Miami, and Mérida; its subsidiary **Aerocaribe** (tel. 987/20503 or 987/20988) flies nonstop from Cancún, while **Aerocozumel** (tel. 987/20877 or 987/20503), another Mexicana subsidiary, has flights from Belize, Cancún, Chichén Itzá, Chetumal, Mérida, and Playa del Carmen.

Between the Airport Taxis can be hired at reasonable fixed rates that run about $5
and Hotels for private cars and $1 for the collective service. Most car rental agencies (*see* Getting Around, below) maintain offices in the terminal.

Arriving and Departing by Ferry, Jetfoil, and Cruise Ship

By Ferry The passenger-only ferry departs from the **Playa del Carmen dock** (no phone) for the 40-minute trip to the pier of the Hotel Fiesta Americana Sol Caribe (tel. 987/20700) in Cozumel. It leaves approximately every two hours between 5:30 AM and 9 PM and costs about $4. Returning to Playa, the service operates roughly 4 AM—8 PM. Verify the regularly changing schedule. The older car ferry from **Puerto Morelos** (tel. 987/20950) is not recommended unless you *must* bring your car. The three- to four-hour trip costs $25 per car or $4 per passenger; there is no Monday service. Again, schedules change frequently, so we advise you to call ahead before planning to leave, but note that tickets go on sale approximately two hours before departure.

By Jetfoil Two waterjet catamarans make the trip between Cozumel (downtown pier, at the zócalo) and Playa del Carmen. This service, operated by **Aviomar** (tel. 987/20477 or 987/21728), costs the same as the ferry and takes as much time, but the vessel is considerably more comfortable and offers on-board movies and refreshments. The boats make at least seven crossings a day, leaving Playa del Carmen approximately every two hours between 5:30 AM and 7:30 PM and returning from Cozumel between 4 AM and 6:30 PM. Tickets are sold at the piers in both ports one hour before departure, but call to confirm the schedule.

By Cruise Ship At least a dozen cruise lines call at Cozumel and/or Playa del Carmen, including, from Fort Lauderdale, **Costa Cruises** (tel. 800/327–2537); from Miami, **Carnival** (tel. 800/327–9501), **Chandris** (tel. 305/576–9900), **Dolphin** (tel. 800/222–1003), **Norwegian** (tel. 800/327–7030), and **Royal Caribbean** (tel. 800/327–2055); from New Orleans, **Commodore** (tel. 800/327–5617); from New York City, **Regency** (tel. 800/388–5500); from Tampa, **Holland America** (tel. 800/426–0327), **Princess Cruises** (tel. 800/446–6690). **Special Expeditions** (tel. 212/765–7740) offers 15-day sailings between the Panama Canal and the "Maya Coast," with passengers disembarking in Cozumel.

Getting Around

By Bus Local bus service runs to the hotel zones north and south of town on the west side, as well as from the main pier out to Chankanaab. The service is irregular but inexpensive (under $1).

By Car Open-air Jeeps and other rental cars, especially those with four-wheel drive, are a good way of getting down dirt roads leading to secluded beaches and small Mayan ruins (although the rental insurance policy may not always cover these jaunts). The only gas station on Cozumel, at the corner of Avenida Juárez and Avenida 30a, is open daily 7 AM–midnight.

Car Rentals Following is a list of rental firms that handle two- and four-wheel vehicles (all the major hotels have rental offices): **Avis** (Calle 20 between Calle Rosada Salas and Calle 3 S, tel. 987/21923; at Hotel Stouffer Presidente, tel. 987/20322), **Budget** (Av. 5a and Calle 2 N, tel. 987/20903; at the cruise-ship terminal, tel. 987/21732; and at the airport, tel. 987/21742), **Cozumel Maya Rent** (Av. Aeropuerto and Av. 30a, tel. 987/20655), **Fiesta Cozumel** (Hotel Mesón San Miguel, tel. 987/21389), and **Hertz** (Av. Juárez and Calle 10, tel. 987/22136). Car rates start at $50 a day.

Mopeds and Motorcycles Mopeds and motorcycles are very popular here, but also extremely dangerous because of heavy traffic, potholes, and hidden stop signs; accidents happen all too frequently. Mexican law now requires all passengers to wear helmets, though this law is not consistently enforced. For mopeds, go to **Fiesta Cozumel**, **Rentadora Caribe** (Calle Rosada Salas 3, tel. 987/20955), or **Rentadora Cozumel** (Calle Rosada Salas 3B, tel. 21429, and Av. 10a S at Calle Rosada Salas, tel. 987/21120). Motorbikes rent for $20 per day.

By Taxi **Taxi service** is available 24 hours a day, with a 25% surcharge between midnight and 6 AM, at the main location (2 Calle N, tel. 987/20041 or 987/20236) or at the *malecón* (the square) at the main pier in town. Fixed rates of about $2 are charged to go between town and either hotel zone and about $4 between the two hotel zones, to the airport, or to San Francisco Beach. However, cruise-ship passengers taking taxis to or from the international terminal are routinely charged about twice as much as tourists staying on the island.

Mail

The local **post office** (Calle 7 S at the malecón, tel. 987/20106), 6
blocks south of the square, is open weekdays 9–1 and 3–6 and
Saturday 9–1. If you are a cardholder, you can receive mail at
the American Express office at **Fiesta Cozumel American Express** (Av. Rafael Melgar 45, tel. 987/20974 or 987/20831) weekdays 8–1 and 5–8 and Saturday 8–5.

Telephones

Long-distance calls can be placed from the designated **booths**
(on Av. 5a N at Calle 2, next to Budget Rent-a-Car, and on Calle 1 S at the main square) daily 8–1 and 4–9.

Guided Tours

Orientation Island tours are offered for about $18 by at least two of
Cozumel's leading travel agencies. The **Intermar Caribe** (tel.
987/20895) version includes swimming at a beach on the windward side, a visit to a "coral factory" in town, and snorkeling
and lunch at Chankanaab. **Turismo Aviomar** (tel. 987/20588)
sells the same tour and a variation: the Mayan ruins at San
Gervasio, swimming at Chen Río beach, and lunch, beach
games, and jetskiing at Playa del Sol (near Palancar Beach, on
the leeward side).

Air Tours **Aviomar** charters three-seater Cessnas for half-hour flights
over the island for about $150. It also sells tours to Chichén
Itzá, Cobá, and Belize.

Specialty **Snorkeling tours** go for anywhere from $18 to $35, depending on
Tours the length, and take in the shallow reefs off Palancar or the Colombia lagoon. Lunch on a beach and equipment are usually included. A tour by **Aviomar** departs from Playa del Sol and
caters particularly to cruise-ship passengers, who are taken directly from the ship to the beach. **Fiesta Cozumel** runs snorkeling tours from its 45-foot catamaran, the *Zorro*. **Diving tour**
rates begin at about $50 per day; snorkelers wishing to accompany dive boats may do so for about $20, but it is much less expensive—about $8 per day—to rent your own equipment at one
of the dive shops in town or out at the beaches (*see* Participant
Sports, below).

Strictly for scuba enthusiasts is the all-inclusive scuba trip to
Banco Chinchorro, a ship graveyard 10 miles off the coast of
southern Quintana Roo, almost due east of Chetumal. This unusual excursion (for professional divers only), offering 100-foot
dives, reef dives, and night dives, takes place aboard the luxurious 100-foot MV *Oceanus*, which houses guests for a minimum of three nights (which costs $600). **Barbachano Tours**
(1570 Madruga Ave., Ph. #1, Coral Gables, FL 33146, tel. 305/
662-5971) sponsors the trip. Glass-bottom-boat trips provided
by Aviomar & CADO (tel. 987/21842) appeal to people who
don't want to get wet but do want to see the brilliant underwater life around the island. Included are snorkeling in the shallow reefs and a meal of fried fish caught in Playa del Carmen.
Larger motorboats tour the more distant reefs.

Off-island tours to Tulum and Xel-Há, run by **Intermar Caribe**
and **Turismo Aviomar,** cost about $35 and include the 30-minute
ferry trip to Playa del Carmen, the 45-minute ride to Tulum,

1½–2 hours at the ruins, entrance fees, guides, lunch, and sometimes a brief stop for snorkeling at black coral reefs, caves, and adjacent cenotes of the Xcaret lagoon.

The Cozumel Museum offers evening **turtle-watching tours** on which visitors aid in the preservation of the endangered turtle species. The tours run between May and September, when the babies hatch. After a slide show, a guide takes participants to the eastern shore of the island, where they seek out and mark nests and collect the eggs, which are the size of ping-pong balls. The expedition ends, following a lecture by biologists at the hatchery, at midnight. Tours are offered on weekends, but special trips can be arranged on other days for a minimum of six people. *Av. Melgar and Calle 4 N, tel. 987/20838. Suggested donation: $10. May–Sept., Fri.–Sat. 8 PM–midnight.*

Exploring

Cozumel is about 53 kilometers (33 miles) long and 15 kilometers (9 miles) wide, but only a small percentage of its roads—primarily those in the southern half—are paved. Dirt roads can be explored, with care, in a four-wheel-drive vehicle. Aside from the 3% of the island that has been developed, Cozumel is made up of vast expanses of sandy or rocky beaches, quiet little coves, palm groves, scrubby jungles, lagoons and swamps, and a few low hills (the maximum elevation is 45 feet).

San Miguel, Cozumel's hub, is simply laid out in characteristically Mexican grid fashion. Avenida Benito Juárez stretches east from the pier for 16 kilometers (10 miles) across the island, dividing north from south. Running perpendicular is Avenida Rafael Melgar (also known as the malecón), the coastal road on the island's leeward side. Avenues, which are labeled "norte" or "sur" depending on where they fall in relation to Juárez, parallel Melgar and are numbered in multiples of five. This means that the avenue after Avenida 5a Sur is Avenida 10a Sur, but if you were to cross Juárez on Avenida 5a Sur it would turn into Avenida 5a Norte.

Numbers in the margin correspond to points of interest on the Cozumel map.

❶ Cozumel's principal town, **San Miguel,** serves as the hub of the island; its malecón (Avenida Rafael Melgar) is the main strip of shops and restaurants. The **Plaza del Sol** (between Avenida Juárez and Calle 1 Sur) houses some government buildings, including the large and modern convention center (used more for local functions than for formal conferences) and the **state tourist office** (tel. 987/20972 or 987/20218); otherwise the plaza is not particularly interesting or striking. Heading inland (east) from the malecón takes you away from the touristy zone and toward the rather ordinary residential sections. The commercial district is concentrated in the 10 blocks between Calle 10 N and Calle 7 S. North of that point, you find almost no development until you reach the stretch of hotels beyond the airport; south of town, development continues almost uninterrupted as far as the Stouffer Presidente.

The **Museo de la Isla de Cozumel** is a good place to begin orienting yourself. Housed on two floors of what was once the island's first luxury hotel are four permanent exhibit halls of dioramas, sculptures, charts, and explanations of the island's history and

96

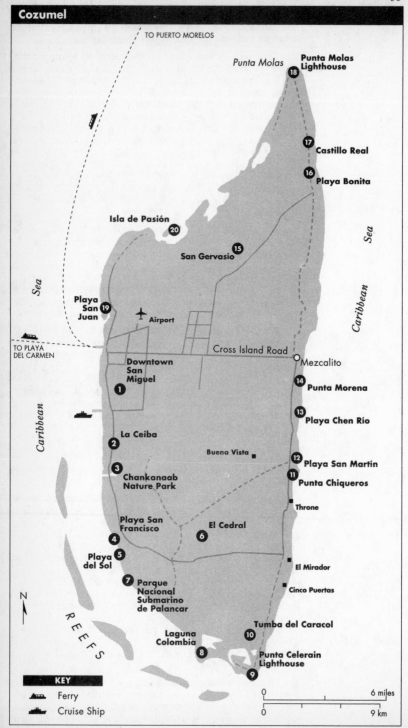

ecosystem. Displays cover Mayan, colonial, and modern times and detail the local geology, flora, and fauna. The museum also presents temporary exhibits, guided tours, and workshops. *Av. Rafael Melgar at Calle 4 N, tel. 987/21545 or 987/21475. Admission free except for special events. Open Tues.–Sun. 9–7.*

Time Out On the terrace off the second floor of the museum, the **Restaurante del Museo** (Av. Melgar and Calle 4 N, tel. 987/20838) sells soft drinks, beer, and full meals of *fajitas* (thin strips of grilled beef), barbecued meat, and grilled red snapper, all enhanced by a great waterfront view.

2 Heading south of town, divers and snorkelers may want to take a plunge off the pier at **La Ceiba:** About 100 yards offshore lie the remains of a small airplane that was placed there in 1977 during the making of a Mexican movie. An underwater trail marks various types of sea life, including sponges and enormous coral formations; visibility is excellent to about 98 feet (about 30 meters). La Ceiba, which is part of the second cluster of hotels and shops south of town, lies adjacent to the international passenger terminal for cruise ships.

3 About a 10-minute drive south of San Miguel you will find **Chankanaab Nature Park** (the name means "small sea"), a lovely saltwater lagoon that the government has made into a wildlife sanctuary, botanical garden, and aquarium. Underwater caves, offshore reefs, a protected bay, and a sunken ship attract droves of snorkelers and scuba divers. The botanical garden boasts about 370 varieties of plant life from more than 20 countries; some 60-odd species of marine life, including fish, coral, turtles, and various crustaceans, reside in the lagoon. Sadly, swimming through the underwater tunnels from the lagoon to the bay is now forbidden, but visitors may walk through the shallow lagoon. Be warned, however, that the bottom is rocky, so wear shoes with rubber soles. As to the bay and its contents, the beach is excellent, and the waters hide crusty old cannons and anchors as well as the statue of a saint. A dive shop, restaurant, gift shop, snack stand, and dressing room with lockers and showers are on the premises. *Carretera Sur, Km 9, no phone. Admission: $2. Open daily 9–5.*

4 South of Chankanaab lies **Playa San Francisco,** an inviting 5-kilometer (3-mile) stretch of sandy beach that's considered one of the longest and finest on Cozumel. Comprising the beaches known as Playa Maya and Santa Rosa, San Francisco gets especially crowded during high season, on weekends (with cruise-ship passengers), and on Sundays (when locals come to eat fresh fish and hear live music). Environmental concerns have halted plans to build five new luxury hotels here. In the meantime, however, the beach has everything beach goers need (though costs run higher here than on other, less frequented beaches): two outdoor restaurants, a bar, dressing rooms, gift shops, volleyball nets, beach chairs, and snorkeling equipment. Divers also use this beach as their jumping-off point for dives to the San Francisco reef and the Santa Rosa wall. Just past San Francisco is **Playa del Sol.** Now open to the public, this beach

5 was once privately owned by the tour operator Aviomar; it has complete facilities, including a restaurant-bar, shops, and snorkeling and jetskiing equipment.

A turnoff at Km 17.5 leads about 3 kilometers (2 miles) inland

6 down a dirt road to the village and ruins of **El Cedral,** once the largest Mayan site on Cozumel and the temple sighted by the original Spanish explorers in 1518. The first Mass in Mexico was reportedly celebrated at this temple, most of which was torn down by the conquistadores. The site was uninhabited as recently as the turn of the century, and the ruined temple was used as a jail. The U.S. Army Corps of Engineers destroyed most of the ruin during World War II to make way for the island's first airport, and now all that remains is a small structure capped by a Mayan arch and covered by faint traces of paint and stucco. A defiant tree grows from its roof. Every May a fair, with dancing, music, and a cattle show, is held at this site.

More interesting than the ruin is the small green contemporary church housing 92 crosses shrouded in embroidered lace mantles. The crosses, which were thought to have oracular qualities, testify to the cult of the "Speaking Cross," which inspired the rebellious Maya during the War of the Castes in the mid-1800s. In this war, the Indians vainly attempted to win back the land that had been wrested from them three centuries before. Families fleeing the mainland settled in San Miguel and made their living off the Colombia hacienda south of San Francisco Beach.

Heading back to the coast but continuing south, you'll come to

7 **Parque Nacíonal Submarino de Palancar,** whose beach, with a gently sloping shore enlivened by palm trees, is far more deserted than San Francisco. Offshore lies the famous **Palancar Reef,** which is practically Cozumel's raison d'être. Because of the diversity of coral formations and the dramatic underwater peaks and valleys, divers rank this reef among the top five in the world.

8 At the island's southern tip is the **Laguna Colombia,** a prime site for jungle aficionados. It is reached by boat. Fish migrate here to lay their eggs, and barracuda, baby fish, and birds show up in great numbers in season. Other popular diving and snorkeling spots can be found offshore in the reefs of **Tunich, Colombia,** and **Maracaibo.**

9 The **Punta Celerain Lighthouse,** surrounded by sand dunes at the narrowest point of land, stands 4 kilometers (3 miles) from the road and affords a misty, mesmerizing view of pounding waves, swamps, and scraggly jungle. Alligators were once hunted nearby; nowadays you may spot a soldier or two from the adjacent army base catching an iguana. On Sundays at noon, the point comes to life when Primo the lighthouse keeper serves fried fish and beer, and locals and tourists gather to chat. A number of secluded beaches trail off to the left.

The east coast of Cozumel, at which you have now arrived, presents a splendid succession of mostly deserted rocky coves and powdery beaches. Swimming can be treacherous here, but there is nothing (except perhaps the lack of changing facilities) to prevent deliciously solitary sunbathing on any of the several beaches. As you follow the dirt road north, you will first pass

10 the **Tumba del Caracol,** another Mayan ruin that may have served as a lighthouse. A few other minuscule ruins in the area—**Buenavista, Cinco Puertas,** and the **Throne**—are accessible only by a dirt road that is nearly impassable during the rainy season.

⑪ **Punta Chiqueros,** a moon-shaped cove sheltered from the sea by an offshore reef, is the next attraction en route. Part of a longer
⑫ stretch of beach called **Playa San Martín,** it has fine sand, clear water, and moderate waves. Not only is the scenery beautiful, but you can also swim and camp here and later dine at a restaurant called **Tortuga Desnuda** (Naked Turtle). A little more than 3 kilometers (2 miles) away, almost at the other end of Playa
⑬ San Martín, is **Playa Chen Río,** another good spot for camping or exploring, where the waters are clear and the surf is not too strong.

Nearly 1 kilometer (½ mile) north of Chen Río along the main
⑭ road is **Punta Morena,** where waves crash on the rocky beach and, on June nights when the moon is full, turtles come to lay their eggs. If you're on the beach then, you may be stopped by soldiers who are stationed here to control poaching and drug traffic. This is also the site of the eastern coast's only hotel, also called Punta Morena, which has a restaurant and bar.

The cross-island road meets the east coast at **Mescalito Café;** here you can turn back to town or continue north. If you choose the latter, you'll have to travel along a dead-end dirt road; eventually you'll have to turn around.

⑮ At this point you may decide to detour inland to the ruins of **San Gervasio,** the largest extant Mayan site on Cozumel. To get there, take the cross-island road west to the army airfield and follow it for 10 kilometers (6 miles) north. Formerly the island's capital and probably its ceremonial center, the classical- and postclassical-style site was continuously occupied from AD 300 to AD 1500. Typical architectural features from the era include plazas limestone and masonry superstructures atop stepped platforms; stelae, bas-reliefs, and frescoes. What remains today are several small mounds scattered around a plaza and several broken columns and lintels that were once part of the main building or observatory. There is a snack bar on the grounds. *Admission: $2. Open daily 8–5.*

An even less maneuverable dirt road leads northeast of San Gervasio back to the unpaved coast road. At the junction is the
⑯ marvelously deserted **Playa Bonita,** where you can camp, though no facilities are available. At the northern end of the
⑰ beach you'll find **Castillo Real,** another Mayan site comprising a lookout tower, the base of a pyramid, and a temple with two chambers capped by a false arch. The waters here harbor several shipwrecks, remnants from the days when buccaneers lay in wait for richly cargoed galleons en route to Europe.

A number of other minor ruins are spread across the northern
⑱ tip of Cozumel, which terminates at the **Punta Molas Lighthouse,** an excellent spot for sunbathing, birding, and camping. This entire area is accessible only by four-wheel-drive vehicles (or by boat), but the jagged shoreline and the open sea offers magnificent views, making it well worth the trip.

Back on the leeward side, north of town, is a long expanse of
⑲ sandy beach known as **Playa San Juan,** which culminates in Punta Norte. The island's northern cluster of hotels occupies the sea side of the highway; across the way are several restaurants. Just beyond Punta Norte, smack in the middle of Abrigo

㉑ Bay, you'll find **Isla de Pasión.** The secluded beaches of this tiny island are now part of a state reserve, and fishing is permitted. Continue along the coast road to return to San Miguel.

Cozumel as a Port of Call

In 1990 Cozumel, Mexico's largest cruise-ship port, hosted more than 540 ships unloading more than 500,000 passengers, many of whom claim that Cozumel is their favorite destination. Generally, boats arrive around 7 AM and depart at 5 PM, though some spend as many as 18 hours in port. Because of the limited amount of time on shore, most cruise visitors opt for shore excursions sold on board and operated exclusively by Aviomar, because these packages are designed to coincide with the ship's itinerary. Going off on one's own may entice the adventurer, but it also may entail greater expense and risk. For example, if taxi drivers become aware that they are your only means of transportation, they may try to take advantage of you; they will sometimes charge cruise ship passengers as much as twice the rate they charge on-island visitors. Similarly, a tour operator who knows you won't be around long enough to file a complaint for unprofessional service may sign you up for some dubious, overpriced tour or snorkeling trip.

The island tours and diving packages sold to ship passengers by Aviomar or Intermar Caribe (*see* Guided Tours, above) survey Cozumel's lagoons, parks, and beaches. Another, considerably cheaper option is to take a taxi to the pier at La Ceiba, Playa San Francisco, or some other beach on the west coast and rent your own snorkeling equipment. You might decide to spend all your time shopping, possibly taking a break for a margarita at Carlos n' Charlies, or seeing the museum. You could hire a taxi for a quick tour around the island's southern point, taking in one of the small ruins or finding a quiet beach on the windward side (ask the driver to wait for you—you don't want to get stranded). Experienced riders may wish to rent a moped for a spin around the island, but bear in mind that accidents are frequent; check with your activities director about liability.

What to See and Do with Children

Chankanaab Nature Park (*see* Exploring, above).

Museo de la Isla de Cozumel (*see* Exploring, above).

Shopping

Shopping is an even bigger industry for Cozumel than diving, principally because of the lucrative trade with cruise-ship passengers. Thousands disembark each year in San Miguel, and consequently prices are relatively high compared to, say, Mérida. The variety of folk art ranges from downright schlocky curios to some excellent silver jewelry, pottery, painted balsawood animals, blown glass, and *huipiles* (embroidered cotton dresses).

As in other Mexican resort destinations, Cozumel's shops accept dollars as readily as pesos, and many goods are priced in dollars. You'll get a better price everywhere on Cozumel if you pay with cash or traveler's checks, although credit cards— MasterCard and Visa more often than American Express or

Diners Club—are widely accepted. If you use plastic, however, you may be asked to pay a surcharge. Authorities and experienced travelers alike warn against buying from street vendors, because the quality of their merchandise leaves much to be desired, although this may not be apparent until it's too late.

Cruise ships traditionally dock at Cozumel on Monday, but there is traffic here almost every weekday, and the shops are fullest from 10 to 11 and 1 to 2. Generally, stores are open 9–1 and 5–9, but a number of them disregard siesta hours and open even on weekends, particularly during high season. Don't pay much attention to written or verbal offers of "20% discounts, today only" or "only for cruise-ship passengers," because they're nothing but bait to get you inside. Similarly, many of the larger stores advertise "duty-free" wares, but these are of greater interest to Mexicans from the mainland than to North Americans since the prices tend to be higher than retail prices in the United States.

A last word of caution: Cruise-ship activities directors tend to push the black coral "factories," but they should be avoided because coral is an endangered species and because it is hard to tell real coral from black plastic.

Shopping Districts/Streets/Malls

Cozumel has three main shopping areas: **downtown** along the waterfront, on Avenida Rafael Melgar, and on some of the side streets around the zócalo (there are more than 150 shops in this area alone); at the **crafts market** (Calle 1 S, behind the plaza) in town, which sells a respectable assortment of Mexican wares; and at the cruise-ship **passenger terminal** south of town, near the Casa Del Mar, La Ceiba, and Sol Caribe hotels. There are also small clusters of shops at **Plaza del Sol** (on the east side of the main plaza), **Plaza de las Garzas** (malecón at Calle 8), and **Plaza Maya 2000** (across from the Sol Caribe). As a general rule, the newer, trendier shops line the waterfront, while the area around Avenida 5a houses the better crafts shops. The **town market** (Calle Rosada Salas, between Avs. 20a and 25a) sells fresh produce and other essentials; the **flea market** (Av. 5a N between Calles 2 and 4) features an eclectic array of shells, coins, bottles, erotic Mayan figurines, Cuban cigars, Cozumel honey, "magic" powders and herbs, antique masks, sharks' teeth, amber, rare coins and stamps, discarded books and magazines, photographs from the Mexican revolution, and other oddities.

Department Stores   **Orbi** (Av. Rafael Melgar S 27, tel. 987/20685) sells everything from liquor and perfume to snorkeling gear and luggage. **Pama** (Av. Rafael Melgar S 9, tel. 987/20090), in the heart of town, features imported food, luggage, snorkeling gear, jewelry, and crystal.

Specialty Stores   **La Fiesta Cotton Country** (Av. Rafael Melgar N 164-B, tel. 987/ *Clothing*   22032), a large store catering to the cruise ships, sells a variety of T-shirts as well as souvenirs.

Several trendy fashion chain stores line Avenida Rafael Melgar (between Calles 2 and 6), including **Esprit, Express, Aca Joe, Benetton,** and **Polo/Ralph Lauren.** Though prices tend to be a bit cheaper here than in the United States, the quality of the merchandise is generally inferior.

Jewelry Jewelry on Cozumel is pricey, but it tends to be of higher quality than the jewelry you'll find in many of the other Yucatán towns. **Van Cleef** (Av. Rafael Melgar, tel. 987/20699) offers a good collection of silver jewelry and gemstone rings.

Another good jeweler, next door to Van Cleef, is **Casablanca** (Av. Rafael Melgar 33, tel. 987/21177), which specializes in gold, silver, and gemstones, as well as expensive crafts.

La Fiesta Silver Country (Av. Rafael Melgar N 164-A, tel. 987/22143 or 987/22054) offers silver, much of it of the cheap, junky variety, but with some nice-looking pieces.

Nothing but fine silver, gold, and coral jewelry—particularly silver bracelets and earrings—is sold at **Joyería Palancar** (Av. Rafael Melgar N, tel. 987/21468).

Alexandra (Av. Rafael Melgar, tel. 987/21609) features earrings of original design as well as gold and gemstones.

Argentium (Av. Rafael Melgar, tel. 987/21609), next to Disco Scaramouche, has a small but fine selection of silver.

Mexican Crafts **La Concha** (Av. 5a S 141, tel. 987/21270), inside a small shopping center half a block south of the zócalo, is one of three such outlets (the others are located at Plaza Maya and the ship terminal) that offer a small but pretty selection of Mexican and Guatemalan folk art.

Na Balam (Av. 5a N 14, no phone) sells high-quality Mayan reproductions, batik clothing, and jewelry.

Xaman-Ek: The Bird Sanctuary (Av. Rafael Melgar, no phone), specializes, as its name implies, in all manner of artificial birds, made of papier-mâché, ceramics, and other materials.

The nearly block-long **Los Cinco Soles** (Av. Rafael Melgar 27, tel. 987/20132) features a wide variety of items, including blue-rim glassware, *talavera* pottery (blue-and-white pottery from Puebla), brass and tin animals from Jalisco, tablecloths and place mats, cotton gauze and embroidered clothing, onyx, T-shirts, papier-mâché fruit, reproduction Mayan art, Mexican fashions, silver jewelry, soapstone earrings and beads, and other Mexican wares.

A large selection of ceramics, brightly painted wooden fish, papier-mâché masks, jewelry, and onyx (including Chinese checker sets) is available from **Bazar del Angel** (Av. Rafael Melgar, 2 blocks south of the zócalo, tel. 987/21791).

Unicornio (Av. 5a S 1, tel. 987/20171) specializes in Mexican folk art, including calcedonia stone picture frames and jewelry boxes. Though you'll find a lot of junk, there are some good talavera sets and ceramic birds, as well as T-shirts and embroidered clothing.

Ruth (Calle 4 N between Avs. 5a and 10a, no phone) has a nice if small choice of crafts.

Gordon Gilchrist (Studio I, Av. 25a S at Calle 15, tel. 987/26159), a local artist, displays—by appointment—his etchings of local Mayan sites.

Hammocks (Av. 5a N and Calle 4, no phone) are made and sold by Manuel Azueta from his front porch.

Sports and Fitness

Most people come to Cozumel to take advantage of the island's water-related sports—particularly scuba diving, snorkeling, and fishing (*see* below), but jetskiing, sailboarding, water-skiing, and sailing remain popular as well. You will find services and rentals throughout the island, especially through major hotels and water-sports centers such as **Del Mar Aquatic** (Costera Sur, Km 4, tel. 987/21900) and **Agua Safari** (Av. Rafael Melgar 39A, tel. 987/20101).

Fishing

The waters off Cozumel swarm with more than 230 species of fish, the numbers upholding the island's reputation as one of the world's best locations for sailfishing and sportfishing. World records are frequently set here for such catch as blue and white marlin (a 670-pound blue marlin was caught in 1990), grouper, dolphin fish, sailfish, and wahoo. Billfish is also a popular catch, especially during migration (late April–June) when these beaky-jawed fish can be hooked within a quarter-mile from shore on the leeward side where the sea bottom descends to 914 meters (3,000 feet). Deep-sea fishing for tuna, barracuda, and kingfish is productive year-round. Aficionados also enjoy Cozumel's bottom fishing (grouper, yellowtail, and snapper) and bonefishing on the shallow sand flats, at the northern end of the island, which harbor tarpon, snook, cubera, and small sharks. The best times to fish are sunrise and sunset, just before a full moon.

Please obey regulations forbidding commercial fishing, sportfishing, spearfishing, and the collection of any marine life between the shore and El Cantil Reef and between the cruise-ship dock and Punta Celerain. U.S. Customs allows you to bring up to 30 pounds of fish back into the country.

Charters High-speed fishing boats up to 100 feet long can be chartered for about $300–$750 per day from the **Club Naútico de Cozumel** (Puerto de Abrigo, Av. Rafael Melgar, Box 341, tel. 987/21135), the island's headquarters for game fishing. Other charters available from Club Naútico include bonefishing and cost about $150 for six hours. Daily charters are easily arranged from the dock or at your hotel, but you might also try **Aquarius Fishing and Tours** (Calle 3 S, tel. 987/21092) for a 4½-hour fishing trip ($125; maximum 3 people). All rates vary with the season. More information can be provided by **Caribbean Nautical Promotions** (tel. 800/423–1666; fax 305/443–9522). Reservations are necessary.

Scuba Diving

With more than 30 charted reefs whose average depths range from 15 to 24 meters (50 to 80 feet) and a water temperature that hits about 75–80°F during peak diving season (June–August, when hotel rates are coincidentally at their lowest), Cozumel is far and away Mexico's number-one diving destination. Sixty thousand divers come here each year to explore the underwater coral formations, caves, sponges, sea fans, and tropical fish. The diversity of options includes deep dives, drift dives, shore dives, wall dives, and night dives, as well as theme dives focusing on ecology, archaeology, sunken ships, and photography. Because there have been a number of recorded diving fatalities in Cozumel, the island has made a serious effort toward safety. About half the operators have banded together to form the **Cozumel Association of Dive Operators** (CADO, Av. Rafael E. Melgar and Av. 5 S, Box 450, Cozumel, 77600, tel. 987/21842; fax 987/21842), an organization designed to establish some operational standards for training boat captains in the science of navigation and training divers in ecotourism. Divers are not required to be certified, but it is strongly advised that they complete a certification course before setting out. About 25 dive operators are also affiliated with the island's **recompression chamber** (Calle 5 S 21B, between Av. Rafael Melgar and Av. 5a S, next to Discover Cozumel, tel. 987/22387), which treats tourists for free through an arrangement with CADO. The recompression chamber, which boasts a 38-minute response time from reef to chamber, treats decompression sickness, commonly known as "the bends," by giving patients oxygen. The sickness occurs when divers surface too quickly and nitrogen is absorbed into the bloodstream. Other injuries treated here include nitrogen narcosis, collapsed lungs, and overexposure to the cold.

Diving requires that you be reasonably fit. It should also go without saying that—particularly if you are new to diving—you should find a qualified instructor. Another caveat: Always stay at least 3 feet above the reef, not just because the coral can sting or cut you, but also because coral is easily damaged and grows very slowly: It's taken 2,000 years for it to reach its present size.

Dive Shops and Tour Operators Most dive shops can provide you with all the incidentals you'll need, as well as with guides and transportation. You can choose from a variety of two-tank boat trips and specialty dives ranging from $45 to $56; three-hour resort courses cost about $60, and 1½-hour night dives, $30. Certification dives cost from $100 to $300, depending on the number of days, while dive-master courses cost as much as $450. Equipment rental is relatively inexpensive, ranging from $5 for tanks or a lamp to about $8 for a regulator or jacket; underwater cameras can cost as much as $35, and videos of your own dive, about $75.

Because dive shops tend to be competitive, it is well worth your while to shop around when choosing a dive operator. In addition to the dive shops in town, many hotels have their own operations and offer dive and hotel packages starting at about $350 for three nights, double occupancy, and two days of diving. For an unusual live-aboard scuba experience, *see* Guided Tours, above. You can also pick up a copy of the *Chart of the Reefs of Cozumel* in any dive shop. The following is a list of recommended shops on the island, all of which are members of CADO: **Aqua Safari** (Av. Rafael Melgar 39a, tel. 987/20101); **Blue Angel** (Hotel Villablanca, tel. 987/21631), for PADI certification; **Blue Bubble** (Box 334, Av. 5a S at Calle 3 S, tel. 987/21865), for PADI instruction; **Caribbean Divers** (Box 191, 5 locations, including Calle 4 N, tel. 987/21080; fax 987/21426), for PADI and NAUI certification; **Del Mar Aquatics** (Costera Sur, Km 4, tel 987/21900; fax. 987/21833); **Dive House** (Av. 1a, no. 6, tel. 987/21953; fax 987/23068); **Dive Paradise** (Av. Rafael Melgar 601 at Calle 3 S, tel. 987/21007; fax 987/21061); **El Clavado**, (Parque Nacíonal Chankanaab, tel. 987/20482 or 987/23058); **Fantasia Divers** (Av.

25, enter at Adolfo Rosado Salas and Av. 35, tel. 987/22840; fax 987/21210); **Scuba, Scuba!** (calle 5 S and Av. Rafael Melgar, tel. 987/21379); **Yucab Reef** (Av. Rosado Salas 11, tel. 987/21842). Although not a CADO member, **Pro Dive** (Calle 3 S at Av. 5a S) is also recommended.

Reef Dives The reefs stretch for 32 kilometers (20 miles), beginning at the international pier and continuing on to Punta Celerain at the southernmost tip of the island. The following is a rundown of Cozumel's main dive destinations.

Colombia Reef This reef—reaching 25–30 meters (82–98 feet)—is excellent for experienced divers who want to take some deep dives. Its underwater structures are as labyrinthine and varied as those of Palancar (*see* below); large groupers, jacks, eagle rays, and even an occasional sea turtle cluster at the mouths of caves and near the overhangs.

Maracaibo Reef Generally considered the most difficult of all the Cozumel reefs for divers, this one—located off the southern end of the island—lends itself to drift dives because of its length. You don't even see the ledge of the reef until you go 37 meters (121 feet) below the surface. Although there are shallow areas, only expert divers who can cope with the strong current should attempt Maracaibo.

Palancar Reef This reef system, situated nearly 2 kilometers (1 mile) offshore, offers about 40 dive locations. Black and red coral and huge elephant-ear sponges and barrel sponges, as well as a sunken cannon and an enormous bronze statue of Christ, are among the attractions at the bottom. The reef, which begins at about 27 meters (89 feet) below the surface, is particularly suitable for drift dives. A favorite of divers is the section called **Horseshoe,** comprising several coral heads at the top of the drop-off. Towering coral columns and deep ravines and canyons make for some of the most sensational dives in the Caribbean.

Paraíso Reef Just north of the cruise-ship pier, about 200 meters (656 feet) offshore and up to 17 meters (56 feet) deep, Paraíso provides a practice spot for divers before they head to deeper drop-offs. Also a wonderful site for night diving, this reef is inhabited by star coral, brain coral, sea fans and other gorgonians, and sponges. From Paraíso you can swim out to the drop-offs called La Ceiba and Villa Blanca.

Plane Wreck This airplane was taken about 91 meters (about 300 feet) off the La Ceiba pier and sunk during a 1977 Mexican motion picture production. Because of its reassuring proximity to the shore and because the average depth of the water is only 9–17 meters (30–56 feet), it has been a favorite training ground for neophyte divers ever since. Enormous coral structures and colorful sponges surround the reef, while an underwater trail guides divers by the marine life.

Santa Rosa Wall Also a renowned spot for deep dives and drift dives, this wall—just north of Palancar—drops off abruptly at 22 meters (72 feet) to enormous coral overhangs and caves below. Sponges are especially populous here, as are angelfish, groupers, and eagle rays—along with a shark or two.

Tormentos Reef Sea fans and other gorgonians and sponges live on this variegated reef, where the maximum depth reaches about 21 meters (70 feet). Tormentos, one of the best locations for underwater photography, hosts sea cucumbers, arrow crabs, and other marine life, which provide a terrifically colorful backdrop.

Yucab Reef About 121 meters (400 feet) long and 9 meters (30 feet) deep, this reef is located less than a mile from shore, near Chankanaab. Coral, sponge, sea whips, and angelfish swim in these waters, where the currents can reach 2 or 3 knots.

Snorkeling

Snorkeling ranks just after diving among the island's popular sports. There is good snorkeling in the morning off the piers at the Stouffer Presidente and La Ceiba, where fish are fed. The shallow reefs in Chankanaab Bay, Playa San Francisco, and the northern beach at the Club Cozumel Caribe also provide clear views of brilliantly colored fish and sea creatures, among them fingerlings, parrot fish, sergeant majors, angelfish, and squirrel fish, along with elk coral, conch, and sand dollars.

CADO members that specialize in snorkeling include **Fiesta Cozumel** (tel. 987/22935 or 987/20974), **Snorkozumel** (tel. 987/20651), and **Turismo Aviomar** (tel. 987/20477 or 987/20942). Locals insist that the best snorkeling trips are aboard the *Zorro* (*see* Guided Tours, above), a 35-passenger, 45-foot catamaran with a huge sun deck, operated by Fiesta Cozumel.

Beaches

Cozumel's beaches vary from long, treeless, sandy stretches to isolated coves and rocky shores. Virtually all development remains on the leeward (western) side, where the coast is relatively sheltered by the proximity of the mainland 19 kilometers (12 miles) to the west. Reaching beaches on the windward (eastern) side is more difficult and requires transportation, but you'll be rewarded if you are looking for solitude. For descriptions of individual beaches, *see* Exploring, above.

Leeward Beaches The best sand beaches lie along the northern half of Cozumel's leeward side, some 5 kilometers (3 miles) long; names have been given to several stretches, including **San Francisco, Santa Rosa, Palancar,** and **Punta Sur.**

The southwestern beaches are the widest and among the most beautiful. One favorite is **Playa del Sol,** 2 kilometers (1 mile) south of Playa San Francisco, which was formerly the private beach of Aviomar but is now open to the public. One drawback, however, is Playa del Sol's popularity with cruise-ship passengers (because of Aviomar's corner on the cruise-ship excursion market). Also lovely and marvelously secluded are the beaches around Punta Celerain, near the lighthouse at the southern point. **Santa Pilar** and **San Juan** beaches, which run along the northern hotel strip, sell soft drinks and rent water-sports equipment.

Windward Beaches On this side you'll find massive, solitary beaches, including **Punta Morena, Chen Río, San Martín, Punta Chiqueros,** and **Playa Encantada.** A couple of them have small snack bars. Swimming on this side is dangerous only if you go out too far or on those rare occasions when a southwestern wind blows. There is a string of nameless beaches on the dirt road leading to **Punta Molas** at the northern tip, which can be reached by Jeep, but you should allow plenty of time for the trip.

Dining

Dining options on Cozumel reflect the nature of the place as a whole, with some harmless pretension at times but mainly the insouciant, natural style of the tropical island. More than 80 restaurants in the downtown area alone offer a broad choice, from air-conditioned, Americanized places serving Continental fare and seafood in semiformal "nautical" settings to sensible, simple outdoor eateries that specialize in fish. For the most part, the more established restaurants accept credit cards, while the café-type places accept only cash. Resort hotels offering buffet breakfasts and dinners are good values for bottomless appetites. Casual dress and no reservations is the rule in most Moderate and Inexpensive Cozumel restaurants. In Expensive restaurants, you would not be out of place if you dressed up, and reservations are advised.

Highly recommended restaurants are indicated by a star ★.

Category	Cost*
Expensive	over $20
Moderate	$10–20
Inexpensive	under $10

per person, excluding drinks, service, and sales tax (15%)

Expensive **Arrecife.** A well-trained staff and impeccably prepared seafood and Continental fare put this hotel restaurant in a class by itself. Tall windows and excellent views of the sea complement the somewhat formal, elegant decor, while jazz quartets—which play regularly—further enhance the romantic mood. *Hotel Stouffer Presidente, tel. 987/20322, ext. 8. AE, DC, MC, V.*

Café del Puerto. The eclectic decor, including wood furniture, wood-paneled walls, and wood palm trees, contributes to the vaguely South Seas–style ambience of this second-floor restaurant overlooking the pier. Nightly specials may include oysters or a grilled seafood platter, and the regular menu features prime rib, ham, and lobster and other seafood, along with a multi-item salad bar. Live piano music accompanies your meal. *Malecón next to El Portal, tel. 987/20316. AE, MC, V. No lunch.*

Donatello's. Pale pink walls, pink marble floors, dim lighting, and garish paintings lend a certain elegance to this place. Although not yet world-class, Donatello's ranks as the most sophisticated restaurant in town; it offers less formal dining in the back garden. Italian accents enhance the menu, which includes such specialties as scampi, lobster, veal, and pasta (including macaroni with salmon). A pianist and mariachis entertain nightly. Exquisite desserts, including coconut ice cream and bananas flambées, nicely round out the meal. *Av. Rafael Melgar S 131, tel. 987/20090 or 987/22586. AE, MC, V. No lunch.*

Morgan's. No longer the big night out it used to be, this restaurant has managed to maintain impeccable service, a quiet atmosphere with the obligatory candlelight, and an international cuisine. Located in the former customs house and done up in honor of its namesake—the seafaring pirate Henry Morgan, who once plied these waters—the restaurant is decorated with ship paneling, portholes, and compasses. The menu offers such appetizers as avocado cocktail and ham with melon, in addition to a selection of steak and fish entrées. *Zócalo, tel. 987/20584. AE, DC, MC, V. Closed Sun. lunch.*

Pepe's Grill. This large, bustling restaurant follows the nautical mode, from the fishnets and ship wheels to the wind vanes covering the walls. Tall windows provide exceptional views of the malecón. You can choose between the quiet air-conditioned setting upstairs and the livelier atmosphere in the open-air dining room downstairs. This restaurant caters to the cruise-ship clientele, so most North Americans will feel right at home, but with the comforts of home come long lines and high prices. Caribbean seafood—lobster, shrimp flambée, shellfish grill, and King Crab—is featured as specials, but the steaks—particularly the chateaubriand in béarnaise sauce, from the state of Chihuahua—are superb. The dolphin fish is fresh and good, as are the Caesar salad and the salad bar. Live music is played daily. *Av. Rafael Melgar S at Calle Rosada Salas, tel. 987/20213. AE, V.*

Moderate   **Carlos 'n' Charlie's & Jimmy's Kitchen.** Rock 'n' roll, a Ping-Pong table, and drinking contests are the status quo here. American-style ribs, chicken, and beef selections taste good, but the drinks are better. You can recognize this place by the red wall just north of the ferry pier. *Av. Rafael Melgar between Calles 2 and 4 N, tel. 987/20191. MC, V.*

★ **El Capi Navegante.** Locals say you'll find the best seafood in town here, where such Caribbean specialties as oysters, grouper, lobster, shrimp, and fish fillet are skillfully prepared. Highly recommended dishes include conch ceviche, deep-fried whole snapper, and stuffed squid. Nautical blue-and-white decor, accented by the life preservers on the walls, adds personality to this place. *Av. 10a S 312 at Calle 3, tel. 987/21730. AE, MC, V.*

★ **Kanpai.** Cozumel's only sushi bar—aptly decorated with bamboo furniture and fans on the walls—offers high-priced (but worth it) sushi, sashimi, tempura, and teriyaki, as well as Thai, Chinese, and Mexican delicacies. *Av. 5a S between Calle Rosada Salas and Calle 3, no phone. MC, V.*

★ **La Cabaña del Pescador.** To get to this rustic hut in a swampland setting, you've got to cross a gangplank, but it'll be worth it if you're looking for fresh lobster. Locals swear food at this glassed-in straw hut is the best on the island; tails are sold by the pound, and "the rest is on the house." In addition to the excellent food, the interior decor—miniature sailboats on the tables and seashells and nets hanging from the walls—creates a relaxing ambience. *Across the street from Playa Azul Hotel, north of town, no phone. No credit cards. No lunch.*

Las Palmeras. The lovely redbrick patios with the requisite potted palms and ceiling fans set the mood at this unpretentious waterfront restaurant. Breakfast is a bargain; for other meals, expect Yucatecán specialties and barbecued ribs. The restaurant also sells margaritas and piña coladas to go. *On the malecón, just across from the pier; tel. 987/20532. AE, MC, V.*

Inexpensive   **El Moro.** This family-run restaurant on the eastern edge of
★ town specializes in cheap local cuisine—seafood, chicken, and meat. Inside, the decor follows the local theme, beginning with Yucatecán baskets hanging on the walls. Divers flock to this place, so you know portions are hearty and the food is delicious.

Ask your taxi driver how to get to the restaurant. *Calle 70, no phone. No credit cards. Closed Thurs.*

El Portal. Located on the malecón just opposite the ferry pier and next to the zócalo, this restaurant offers a breezy, agreeable ambience for breakfast, lunch, or dinner. The informally decorated interior, highlighted by the central fountain and red tile ceiling, is brightened by potted plants. Entrées include ceviche, *pescado veracruzano* (fish served in a sauce of tomatoes, onions, and green peppers), *sopa de lima* (lime soup), enchiladas, and Yucatecán specialties. *Av. Rafael Melgar, tel. 987/20316. MC, V.*

La Choza. Home-cooked Mexican food—primarily from the capital and among the best in town—is the order of the day at this family-run establishment, which dispenses with menus. The informal outdoor setting is enhanced by a palapa; inside, wood furniture and simple, colored tablecloths, which nicely set off the hand-painted pottery dishes, keep in step with La Choza's down-home feel. *Av. 10a S at Calle Rosada Salas, tel. 987/20958. No credit cards.*

La Cosa Nostra. This modestly decorated restaurant, with a long bar, wood tables, and white walls with paintings of Cozumel, attracts locals who gather here on the weekends to hear live organ music and meet with friends. The cooking's not bad, either: La Cosa Nostra excels in homemade Italian fare, from the fettuccine Giovanna (pasta with shrimp in a rich cream sauce) to pizza sold by the slice. There is a happy hour from 6 to 7. *Av. 15a S 548, between Calles 5 and 7, no phone. AE, MC, V. No lunch.*

Mr. Papa's. This place offers 100 types of stuffed potatoes, as well as burgers, ribs, chicken, other North American dishes, and some standard Mexican fare such as guacamole, nachos, and tacos in a jovial air-conditioned setting with wood tables, green carpets, and walls painted different shades of purple. Between the hours of 2 and 4 and 7 and 8, you get all you can eat and all the beer you can drink for about $10, *Calle Rosada Salas 30-A, opposite Scaramouche, tel. 987/21882. MC, V.*

Plaza Leza. If you're craving the low-key, unpretentious atmosphere of a Mexican sidewalk café, stop here, where you can dawdle for hours over a cup of coffee or a beer. Choose a table on the plaza; or for more privacy, go indoors to the somewhat secluded, cozy inner patio. Plaza Leza serves everything from *tacos de bistec* (beef tacos), enchiladas, and lime soup to chicken sandwiches and coconut ice cream. *On the main plaza, tel. 987/21041. AE, MC, V.*

Santiago's Grill. Beautiful American cuts of meat, including T-bones and sirloins, as well as beef brochettes and fresh shrimp, draw long lines nightly. Because this small outdoor restaurant, with only 10 tables, is included on a list given to cruise-ship passengers, it is particularly popular with these tourists. *Calle Rosada Salas 299 at Av. 15a S, tel. 987/20175. No lunch. AE, MC, V.*

Lodging

Cozumel's hotels are located in three main areas, all on the island's western or leeward side: in town and north and south of town. Because of the proximity of the reefs, divers and snorkelers tend to congregate at the southern properties. Sailors and anglers, on the other hand, prefer the hotels to the north, where the beaches are better. Most budget hotels—with various architectural styles—are located in town.

Cozumel offers about 2,700 hotel rooms in 50 properties. Before booking you should call around, because you will find many bargains in the form of air, hotel, and dive packages, especially off-season; some packages offered combine Cozumel-Cancún stays, with free airfare between the two. Christmas reservations must be made at least three months ahead of time. The majority of the resort hotels (located north and south of town) are affiliated with international chains and offer all the usual amenities; they also generally rent water-sports equipment and can arrange excursions. All hotels have air-conditioning unless otherwise noted.

The **Cozumel Island Hotel Association** (Box 228, Cozumel, QR 77600, tel. 987/21097; fax 987/21599 or 987/20016), to which 15 properties belong, functions unofficially as the island's tourist information bureau. Barbachano Tours, one of Cozumel's leading tour operators, has recently launched a new toll-free **Cozumel Central Reservations service** (tel. 800/327–2254). All properties have a 77600 postal code.

Highly recommended hotels are indicated by a star ★.

Category	Cost*
Very Expensive	over $100
Expensive	$75–$100
Moderate	$40–$75
Inexpensive	under $40

All prices are for a standard double room, excluding service charges and the 15% tax.

Very Expensive **Fiesta Americana Sol Caribe.** This enormous hotel, situated south of town, just across the street from its own vast beach (accessible by underground footpath), incorporates a "neo-Mayan" design into the large white stones and a wood roof, surrounded by lots of lush greenery. Access to the 10 stories is by a glass-encased elevator that overlooks the huge and sinuous pool, the breezy lobby bar, the waterfall, and the swim-up bar at pool level. Spiffily decorated rooms, highlighted by pastel colors and furnishings with rattan details, include writing desks, chairs, and stylish reading lamps. The bathrooms, though satisfactory, could use a face-lift, and the rooms in the main building lack balconies. At press time accommodations in the new tower—which are to feature balconies and luxury amenities—are scheduled to open in late 1991, though most of these suites will be sold as time-shares. Live music is played nightly in the lobby bar, and the Mexican fiesta on Wednesday and Saturday nights appeals to North Americans. *Box 259, Playa Paraíso, Km 3.5, tel. 987/20700 or 800/FIESTA–1; fax 987/21301. 321 rooms. Facilities: 3 restaurants, 2 bars, satellite TV, minibars, pool, private dock, 3 tennis courts, water sports, travel agency, motorcycle and car rental, dive shop, boutiques, beauty salon. AE, DC, MC, V.*

Fiesta Inn. This three-story motel, on the south side of town across the street from the beach, has all the trademarks of the Fiesta brand name: a comfortable lobby with a fountain and

garden, brightly decorated modern rooms with Moorish archways, a large pool, and an international dining facility. The
white stucco building features flat roofs made of red tiles.
Rooms are painted light blue, with blue carpets, cream-color
wicker furniture, and private balconies. *Costera Sur, Km 1.7,
Carretera a Chankanaab, tel. 987/22900, 987/22899, or 800/FI-
ESTA–1; fax 987/22154. 180 rooms. Facilities: restaurant, 2
bars, beach club, water sports, pool. AE, DC, MC, V.*

★ **Melia Mayan Cozumel.** Located to the north of town, this picturesque hotel conveys an intimate, quiet, and uncluttered feel
from the moment you enter the handsome tiled walkway. The
pleasant lobby is decorated in soothing ivory and coral colors
from the stucco walls to the lampshades and wicker chairs. Its
windows face the sea, allowing you to observe the water sports
and diving. Though the main pool is small, the hotel's beach,
with palapas and a snack bar, draws the guests. Superior
rooms, with their luxurious white decor, have their own balconies overlooking the water. The smaller standard rooms have
small patios—complete with chairs and tables—that open onto
the beach. Ask for one with a sea view (rooms with a garden
view are in a separate building and overlook a swamp). Suites
are also available. *Box 9, Carretera a Sta. Pilar 6, tel. 987/
20072, 987/20411, or 800/336–3542; fax 987/21599. 200 rooms.
Facilities: restaurant, café, 2 bars, beach, 2 pools, water-sports
center, 2 tennis courts, minibars, in-room safety deposit
boxes, shops. AE, MC, V.*

★ **Stouffer Presidente.** This hotel, dramatically refurbished since
the 1988 hurricane, exudes luxury, from the courteous,
prompt, and efficient service to the tastefully decorated interi-
or. The Stouffer is famed not only for possessing one of the best
gourmet restaurants on the island, Arrecife (*see* Dining,
above), but also for its respectable and professional water-
sports center. Located on its own beach at the southern end of
the hotel zone, the property ranks among the best on the island
for snorkeling. Deluxe rooms—handsomely decorated with
pine trim, white walls, and pink, blue, and purple touches, and
with their own private terraces fronting the pool or beach—
are well worth the extra money. *Carretera a Chankanaab, Km
6.5, tel. 987/20322, 987/21520, or 800/HOTELS–1; fax 987/
21360. 259 rooms. Facilities: 2 restaurants, 2 bars, 2 pools, 2
lighted tennis courts, dive shop, water-sports center, boutique,
car and motorcycle rental, travel agency. AE, DC, MC, V.*

Expensive **Casa del Mar.** Located just south of town near several boutiques, sports shops, and restaurants, this three-story hotel is
frequented by divers. The unpretentious, tasteful lobby, which
has natural wood banisters and overlooks a small garden of potted plants, exemplifies the overall simplicity of this place.
Clean and modern suites come complete with bathtubs, small
balconies, and views of the pool or the sea. *Carretera Costera,
Km 1.5 (Box 129), 21900, tel. 987/21855 or 800/621–6830; fax
987/21855. 97 rooms, 7 cabanas. Facilities: 2 restaurants, 2
bars, pool, Jacuzzi, dive shop, car rental. AE, MC, V.*

Galápago Inn. This pretty white stucco hotel just south of town
is a favorite with divers, because several diving excursions
(which include three meals a day) are offered as packages with
your stay. The central garden, with tiled benches and a small
fountain, contributes to the inn's homey feel. *Av. Rafael
Melgar 141, tel. 987/20663 or 800/847–5708. 31 rooms. Facilities: restaurant, bar, pool, beach. MC, V.*

Plaza Las Glorias. Mediterranean architecture prevails inside and out here, with Mexican tiles, marble floors, and stucco walls. This pertly modern, all-suites, motel-style property, situated within walking distance of town, has private terraces and ocean views from each unit. *Box 435, Av. Rafael Melgar, Km 1.5, tel. 987/22000 or 800/342–AMIGO; fax 987/21937. 180 suites. Facilities: 2 restaurants, 2 bars, evening entertainment, minibar, in-room safe, hair dryers, dive center, water sports, pool, shopping arcade. AE, MC, V.*

Moderate **Bahía.** The lobby here is small but the hallways are pleasant enough, with white walls and red tile floors. The large rooms, decorated with the standard stucco, wood, and tile, come with sofabeds and kitchenettes. Ask for a room with a sea view; the balconies overlook the malecón and go for the same price as those facing town. Two penthouse suites are available. *Av. Rafael Melgar and Calle 3 S, tel. 987/20209. 27 rooms. Facilities: kitchenettes. AE, MC, V.*

Playa Azul. This Best Western–managed property north of town—just opposite the Cabaña del Pescador lobster house—is a nondescript pink concrete low-rise structure whose best feature may be its small, pleasant, and unpretentious lobby, decorated in white, pink, and aqua tones. Mexican families stay here, enjoying the garden and its coconut palms, which soften the effect of the concrete exterior. Hurricane damage from 1988 has not yet been repaired, although the hotel was recently remodeled. Choose between suites or bungalow-like villas near the pool (but without sea views or phones). *Carretera San Juan, Box 31, tel. 987/20033, 987/20043, or 800/528–1234; fax 987/21915. 64 rooms. Facilities: restaurant, bar, pool, dive shop, water sports. AE, DC, MC, V.*

★ **Villas Las Anclas.** Rated as a three-star hotel, these villas are actually furnished apartments for rent by the day, week, or month. Conveniently located parallel to the malecón, the duplexes include a kitchenette and sitting room downstairs, while up the spiral staircase you will find a small bedroom with a large desk (but no phone), water purifier, and inset shelves over the double bed. Spanking-white modern decor brightens the rooms, and the fresh-ground coffee sold at the front desk gives you a lift in the morning. *Av. 5a S 325, Box 25, tel. and fax 987/21403. 7 units. Facilities: kitchenettes. No credit cards.*

Inexpensive **Bazar Colonial.** This attractive modern three-story hotel, located over a small cluster of shops, has pretty red tile floors and bougainvillea, which add splashes of color. Natural wood furniture, kitchenettes, bookshelves, sofabeds, and an elevator make up for the lack of other amenities, such as a restaurant and a pool. *Av. 5a S 9, tel. 987/20506; fax 987/30309 or 987/21387. 28 rooms. Facilities: shops, kitchenettes. AE, MC, V.*

Mary Carmen. Functional and clean, this hotel offers rooms (but no phones) on the ground floor with both air-conditioning and ceiling fans; on the first floor, only air-conditioning is offered. Although the room decor is unimpressive, the functional double bed and two chairs (with a 1970s-style plastic flower arrangement) suffice. *Av. 5a S 4, tel. 987/20581. 27 rooms. No facilities. MC, V.*

★ **Mesón San Miguel.** Situated right on the square, this hotel sees a lot of action because of the accessibility of its large public bar and outdoor café, which are often filled with locals. The architecturally eclectic San Miguel, with four stories and an elevator, features such flourishes as brown, black, and white art deco floor tiles and thick art deco glass bricks set in the walls. The remodeled rooms are clean and functional, with balconies overlooking the zócalo—a good bet for your money. *Av. Juárez 2 bis, tel. 987/20323 or 987/20233. 97 rooms. Facilities: restaurant, bar, café, small pool, game room. AE, MC, V.*

Suites Elizabeth. This basic and functional hotel offers two types of rooms: with fans and with air-conditioning. The latter include large balconies with a view of the rooftops, and all rooms come with refrigerators and stoves (but no phones). The vintage '70s furnishings, including linoleum floors and yellow-orange bedspreads and curtains, look outdated but are still functional. *Calle Rosada Salas 44, Box 70, tel. 987/21388. 37 rooms. No credit cards.*

The Arts and Nightlife

The Arts

Although Cozumel doesn't have much in the way of highbrow performing arts per se, it does offer the visitor an opportunity to attend performances that reflect the island's heritage, including Maya Night on Monday and Fiesta Mexicana on Thursday, both at 7 PM at the **Melía Mayan Cozumel** (tel. 987/20072); Viva México, Wednesday (and Saturday during high season) at 6 PM at the **Fiesta Americana Sol Caribe** (tel. 987/20700); or Caribbean Night on Sunday at the **Stouffer Presidente** (tel. 987/20322). They all feature different variations on the theme of folkloric dances, mariachis, games, and dancing to live tropical music with—of course—a copious open bar and a buffet dinner. The price is not cheap.

Nightlife

Cozumel offers enough daytime activities to make you want to retire early, but the young set keeps the island hopping late into the night. There is plenty of nightlife, but a word to the wise: Avoid the temptation to buy or use drugs here. Local police are putting more effort into controlling drug trafficking, and a foreigner involved with drugs will have a particularly difficult time with the Mexican authorities.

Bars Bar-hoppers like **Carlos 'n' Charlie's & Jimmy's Kitchen** (Av. Rafael Melgar, between Calles 2 and 4 N; tel. 987/20191) and **Chilis** (tel. 987/21832), both on the waterfront north of the plaza.

Discos **Carlos 'n' Charlie's** (Av. Rafael Melgar between Calles 2 and 4 N, tel. 987/20191) is the in spot for partying; **Scaramouche** (Av. Rafael Melgar at Calle Rosada Salas, no phone), recently remodeled, features a fantastic laser show; and **Neptuno** (Av. Rafael Melgar at Calle 11 S, tel. 987/21537), preferred by the teenage set and locals, can be loud and fun.

Live Music Sunday evenings bring locals to the zócalo to hear mariachis and island musicians playing tropical tunes. The piano bar in **La Gaviota** (Carretera a Sta. Pilar, tel. 987/20700, ext. 251), a restaurant at the Sol Caribe, is well attended, and trios and mariachis perform nightly in the lobby bar from 5 to 11.

Movies San Miguel has two theaters: **Cine Cozumel** (Av. Rafael Melgar between Calles 2 and 4 N, tel. 987/20766) and **Cine Cecilio**

Borges (Av. Juaréz s/n, at Av. 35, tel. 987/20402). Both show films in English (generally with subtitles) and Spanish nightly at 9:15.

6 Mexico's Caribbean Coast

Introduction

Above all else, beaches are what define the eastern coast of the Yucatán peninsula. White, sandy strands with offshore coral reefs, oversize tropical foliage and jungle, Mayan ruins, and abundant wildlife make the coastline a marvelous destination for lovers of the outdoors. The scrubby limestone terrain is mostly flat and dry, punctuated only by sinkholes, while the shores are broken up by freshwater lagoons, underwater caves, and cliffs.

The coast consists of several destinations, each catering to different preferences. The lazy fishing villages of Puerto Morelos and Playa del Carmen so far have been only slightly altered to accommodate foreign tourists. Rustic fishing lodges on the even more secluded strip of land known as Boca Paila are gaining a well-deserved reputation for flat fishing and fly-fishing. The beaches, from Punta Bete to Akumal—beloved of scuba divers, snorkelers, birders, and beachcombers—offer accommodations to suit every budget, from campsites and bungalows to condos and luxury hotels. Ecotourism is on the rise, with special programs designed to involve visitors in preserving the threatened sea turtle population. Then, too, there are the Mayan ruins at Tulum, superbly situated on a bluff overlooking the Caribbean, and Cobá—a short distance inland—whose towering pyramids evoke the magnificence of Tikal in Guatemala. At the Belizean border is Chetumal—a modern port and the capital of Quintana Roo—which, with its dilapidated clapboard houses and sultry sea air, is more Central American than Mexican. The waters up and down the coast, littered with shipwrecks and relics from the heyday of piracy, are dotted with mangrove swamps and minuscule islands where only the birds hold sway.

The wildlife on the Caribbean coast is unsurpassed in Mexico, except perhaps in Baja California. Along the more civilized stretches of road, wild pigs, turkeys, monkeys, iguanas, lizards, and snakes appear in the clearings. Jaguars, stags, armadillos, tapirs, wild boars, peccaries, ocelots, raccoons, and badgers all inhabit the rich tropical jungle. The reefs, lagoons, cenotes, and caves along the Caribbean and down the Hondo River— which runs along the borders between Mexico, Belize, and Guatemala—are filled with alligators, giant turtles, sharks, barracuda, and manatees. During July and August sea turtles throng the beaches, laying thousands of eggs. Birders come to stare into the jungle for glimpses of parrots, toucans, and the long red-and-green feathers of the rare and sacred quetzal. Onlookers are entertained by yellow, blue, and scarlet butterflies, singing cicadas and orioles, sparkling dragonflies, kitelike frigates, and night owls nesting in the trees. Colorless crabs scuttle sideways toward the coconut groves—whose numbers are being diminished by a blight imported from Florida—over pale white limestone and sand that seldom burns the soles of your feet. Tiny mosquitoes and gnats, impervious to mild repellents, bore through the smallest rips in window screens, tents, and mosquito nets.

The music, food, and cultural traditions of the northern Caribbean coast are Yucatecan. Cancún's transformation into a world-class resort has brought an international flair to the region, where Continental restaurants and local handicraft boutiques flourish a short distance from small Mayan villages whose whitewashed huts are covered with dried palm fronds (palapas). The central part of the Yucatán coastline is more purely Mayan: Seaside fishing collectives, jungles, and close-knit communities of Mexican Indians and Guatemalan refugees carry on ancient traditions. The south, particularly Chetumal, is influenced by its status as a seaport and its proximity to Belize and Guatemala.

Quintana Roo entered the modern era in the 1970s, when Mexico City decided to develop the area for tourism (it did not become a state until 1974). With the advent of Cancún, huge resorts and time-share complexes began to appear, and now they are slowly spreading south. But thanks to the federal government's foresight in setting aside huge tracts as wildlife reserves, vast pockets of undeveloped land remain along the Caribbean coast. This is one of the last stretches of coastline to be developed in North America, and for that reason the coast is attracting more and more travelers who are eager to experience its tranquility and beauty.

Essential Information

Important Addresses and Numbers

Tourist Information *Chetumal*
The main tourist office (Palacio del Gobierno, 2nd floor, tel. 983/25073; fax 983/20855) is open weekdays 9–2:30 and 6:30–9:30. The tourist information booth (no phone) on Avenida Héroes, just opposite Avenida Efraín Aguilar, will give you *Guía Turística Pasaporte*, the free monthly brochure you can find at many hotels.

Playa del Carmen The tourist office, located one block from the beach on Avenida Quinta (tel. 987/21230, then ask for tourist office), is open Monday–Saturday 7–2 and 3–9, Sunday 7–2. The tiny *Playa Maya Tourist Bulletin*, which you can pick up free in any shop in town, consists mostly of ads but includes some useful schedules and a little map.

Emergencies *Chetumal*
Police (Av. Insurgentes and Av. Belice, tel. 983/20809); **Red Cross** (Av. Efraín Aguilar at Av. Madero, tel. 983/20571); **Highway patrol** (Carretera Chetumal–Bacalar Km 4, tel. 983/20193).

Playa del Carmen **Police** (Av. Juárez between Av. 15a and Av. 20a, next to the Post Office, no phone); **Red Cross** (Av. Héroes de Chapultapec con Independencia, tel. 983/20571).

Medical Clinics *Playa del Carmen*
Centro de Salud (Av. Juárez at Av. 15a, tel. 987/21230, ext. 147).

Chetumal **Hospital General** (Av. Andres Quintana Roo, tel. 983/21932).

Pharmacies *Chetumal*
Farmacia Social Mechaca (Av. Independencia 134C, tel. 983/20044).

Banks *Chetumal*
Banco del Atlántico (Av. Héroes 37, tel. 983/20630 or 983/20631) and **Bancomer** (Av. Alvaro Obregón 222 at Av. Juárez, tel. 983/25300 or 983/25318) provide banking services, including foreign currency exchange.

Playa del Carmen **Banco del Atlántico** (corner of Av. 10a and Av. Juárez, no phone) is open weekdays 10–noon.

English-language **Bookstores**	In Playa del Carmen, a small selection of magazines and books, some of them in English, is sold at **Papaya Tropical** (Av. 5a at Calle 6). Hours are daily 9:30–1 and 5–9.
Gas Stations	There are gas stations in Puerto Juárez, Puerto Morelos, Cancún, Playa del Carmen, Tulum, Felipe Carrillo Puerto, and Chetumal.
Travel Agencies **and Tour Operators** *Chetumal*	**Chetumal Caribe** (Hotel Del Prado, Av. Héroes 138, tel. 983/20544) and **Turismo Maya Internacional** (Hotel Continental Caribe, Av. Héroes 171, tel. 983/20555 or 983/21080) arrange tours throughout the area.
Playa del Carmen	**Rent-a-Car** (Av. Juárez between Avs. 10a and 15a, no phone) also functions as Playa's principal telephone operator and car rental service and is open weekdays 8–1 and 5–7, weekends 8–1.

Arriving and Departing by Plane, Ferry, Car, and Bus

By Plane *Playa del Carmen*	**Aerocozumel** (tel. 983/26675) runs 20-minute flights to and from both Cancún and Cozumel.
Chetumal	The Chetumal airport is located on the southwestern edge of town, along Avenida Alvaro Obregón where it turns into Route 186. **Aerocozumel** has a daily nonstop flight to Mérida and a connecting flight to Cozumel (via Mérida and Chichén Itzá).
By Ferry	Ferries and jetfoils—which can be picked up at the dock—run between Playa del Carmen and Cozumel about every 2 hours and take about 40 minutes. The fee varies depending on which boat you choose, but the one-way trip costs between under $1 and about $3.50.
By Car	The entire coast, from Punta Sam to the main border crossing to Belize at Chetumal, is traversable on Route 307. This straight road is entirely paved, although at present it has only two lanes. Gas stations, however, are few and far between, so you should gas up whenever you can. Good roads that run into Route 307 from the west are Route 180 (from Mérida and Valladolid), Route 295 (from Valladolid), Route 184 (from central Yucatán), and Route 186 (from Villahermosa and, via Route 261, from Mérida and Campeche). Approximate driving times are as follows: from Cancún to Felipe Carrillo Puerto, 3 hours; from Cancún to Mérida, 4½ hours; from Carrillo Puerto to Chetumal, 2 hours; from Carrillo Puerto to Mérida, about 4½ hours; from Chetumal to Campeche, 6½ hours.
By Taxi	Taxis can be hired to go as far as Playa del Carmen, Tulum, or Akumal, but the price is steep unless you have many passengers. Fares run about $32 or more to Playa alone; between Playa and Tulum or Akumal, expect to pay at least $25.
By Bus *Playa del Carmen*	There is first-class service on the ADO line (Av. Juárez, 1 block from the beach, no phone) between Playa and Cancún, Valladolid, Chichén Itzá, and Mérida at least seven times daily; between Playa and Tulum, Xel-Há, and Chetumal twice daily; between Playa and Valladolid once a day; and between Playa and Mexico City seven times daily. One-way fare to Mérida runs about $7, less to the closer destinations on the Yucatán peninsula.

Chetumal The bus station (Av. Juárez, between Calles Juarez and Belize, tel. 983/21547) is served by ADO and other lines. Buses run regularly from the Central Camionera, in the north of the city near Avenida Belice and Avenida Insurgentes, to Cancún, Villahermosa, and Mexico City; Mérida; Campeche; and Veracruz.

Telephones

Electricity and telephones are the exception rather than the rule in this region, although most hotels have radio communication with the outside world.

Chetumal The government-run telephone office, **TELMEX**, is located at Avenida Juárez and Lázaro Cárdenas. For long-distance and international calls, you might also try the booths on Avenida Héroes: One is on the corner of Ignacio Zaragoza and the other is just opposite Avenida Efraín Aguilar, next to the tourist information booth.

Playa del Carmen At this writing, Playa residents are still eagerly awaiting the arrival of a true phone service; presently there are only three phone lines in the entire town. The long-distance phone booth, under the orange-and-white tower just off the zócalo, is open daily 8–1 and 3–8; you may also be able to use the phone in Playa's only travel agency (Av. Juárez between Av. 10a and Av. 15a), which is open Monday–Saturday 7–2 and 3–9, Sunday 7–noon.

Mail

Chetumal The post office (Plutarco Elias Calles, tel. 983/22578) is open Monday–Saturday 8–1 and 3–6.

Playa del Carmen The post office (Av. Juárez, next to the police station, no phone) is open weekdays 9–1 and 3–6, Saturday 9–1.

Guided Tours

There are few major travel agencies or tour operators up and down the coast, so organized tours are best arranged from Cancún or Cozumel. However, because most of the sights you would wish to see along this stretch are natural, there is little point in spending the money for a guided tour unless you don't want to drive. If you are interested in the ruins, you can hire guides at the sites. The roads are generally quite good, so renting a car is probably the most efficient and enjoyable way of touring.

Exploring

Numbers in the margin correspond to points of interest on the Caribbean coast map.

Route 307 parallels the entire coastline for the 382 kilometers (233 miles) from Cancún to Chetumal. The highway is straight and flat, but since at most points it is 1 or 2 kilometers inland from the coast, there is little in sight but dense vegetation, an occasional hut, assorted billboards, painted tires, and road signs marking the dirt-road entrances to the ruins, resorts, beaches, and campgrounds that are hidden from sight. It won't stay that way for long, however, because the Mexican government has already begun to develop the 130-kilometer (81-mile) stretch of coastline known as the **Cancún–Tulum Corridor**. Each year more picture-coded international tourist signs appear, pointing the way to restaurants, gas stations, and hotels. Though buses do traverse the region and are popular with backpackers, a rental car or four-wheel-drive vehicle allows you to explore more thoroughly and creatively without ending up alone in the jungle after dark or in the torrential rains that soak the coast from May to September. Huge Mayarama tour buses from Cancún appear regularly at the ruins, parks, and beaches with their loads of sightseers.

Once you get beyond Tulum and detour inland to the ruins of Cobá, the landscape changes: The road becomes noticeably deserted, and the remaining traffic consists mostly of large, fume-ejecting trucks and an occasional passenger car speeding to the border crossing with Belize. Generally speaking, the only people who venture farther south are en route to Belize, since otherwise there is little to entice them in the way of historic sites or beaches. On the highway south of Tulum, the scenery is monotonous until you reach the beautiful and enormous Laguna Bacalar just north of Chetumal. When you get there, however, you may wonder why the magnificence does not attract more visitors.

Our north–south exploration of the Caribbean coast takes you from Puerto Morelos to Chetumal, with brief detours inland to ➊ the ruins of Cobá and Kohunlich. **Puerto Morelos,** a small coastal town about 36 kilometers (22 miles) south of Cancún, is home to the car ferry that travels to Cozumel. Though the town is a bit seedy, each year more and more tourists stop here to take in its easygoing pace, cheap accommodations, and convenient oceanside location near a superb offshore coral reef. For obvious reasons this place is particularly attractive to divers, snorkelers, and anglers. The reef at Morelos—about 550 meters (1,800 feet) offshore—has claimed many ships over the centuries, and nowadays divers visit the sunken wrecks. Snorkeling gear, fishing tackle, and boats can be rented from the **Ojo de Agua Dive Shop** (no phone) at the hotel of the same name, north of town.

Once the point of departure for Mayan women making pilgrimages by canoe to Cozumel, the sacred isle of the fertility goddess, today Morelos is not very different from many backwater towns in the Spanish-speaking Caribbean, with not much to it beyond a gas station, a central square, and auto repair shops. About 30 years ago it consisted only of a cluster of huts and a wooden jetty; the railroad ran through town en route from Leona Vicario, a point on Route 180 that barely merits inclusion on the Yucatán map. Nature endowed Puerto Morelos with a fine deep-sea port (the principal port for the area until the road to Puerto Juárez was built), so today cruise ships call regularly, and most of the action is centered on the long pier south of the square, where vehicles line up for hours waiting for the ferry to depart. The mainstay resorts—La Ceiba and Playa Ojo de Agua, which normally cater to divers—are still recovering from Hurricane Gilbert, but their restaurants are quite good. Three lighthouses from different eras break up the long stretch of beach, and boats to take out to the surrounding reefs can be rented along the way.

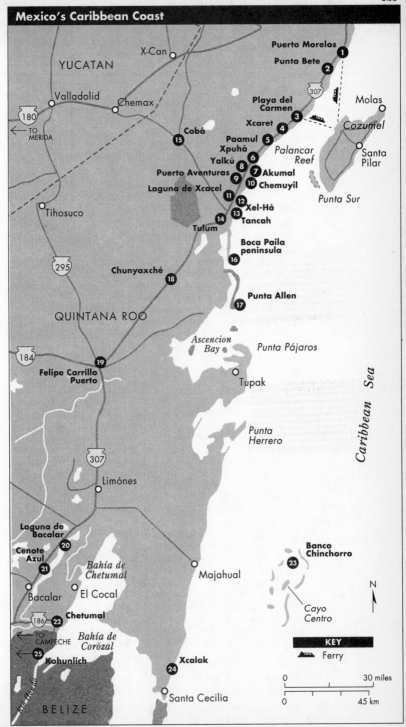

Mexico's Caribbean Coast

About 32 kilometers (20 miles) south of Puerto Morelos is
② **Punta Bete,** a 6½-kilometer (4-mile) white sand beach between
rocky lagoons. The point is the setting for several bungalow-
style hotels, which have almost become cult places for travelers
who love being in or on the water. All the properties, including
several campgrounds, are set off from Route 307 at the end of a
2 ⁹⁄₁₀-kilometer (1⅘-mile) rutted road, but the main entrance
should be used by guests and those arriving for dinner.

③ A 10-minute drive farther south will take you to **Playa del
Carmen,** a once-deserted beach where only 25 years ago Indian
families raised coconut palms to produce copra. Nowadays its
alabaster-white beach and small offshore reefs lend themselves
to excellent swimming, snorkeling, and turtle-watching, and
the town has recently become the preferred destination of hip
young Europeans who want to skip Cancún and go on to see the
archaeological sights of Yucatán.

The 10-block-long, 8-block-wide village is not particularly
charming, since it lacks scenery and its buildings have become
somewhat shabby, but to its credit it has not yet been commer-
cialized beyond recognition. Instead it has a slew of inexpensive, funky bungalow-style hotels; equally eccentric, low-key
restaurants; and all the basics for a short or extended stay, including an auto parts shop, a drugstore, a bank, fresh fruit and
ice cream stands, liquor and food stores, a movie theater (showing Spanish-language films), and a travel agency, which also
rents cars. A dive shop next to the pier rents snorkeling and
scuba equipment, and plenty of young boys and men on the
beach will gladly rent their boats for jaunts to the reefs and
coves to the south.

The busiest parts of Playa are down by the **ferry pier** and at the
zócalo. Take a stroll north from the pier along the beach and
you'll see the essence of the town: simple restaurants roofed
with palapa, where people sit around drinking beer for hours;
two campgrounds; and lots of hammocks. At the far north, just
past the hotel under construction next to the Blue Parrot Inn,
is the nude beach, but sun worshippers may lose some of their
freedom when the hotel is completed. Now head all the way
south, along Avenida 5a (the first street in from the beach), a
street lined with *tienditas* (little shops) selling crafts and groceries; the crafts stands are concentrated especially at the
south end, where the street meets the ferry ramp. On the south
side of the pier is the Playacar, an unfinished monolithic hotel.
If you walk away from the beach, you'll come upon the affluent
section: several condominium projects with stucco walls; homes
with red tile roofs, rustic wooden balconies, security gates and
guards, and well-tended gardens and lawns that can be be seen
from the street. From here, only the sandy streets, the insignificant vestiges of Mayan structures, and the stunning turquoise sea on the horizon suggest you're in the tropics. The
streets at both ends of town peter out into the jungle. Playa is
slowly acquiring the confident veneer of an up-and-coming
beach destination, attributable, in part, to the amiability of the
locals (including the growing number of expatriates who manage many of the hotels and restaurants). As always, however,
popularity inevitably means that prices increase.

④ Six kilometers (4 miles) south of Playa is a dirt road leading to
Xcaret, a small clearing of Mayan shrines still under excava-

tion. A flight of steps leads to a doorway to nowhere, since only one wall of the site's largest structure remains. Like many of the ruins on the Caribbean coast, these can be seen in about five minutes, but the real reason to come is for the moment's tranquility you'll find at the **Xcaret cove.** Divers find the lagoons particularly enticing, because the caves are filled with spring water, and fresh water and seawater mingle around rocky inlets, creating an unusual blend of greens and blues. Slightly north of the most popular diving area are a sacred cenote and Mayan altar inside a cave. For a snack, there's a café that faces the bay.

Time Out If you're hankering for fresh fish, you may want to go back to **Restaurant Xcaret** (no phone), just off the highway before town.

❺ Beachcombers and snorkelers are fond of **Paamul** (10 kilometers/6 miles south of Xcaret), a crescent-shape lagoon with clear, placid waters sheltered by the coral reef at the lagoon's mouth. Shells, sand dollars, and even glass beads—some from the sunken pirate ships at Akumal—wash onto the sandy parts of the beach. Trailer camps, cabañas, and tent camps are scattered along the beach; a restaurant sells cold beer and fresh fish; and in the summer visitors may view one of Paamul's chief attractions: sea turtle hatchlings on the beach. You can also take the jungle path to the north, which leads to a lagoon four times the size of the first and even more private.

❻ Nine kilometers (5½ miles) south of Paamul, along a narrow path is a little fishing community called **Xpuhá,** where residents weave hammocks and harvest coconuts. Some small, overgrown pre-Hispanic ruins in the area still bear traces of paint on the inside walls.

❼ **Akumal,** a stretch of the coast that presently houses four deluxe hotels and is the site of the developing megaresort Puerto Aventuras (see below), lies about 35 kilometers (22 miles) south of Playa del Carmen. People come here to dive or simply to walk on the deliciously long beaches filled with shells, crabs, flying fish, and migrant birds. The name, meaning "Place of the Turtle," recalls ancient Mayan times, when the beach was the nesting ground for thousands of turtles. Later Akumal became part of a coconut plantation, and the area is still suffused with the glow of red-and-yellow bromeliads and orchids. It first attracted international attention in 1926, when explorers discovered the Mantanceros, a Spanish galleon that sank in 1741. Three decades later, Akumal became headquarters for the Mexican Underwater Explorers Club (CEDAM) and a resort for wealthy underwater adventurers who flew in on private planes and searched the waters for sunken treasures.

The long curved bay and beach are rarely empty now; most of the time the beach—with rows of sunbathers—recalls those in Cancún. But this beautiful, secluded area is superior, and because of the proximity of the Belize Reef, the marine life is richer. Although Akumal can be crowded—especially at lunchtime, when tour buses stop here en route from Tulum—it is also expansive and generally much less developed than Cancún. Those who stay are seeking the comforts of an international resort without the high rises, and Europeans—who tend to gravitate toward Mexico's quieter side—are coming in ever greater numbers.

First and foremost, however, Akumal is famous for its diving. Area dive shops sponsor resort courses and certification courses, and luxury hotels and condominiums offer year-round packages comprising airfare, accommodations, and diving (hotel rooms are at a premium during the high season, and reservations should be made well in advance). The reef, which is about 130 meters (425 feet) offshore, shelters the bay and its exceptional coral formations and sunken galleon; the sandy bottom invites snorkelers to wade out at the rocky north end, where they can view the diverse underwater topography. Deep-sea fishing for giant marlin, bonito, and sailfish is also popular.

A small **marine museum** (no phone), on the grounds of the Club Akumal Caribe, exhibits treasures from the galleons that sank off the coast, and an **underwater museum** (no phone) at Puerto Aventuras (see below) gives snorkelers and divers the chance to examine the wreckage. Added attractions include a small Mayan site opposite the detour to the Club Akumal Caribe and discos that entertain guests at night.

8 Devoted snorkelers may want to walk to **Yalkú,** a practically unvisited lagoon just north of Akumal along an unmarked dirt road. Wending its way out to the sea, Yalkú hosts throngs of parrot fish in superbly clear water with visibility to 16 feet, but it has no facilities.

9 Just south of Akumal and 60 kilometers (37 miles) south of Cancún is **Puerto Aventuras** (Box 1341, Cancún, Quintana Roo 77500, tel. 987/22344 or 988/22322, fax 988/32134), an enormous, imitation Cancún in progress, which will comprise condominiums, a 220-slip marina, a tennis club, a beach club, a dive center, an 18-hole golf course, a shopping mall, a movie theater, and—eventually—five deluxe hotels with a total of 2,000 rooms. At this writing, only the **CEDAM underwater archaeology museum** (open daily 9–6), where old ships, coins, and nautical devices are exhibited; the 30-room beach club; and nine holes of the golf course were operating. By 1993, however, Puerto Aventuras— which will follow a design that is a combination of Mediterranean, Caribbean, and Mexican architectural styles—may be siphoning off tourist business from its more established neighbor to the north. Billing itself as "the new Mexican Caribbean destination," this resort is aggressively pursuing the time-share market.

10 In stark contrast to the man-made finery of Akumal is the beautiful little cove at **Chemuyil,** about 5 kilometers (3 miles) south, where you can stop for lunch and a swim. The crescent-shaped beach, with coconut palms swaying gracefully in the breeze, is small and secluded, imbued with tranquility; with any luck, you'll encounter few other visitors (except in winter and on weekends).

Time Out   In Chemuyil a circular, open-air bar and restaurant, **Marco Polo,** is run by friendly owners who whip up excellent *limonada* and prepare shellfish as you sit on a bar stool or lounge in a hammock cooled by ceiling fans. They also have a glass-bottom boat and can take you out to see the cenotes, to go fishing or snorkeling, or to visit yet another solitary beach at **Punta Solimán,** where the cave is populated with oysters and manatees.

Continue south for a couple of kilometers along Route 307 to
⑪ the **Laguna de Xcacel,** which sits on a sandy ridge overlooking yet another long white beach. The calm waters provide excellent swimming, snorkeling, diving, and fishing; birders and beachcombers like to stroll in the early morning. Camping is permitted, and a restaurant (closed on Sunday) is on the site. Tour buses full of cruise-ship passengers stop here for lunch, and the showers and dressing rooms get crowded at dusk.

A natural aquarium cut out of the limestone shoreline 6 kilo-
⑫ meters (4 miles) south of Akumal, **Xel-Há** (pronounced shel-ha) national park consists of several interconnected lagoons where countless species of tropical fish breed; the rocky coastline curves into bays and coves in which enormous parrotfish cluster around an underwater Mayan shrine. Several low wooden bridges over the lagoons have benches at regular points, so you can take in the sights at leisure. Though much of the fauna has been threatened by suntan oil and garbage, the waters are still remarkably clear and they teem with brilliantly colored fish. Certain areas are off-limits to swimmers, but because the lagoons are quite large, in places you can swim fairly far out, or you can explore one of the underwater caves or the cenotes deep in the jungle. Glass-bottom boats travel to the far side of the lagoon, where stingrays and nurse sharks may be hovering beneath the surface. Lockers and dressing rooms are available, and you can rent snorkel gear and underwater cameras (the $18 fee includes a roll of film). Those who choose not to snorkel can rent chaise longues for sunbathing.

The park holds other attractions as well. At the entrance stands a shrine, and there are also other Mayan ruins, including one named for a yellow jaguar painted on the wall; a huge but overpriced souvenir shop; food stands; and a small museum housing 10,000 artifacts from pre-Hispanic days, 16th- and 17th-century shipwrecks (including coins and cannons from the *Mantanceros*), and present-day displays. The enormous parking lot attests to the number of visitors who come here; you should plan to arrive in the early morning, before all the tour-bus traffic hits. For a pleasant breakfast or lunch, you may want to try the restaurant, which serves reasonably good ceviche, fresh fish, and drinks. *Admission: P$20,000. Open Tues.–Sun. 8–5; closed Mon.*

About 9½ kilometers (6 miles) south of Xel-Há in the depths of the jungle stands a small grouping of pre-Hispanic structures covering 10 square kilometers (4 square miles); these once
⑬ served as a satellite city of Tulum. **Tancah,** as the place is known, has still not been fully explored, and while the buildings themselves may not warrant much attention, a curious bit of more recent history does. In the 1930s an airstrip was built here; Charles Lindbergh, who was making an aerial survey of the coast, was one of the first to land on it.

A couple of kilometers farther south lies one of the Caribbean
⑭ coast's biggest attractions: **Tulum,** the most visited Mayan ruin, is the only Mayan city built on the coast, and the spectacle of those amber-gray stones etched against the fiercely blue-green Caribbean waters is nothing less than riveting. Almost Grecian in its stark, low grayness, and vaguely medieval in the

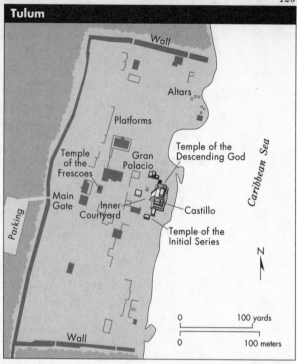

Tulum

Wall

Altars

Platforms

Temple of the Descending God

Temple of the Frescoes

Gran Palacio

Main Gate

Inner Courtyard

Castillo

Parking

Temple of the Initial Series

Caribbean Sea

N

| 0 | | 100 yards |
| 0 | | 100 meters |

Wall

forbidding aspect of its walls, this site surpasses all others for the sheer majesty of its setting.

Resting about 130 kilometers (80 miles) south of Cancún, Tulum comprises 60-odd structures, most of which date from the 12th to the 15th centuries. Only about three structures merit visiting, so you can see the site in two hours, but you may wish to allow extra time for a swim or a stroll on the beach. A path leads from the cliff down to the sea, where it's likely that the ancient Maya beached their canoes.

Tulum—which means "City of the New Dawn," and which the ancient Maya called Zama ("sunrise")—is the only Mayan city known to have been inhabited when the conquistadores arrived. Juan de Grijalva and his men, who spotted it from their ships in 1518, were so intimidated by the enormity of its vivid 25-foot-high, blue, white, and red (the only walled Mayan site) citadel that they were reluctant to land. What they had seen was four towns so close to one another as to appear to be one continuous metropolis. The Postclassical (AD 900–1541) architecture at Tulum evinces strong Toltec and Mixtec (a tribe from the Oaxacan Plateau) influences, because by the early 1500s the peninsular Maya had been absorbed into the empires of central and southern Mexico. Although artistic refinements found elsewhere in the Mayan world are missing here, the structure is extraordinarily well preserved. A 3,600-foot-long, 23-foot-thick wall—punctuated by five gateways and enclosing a dozen or so structures within 16 acres—surrounds Tulum on three sides.

Its largest building, the **Temple of the Descending God**—so called for the carving of a winged god plummeting to earth over the doorway—has skillfully rendered stucco masks in the corners. The deity they represent is thought either to be Ah Muzen Cab, the bee god, or to be associated with the planet Venus, guardian of the coast and of commerce.

The impressive **Castillo** (castle) looms over a 40-foot limestone cliff; atop the castle, at the end of a broad stairway, sits a temple, with stucco ornamentation on the outside and fine frescoes inside the two chambers. The lordly Castillo retains carved traces of the Descending God and columns depicting the plumed serpent god, Kukulcán, who was introduced by the Toltecs. Its summit overlooks an expanse of dense jungle and cactus to the west and the sea to the east. Until the 1940s, modern-day Maya from the Chan Santa Cruz group held an annual eight-day celebration honoring the sanctity of the place.

Tulum has long held special significance for the Indians. A key city in the League of Mayapán (987–1194), it was never conquered by the Spaniards, although it was abandoned about 75 years after the Conquest. For 300 years thereafter, it symbolized the defiance of an otherwise subjugated people; it was one of the last outposts of the Maya during the 1840s War of the Castes. Uprisings continued intermittently until 1935, when the Maya ceded Tulum to the government.

Most of the Chan Santa Cruz Indians are gone now, but some of their beliefs still prevail. For example, they thought that Tulum was connected to Cobá and other ruined cities by a living rope that was actually a road suspended in the sky. In fact, Tulum is linked to several other ancient Mayan sites by sacbeob, white stone causeways once used for ceremonial purposes and as trade arteries. One sacbe led from the northeast gateway to Xel-Há and then to Cobá, 42 kilometers (26 miles) west. Especially in its final days, Tulum functioned as a trading center, providing the much larger city of Cobá with an outlet to the sea and hence the control of commerce with Central America. Tulum's fortifications attest to its military importance. It may once have been home to 2,000 people living in houses set on man-made platforms along the main artery.

The blue-green frescoes outlined in black on the inner and outer walls of the two-story **Temple of the Frescoes** also refer to ancient Mayan beliefs. Reminiscent of the Mixtec style, the frescoes depict the three worlds of the Maya and their major deities, and are decorated with stellar and serpentine patterns, rosettes, and ears of maize and other offerings to the gods. One scene portrays the rain god seated on a four-legged animal—probably a reference to the Spaniards on their horses.

Entrances in Tulum are very low, even for the Maya, who are typically short of stature. Apparently the design forced those who entered to bow in deference to the divinities within. Vaulted roofs and corbeled arches, such as the ones on the Temple of the Frescoes, are examples of Classical Mayan architecture. By contrast, flat roofs resting on wood beams and columns, the generally second-rate sculpture, and the urban layout of straight streets flanked by buildings on either side bear the mark of outside influence that typified the city's later years of decline. *Admission: P$10,000. Open daily 8–5.*

There is also a present-day village of Tulum, just off Route 307 and about 4 kilometers (2½ miles) south of the ruins. This small, evidently poor community has a market, a butcher shop, a taco stand, and a small central square where pigs and dogs roam free. Outsiders are still something of a curiosity until you reach the crossroads (El Crucero) between the highway and the turnoff to the ruins, marked by a couple of restaurants and small hotels. At the parking lot by the ruins, souvenirs, handicrafts, and snacks are sold from a semicircular row of stands, but prices tend to be excessive. You will also encounter unofficial guides who profess various degrees of expertise on Mayan archaeology. Using their services will help the local economy, but you should take their stories with a grain of salt. Tour buses arrive at the ruins by midmorning, so it is wise to get there early.

⓯ Beautiful but barely explored, **Cobá** is a 35-minute drive northwest of Tulum down a well-marked and well-paved road leading straight through the jungle. Two tiny pueblos—Macario Gómez and Balché, clusters of thatched-roof white huts—are the only signs of habitation en route. Once one of the most important city-states in the entire Mayan domain, Cobá now stands in solitude; the spell this remoteness casts is intensified by the silence at the ruins, broken occasionally by the shriek of a spider monkey or the call of a bird. Processions of huge hunter ants cross the footpaths, and the sun penetrates the tall hardwood trees, ferns, and giant palms with fierce shafts of light. Cobá exudes the still, eerie ambience of a dead city.

Archaeologists estimate the presence of some 6,500 structures in the area, but only 5% have been uncovered, and it will take decades before the work is completed. Discovered by Teobert Maler in 1891, Cobá was subsequently explored in 1926 by the Carnegie Institute but not excavated until 1972, when the road from Tulum was built. At present there is no restoration work under way.

The city flourished from AD 400 to 1100, probably boasting a population of as many as 40,000 inhabitants. Its temple-pyramids (one of them is 138 feet tall, the largest and highest in northern Yucatán), situated on five lakes between coastal watchtowers and inland cities towered over a vast jungle plain. Cobá (meaning "ruffled waters") exercised economic control over the region through a network of at least 16 sacbeob, one of which, at 100 kilometers (62 miles), is the longest in the Mayan world. In the elegance of its massive, soaring structures and in its sheer size—the city once covered 210 square kilometers (81 square miles)—Cobá strongly resembles Tikal in northern Guatemala, to which it apparently had close cultural and commercial ties.

The main groupings are separated by several miles of intense tropical vegetation, so the only way to get a sense of the immensity of the city is to scale one of the pyramids. The map of the site available at the Villa Arqueológica will not be of much help because of all the unmarked paths, so you may want to hire one of the local men, such as Jacinto May Hau, who serve as unofficial guides. Hau, who is self-taught, has a guide's license and has worked on various excavations. When you go, bring plenty of bug repellent, and if you plan to spend some time

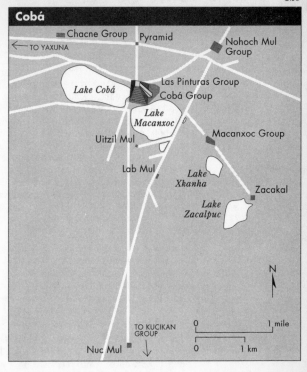

Cobá

Chacne Group Pyramid
← TO YAXUNA
Nohoch Mul Group
Lake Cobá
Las Pinturas Group
Cobá Group
Lake Macanxoc
Uitzil Mul
Macanxoc Group
Lab Mul
Lake Xkanha
Zacakal
Lake Zacalpuc
N
TO KUCIKAN GROUP
0   1 mile
0   1 km
Nuc Mul

here, bring a canteen of water (you can also buy sodas and snacks at the entrance).

The first major grouping, off a path to your right as you enter the ruins, is the **Cobá Group,** whose pyramids are built around a sunken patio. At the near end of the group, facing a large plaza, you'll see the 79-foot-high Iglesia (church), where the Indians place offerings and light candles in hopes of improving their harvests. If you have strong legs and want a great view, scale this ruin—unless you want to to save your energy for the far taller Nohoch Mul (*see* below).

Farther along the main path to your left is the **Chumuc Mul Group,** little of which has been excavated. The principal pyramid here is covered with the stucco remains (*chumuc mul* means "stucco pyramid") of vibrantly painted motifs. A kilometer (³⁄₁₀ mile) past this site is the **Nohoch Mul** (meaning "large hill") **Group,** the highlight of which is the pyramid of the same name, the tallest at Cobá. The pyramid has 120 steps—equivalent to 12 stories— and shares a plaza with Temple 10. The Descending God (also seen at Tulum) is depicted on a facade of the temple atop Nohoch Mul, from which the view is excellent; the temple seems to have been erected much later than the pyramid itself. It was from the base of this pyramid that the longest sacbe started; it extended all the way to Yaxuná, 20 kilometers (12 miles) southwest of Chichén Itzá. These sacbeob had widths of up to 33 feet, and there is considerable speculation about their function, since the Maya had no beasts of burden but carried all cargo on their own backs. The sacbeob's width, which may have been designed to allow people to walk abreast in processions, suggests that the roads played a role in religion as well as in trade. The unrestored **Crossroad Pyramid** opposite Nohoch Mul was the meeting point for three sacbeob.

Beyond the Nohoch Mul Group is the Castillo (castle); its nine chambers are reached by a stairway. To the south are the remains of a ball court, including the stone ring through which the ball was hurled. From the main route follow the sign to **Las Pinturas Group**, named for the still discernible polychromatic friezes on the inner and outer walls of its large, patioed pyramid. An enormous stela here depicts a man standing with his feet on two prone captives. Take the minor path for a kilometer to the **Macanxoc Group**, not far from the lake of the same name. The main pyramid at Macanxoc is accessible by a stairway. The portal of the temple at its summit is divided by a column; there are also a molded lintel and the remains of a stucco painting. Many of the stelae here are intricately carved with dates and other symbols of the history of Cobá.

Devotees of archaeology may wish to venture farther to the small **Kucikán Group,** one of the larger satellites of Cobá, positioned just 5½ kilometers (3½ miles) south of the Cobá group. Only five structures remain, but they are among the more puzzling ruins in the Mayan world. The three-story temple is particularly intriguing because it is the only Mayan structure in which the top story does not rest on filled-in lower stories.

Cobá can be comfortably visited in a half-day, but if you want to spend the night, opt for the Villa Arqueólogica (*see* Lodging, below), operated by Club Med and only a three-minute walk from the site along the shores of Lake Cobá, where common sights are women carrying pails of water on their heads and fishermen poling through the tall reeds. Even on a day trip, consider taking time out for lunch and a swim at the Villa—an oasis of French civilization—after the intense heat and mosquito-ridden humidity of the ruins. *Admission: P$10,000; free on Sun. Open Tues.–Sun. 9–6; closed Mon.*

Return to the coastal road heading south Tulum and continue to the Boca Paila turnoff from Route 307. Several kilometers south, past a few bungalows and campsites, the paved road ends, and a rope over the sand marks the entrance to the **Sian Ka'an Biosphere Reserve.** The reserve includes the 1.3-million-acre **Boca Paila peninsula,** a secluded 35-kilometer (22-mile) strip of land established by the Mexican government in 1986 as one of UNESCO's internationally protected areas and named a World Heritage Site by UNESCO in 1987. The Man and the Biosphere program, of which this is part, was created to preserve threatened areas of the Earth's surface and their natural resources. The reserves are particularly important in developing countries, where dwindling resources often represent the only form of subsistence for large segments of the population. Maintaining the ecological diversity of these areas while providing the local people with food and livelihoods is the challenge of the biosphere program, which has had great success at Sian Ka'an. Under the program, the land is divided for various purposes, including research, preservation, and economic activities in conjunction with conservation. Assisted by scientists, the local population lives off fishing, lobster harvests, coconuts, and small farming, and receives support from the low-impact tourism, biological research, and sustainable development programs under way.

The reserve constitutes 10% of the land in Quintana Roo and covers 100 kilometers (62 miles) of coast. Freshwater and coastal lagoons, mangrove swamps, watery cays, savannahs, tropical jungles, a barrier reef, hundreds of species of exotic migratory birds, fish, other animals and plants, and about 1,000 local residents—primarily Maya—share this area, one of the last undeveloped stretches of coastline in North America. About 20 ruined sites are scattered about; they are linked by a canal system—the only one of its kind in the Mayan world. Boca Paila is not easily reached, but those who take the time to get here feel rewarded.

Sian Ka'an, meaning "where the sky is born," was first settled by the Xiu tribe from Central America in the 5th century. The area once flourished with countless species of wildlife, many of which have fallen into the endangered category, but the waters here still teem with banana fish, bonefish, mojarra, snapper, shad, permit, sea bass, and alligator. Flat fishing and fly-fishing are especially popular, and the peninsula's few lodges run deep-sea fishing trips as far away as **Ascensión Bay,** two hours south near Chetumal. Birders take launches out to **Cajo Colibrí** (Hummingbird Cay) or to **Isla de Pájaros** to view the pelicans, frigate birds, woodpeckers, sparrow hawks, and some 350 other species of birds that roost on the mangrove roots or circle overhead. The beaches are wide and white, and although many of the palms have succumbed to the yellowing palm disease imported from Florida, graceful (but ecologically destructive) sea pines are growing up to take their place. The more adventuresome travelers can explore the caves with which the waterways are riddled or trek out to the tiny ruins of Chunyaxché (*see* below).

The narrow, rough dirt road across Boca Paila (meaning "mouth of the river") is dotted with campgrounds, fishing lodges, and deserted palapas and copra farms. It ends at **Punta Allen,** a fishing village whose main catch is the spiny lobster, and the site of a small guest house. In 1990 some muggings involving tourists took place on the Boca Paila road, but they seem to have been isolated events. In any case, you should travel by car or private plane, or charter a flight from Playa del Carmen or Cozumel.

Continue along the main route to the extensive archaeological site of **Chunyaxché**—known in ancient times as Muyil—which is currently under excavation by Tulane University and the Mexican government, with the help of local Maya and the latest laser and satellite technology. Dating from the Late Preclassical era (300 BC–AD 200), it was connected by road to the sea and served as a port between Cobá and the Mayan centers in Belize and Guatemala. A 15-foot-wide sacbe, built during the Late Postclassical period (1250–1600), extended from the city to the mangrove swamp (today it gets flooded during the rainy season). Structures were erected at 400-foot intervals along the white road, and almost all of them faced west. At the beginning of this century, the ancient stones were used to build a chicle plantation, which was managed by one of the leaders of the War of the Castes. Today all that stands are the remains of a 56-foot **temple-pyramid**—one of the tallest on the Quintana Roo coast—at the center of a big patio. From its summit you can see the Caribbean, 15 kilometers (9 miles) in the distance. Chunyaxché sits on the edge of a deep blue lagoon and is surrounded by a nearly impenetrable jungle inhabited by wild-cats, white-tailed deer, wild boars, raccoons, badgers, pheas-ants, wild turkeys, ducks, herons, and parakeets. You can swim or fish in the lagoon, and there is a small restaurant on the highway next to the dirt road leading to the ruins. *Admission: P$10,000. Open Tues.–Sun. 9–6; closed Mon.*

Twenty-four kilometers (15 miles) to the south, at Km 73 on Route 307, is **Felipe Carrillo Puerto,** named for a local hero who preached rebellion. In 1920 Carrillo Puerto eventually became governor of Yucatán and instituted a series of reforms that led to his assassination by the henchman of a presidential candi-date of an opposing party. This town, formerly known as Chan Santa Cruz, also played a central role in the 19th-century War of the Castes, during which it was not only a significant politi-cal and military center but also a religious capital. It was here that the "Talking Cross" first appeared—carved into a cedar tree near a cenote. The Indian priest Manuel Nahuat, translat-ing from behind a curtain, interpreted the cross as a sign for the Indians to attack the *dzulob* (white Christians) under the protection of the cross. Although Mexican soldiers cut down the tree and destroyed the cross, the Indians made other crosses from the trunk and placed them in neighboring vil-lages, including Tulum. The last messages were given in 1904; by then half the local population had been annihilated in the war. Today the town exists primarily as the hub of three high-ways, and the only vestige of the momentous events of the last century is the small, uncompleted temple (located on the edge of town in an inconspicuous, poorly marked park) begun by the Indians in the 1860s and now formed a monument to the War of the Castes. The church where the Talking Cross was originally housed also stands. Several humble hotels, some good restau-rants, and a gas station may be incentives for stopping here on your southbound trek.

Route 307, a dreary and monotonous road to Belize, continues south for another 112 unremarkable kilometers (69 miles), till the sudden appearance of the spectacularly vast and beautiful **Laguna de Bacalar.** Also known as the Lake of the Seven Col-ors, this is the second largest lake in Mexico (56 kilometers/35 miles long) and is frequented by scuba divers and other lovers of water sports. Seawater and fresh water mix in the lake, in-tensifying the aquamarine hues, and the water contrasts stark-ly with the dark jungle growth. If you drive along the lake's southern shores, you'll enter the affluent section of the town of Bacalar, with elegant turn-of-the-century waterfront homes. Also in the vicinity are a few simple hotels and campgrounds. Bacalar—which appears to be the oldest settlement in Quinta-na Roo, having been founded in AD 435—is the site of beautiful formal gardens. Of some historical interest is the **Fuerte de San Felipe,** a stone fort built by the Spaniards during the 18th cen-tury to ward off marauding pirates and Indians and later used by the Maya during the War of the Castes. The monolithic structure is right on the zócalo and overlooks the lake. Present-ly it houses government offices and a museum with exhibits on local history. *Admission free. Open daily 8–5.*

Just beyond Bacalar exists the largest sinkhole in the world, the **Cenote Azul,** 607 feet in diameter, with clear blue waters that afford unusual visibility even at 200 feet below the surface. Surrounded by lush vegetation and underwater caves, the cenote attracts divers who specialize in this somewhat tricky type of dive. Other recreational areas on the water are to be found at **Laguna Milagros,** a lovely lagoon with an island in the center and a shoreline graced by palms and bougainvillea, and at **Xul-Ha,** a rustic spa. Restaurants and rental shops are in the vicinity, too.

㉒ **Chetumal**—38 kilometers (24 miles) farther along Route 307— is the last Mexican town on the southern Caribbean. It was founded in 1898 as Payo Obispo in a concerted and only partially successful effort to gain control of the lucrative traffic in the region's precious hardwoods, arms, and ammunition, and also to put down the rebellious Indians. The city, which overlooks the Bay of Chetumal at the mouth of the Río Hondo, was devastated by a hurricane in 1955 and rebuilt as a modern state capital and major port. Because of its status as a free port (in the past it was a haven for smugglers), Mexican merchants come to buy imported goods not found elsewhere in the country. In ancient times it was one of the major Mayan ports.

Overall, Chetumal feels more Central American than Mexican; this is not surprising, given its proximity to Belize, with which there is both commercial and tourist traffic. Chetumal's streets are also vaguely reminiscent of some parts of the American South, with monotonous rows of rundown (but often charming) clapboard houses interspersed with low-lying ramshackle commercial establishments. The mixed population includes many black Caribbeans and Middle Easterners, and the arts reflect this eclectic mix—the music includes reggae, salsa, calypso, and Belizean bruckdown; there is not much mariachi. The cuisine represents an exotic blend of Yucatecan, Mexican, and Lebanese.

The town's most attractive thoroughfare, the wide **Boulevard Bahía,** runs along the waterfront and is a popular gathering spot at night (though on the weekend Chetumal practically shuts down). The main plaza sits between the boulevard and Avenidas Alvaro Obregón and Héroes; unremarkable modern government buildings and some especially bland patriotic statues and monuments to local heroes wall in the plaza on two sides. Brackish bay waters lapping at the dock create a melancholy rhythm, but if you sit at one of the sidewalk cafés by the square, you will have an appealing view of this huge, placid bay.

Downtown Chetumal contains a small a zoo, a few discos, and a cultural institute; the reasonably priced hotels, which seem to cater mostly to the modest needs of traveling salesmen, are generally clean. For shopping, you can stroll along Avenida Héroes, where most of the stores are located, but the merchandise tends to be a humdrum, functional miscellany. Although Chetumal's provisions are modest, the town presents a pleasant waterfront, since the city is surrounded by water on three sides. The area's clean, white bayfront beaches can compete with any of the beaches along the coast.

Surrounding attractions offer alternatives to downtown Chetumal. Eight kilometers (5 miles) north of town, you'll find excellent swimming at **Banco Chinchorro,** a 42-kilometer (26-mile) coral atoll and national park (fishing prohibited) situated two hours offshore and littered with shipwrecks. The reef, which is popular with divers, is accessible by boat from the fishing village of **Xcalak,** at the tip of the peninsula, which divides the bay from the ocean. This area is full of mangrove swamps, tropical flowers, birds and other wildlife, and wonderfully deserted beaches. Windsurfing is popular in both the bay and the lagoon. It is possible to camp on the fine sandy beaches at **Cayo Lobos** and **Cayo Centro,** extensions of the reef.

Chetumal's major water attractions, however, sit farther inland. The **Río Hondo** runs alongside the borders between Mexico and Belize and Guatemala; in its wildest parts, alligators roam the riverbeds and manatees breed. The **Palmar** and **Obregón** springs by the river, just outside Chetumal, have rustic resorts.

Time Out   Leave your car behind (you cannot take it to Belize) and take the rickety bus from Chetumal 16 kilometers (10 miles) across the border to **Tony's Motel** (South End, Corozal Town, tel. 501/22055; fax 04/22829) in Corozal, where you can get a good shrimp lunch and a fair sense of the wildness of Belize.

Sixty-eight kilometers (42 miles) west of Chetumal, off Route 186, lies **Kohunlich,** one of the more recently discovered Mayan ruins—renowned for the giant stucco masks on its principal pyramid, for one of the oldest ball courts in Quintana Roo, and for the remains of a great hydraulic system at the Stelae Plaza. The masks—about 5 feet tall—are set vertically into the wide staircases; apparently they played a part in ceremonies dedicated to the sun god. The sculpture here is massive and totemlike, yet exceptionally fine, with realistic depictions of the figures' nose rings, mustaches, mutilated teeth, and deepset eyes adorned with hieroglyphs. The three-story pyramid is thought to contain the tomb of a Mayan ruler, but no investigations have as yet been made. Archaeologists believe that Kohunlich was built and occupied during the Early Classical period, about AD 300–600. This site is usually deserted, and in the vicinity are scores of unexcavated mounds, stelae, and thriving flora and fauna. *Admission: P$10,000. Open daily 8–5.*

What to See and Do with Children

Croco-cun, near Playa del Carmen, is a crocodile farm located 29 kilometers (18 miles) south of Cancún. It has a snack bar and a gift shop. *Rte. 307 at Km 30, tel. 988/41709. Admission: P$8,000. Open Tues.–Sun. 9–6; closed Mon.*

Shopping

There aren't many high-quality crafts available along the Caribbean coast, although stands on the road leading to the ferry in Playa del Carmen and in the parking lot at the Tulum ruins do their best to unload a mediocre and overpriced selection of embroidered clothing, schlock reproductions of ancient carvings and statues, knickknacks made from shells, and hammocks. If you drive, stock up on groceries, pharmacy items, hardware, and auto parts in Puerto Morelos, Playa del Carmen, Felipe Carrillo Puerto, or Chetumal. Gift shops at the resort hotels in Akumal sell the usual postcards, film, and some handicrafts, at resort prices. As for Chetumal, while Mexicans go there to buy imported and black-market appliances, North Americans will find the merchandise inferior and the prices no bargain. Save your shopping dollars for Mérida or Cozumel.

Sports and Fitness

Water Sports Diving, snorkeling, and fishing are among the most popular activities along the coast. Quintana Roo attracts scuba divers and snorkelers to transparent turquoise and emerald waters strewn with rose, black, and red coral reefs and sunken pirate ships. Schools of black, gray, and gold angelfish, luminous green-and-purple parrotfish, earth-colored manta rays, and scores of other jewel-toned tropical species seem oblivious to the clicking underwater cameras. The visibility in these waters reaches 100 feet, so you can see the marine life and topography without even getting wet. There is particularly good diving in Akumal and Laguna de Bacalar. For details, *see* Exploring, above.

For fly-fishing, boats can be rented from locals who run beachside stalls. If you're interested in deep-sea fishing in the Caribbean, where catches such as marlin, bonito, and sailfish can be found, many local marinas run charters. Generally, larger hotels have dive shops on the premises. The following is a brief list of outfitters. For details about where to dive, *see* Exploring above.

Akumal **Akumal Caribe** (tel. 800/351–1622) and **Akumal Dive Shop** (tel. 987/22453 or 987/22567) rent diving equipment.

Chetumal **Casa Lucy** (Av. Héroes No. 52, between Plutarco Elias and Ignacio Zaragoza) rent diving gear.

Playa del Carmen **La Posada del Capitan Lafitte** and **Shangri La Caribe** (tel. 800/538–6802 for both), located on Carretera 307 just north of Playa del Carmen, run deep-sea fishing trips and have full-service dive shops on the premises.

Puerto Morelos Scuba gear is available from the **Ojo de Agua Dive shop** (no phone).

Xel-Ha For diving equipment rentals and deep-sea fishing chargers call **Juan Jose González** and **Demas Calderón** (tel. 987/21717 or 987/22001).

Xcalak Situated about 164 kilometers (100 miles) from Chetumal, and reached by boat, plane, or car, the little fishing village of Xcalak makes a good point of departure for deep-sea fishing. The **Costa de Cocos Hotel** (no phone) runs trips.

Dining and Lodging

Dining Most of the restaurants along the Mexican Caribbean coast are simple beachside affairs with outdoor tables and palapa roofs. Little attention is paid to the niceties of decor you find in such resort destinations as Cancún, Cozumel, and even Isla Mujeres. In addition to their generally casual ambience, restaurants here offer bargains, especially when it comes to seafood, provided it is fresh and local, such as grouper, mojarra, snapper, shad, seabass, shrimp, and lobster. Shrimp, lobster, oysters, and other shellfish are usually flown in frozen from the

Gulf or Pacific coast, and often you can taste the difference. Where tourists congregate, especially in Playa del Carmen and Akumal, a number of places that cater to the North American palate have sprung up; their menus include such items as pizza and spaghetti. The few luxury hotels in the area have fancy restaurants offering Continental cuisine, elegant service, and of course high prices—almost as high as those in Cancún. Many of the restaurants in Playa del Carmen close down in summer (off-season), and the restaurants in the Punta Bete hotels close for the hurricane season (September–November). Generally, all restaurants maintain a casual dress code and do not accept reservations.

Highly recommended restaurants are indicated by a star ★.

Category	Cost*
Expensive	over $10
Moderate	$5–$10
Inexpensive	under $5

per person, excluding drinks, service, and sales tax (15%)

Lodging Accommodations on the Caribbean coast run the gamut from campsites to simple palapas and bungalows to middle-range functional establishments to luxury hotels and condominiums. Many of these hotels include two or three meals in their prices. Unless it is necessary to board on site, there is little reason to stay in Tulum, since much better accommodations can be found less than an hour away at Punta Bete or Playa del Carmen.

In Chetumal, you will probably not find much to impress you in the way of accommodations. Hotels tend to be older, functional, and lacking in character or endearing idiosyncrasies. Accommodations reflect the town's origin as a pit stop for traders en route to or from Central America.

Highly recommended hotels are indicated by a star ★.

Category	Cost*
Very Expensive	over $150
Expensive	$110–$150
Moderate	$40–$110
Inexpensive	under $40

All prices are for a standard double room, excluding service and the 15% tax.

Akumal **Restaurant Zacil.** Seafood, Mexican dishes, and international
Dining cuisine are prepared at this eatery, one of the few comparatively inexpensive beach restaurants in Akumal. You'll find it on the north end of the beach, next to Bungalows Akumal Caribe. A giant palapa covers the dining area, which overlooks the sea through arched windows. The only drawback may be that cruise-ship passengers come here in droves. *North end of beach, no phone. No credit cards. Moderate.*

Lodging **Club Aventuras Akumal-Cancún.** An all-inclusive luxury hotel managed by the Spanish hotel group Oasis, this sprawling property started as the private preserve of millionaire Pablo Bush Romero, a friend of Jacques Cousteau. Ten years ago the property was transformed into one of the largest resorts along the Cancún–Tulum corridor; today the beautiful beach—protected by an offshore reef—and the pier are used as the starting point for canoeing, snorkeling, diving, fishing, and windsurfing jaunts. The U-shaped building, with nautical decor, features handsome mahogany furniture and sunken blue-tile showers between Moorish arches (no doors!). All rooms have balconies (you can choose a sea view or a garden view) and air-conditioning or ceiling fans (same price). The condominium units are much larger and include living rooms and kitchenettes. Recently renovated, Club Aventuras is well maintained, and it rates high for amenities: In addition to the CEDAM dive school on the premises (founded by Cousteau), there are two pools, a grill bar on the beach, and ambitious nightly entertainment that features music and dance. The clientele consists exclusively of Americans and Canadians on package deals led by Adventure Tours. *For reservations: Adventure Tours, 111 Avenue Rd., 5th floor, Toronto M5R 3J8, tel. 416/967–1112 or, in Akumal, 987/22887. 44 rooms plus 49 condominium units and penthouses. Facilities: restaurant, indoor and outdoor bar, beach, 2 pools, game room, dive shop, tennis court, boutiques, travel agency, car rental. AE, MC, V. Very Expensive.*

Akumal Cancún. This large, multistory modern resort has all the attractions of a Cancún property, including American-style service and such amenities as elevators and air-conditioning. The main building is right on the water, and all rooms have a sea view, terrace, and rattan furniture. *For reservations: Av. Bonampak y Cobá, Suites Atlantis, Local 10, Cancún, Quintana Roo 77500, tel. 988/42272. 81 rooms, 11 villas. Facilities: restaurant, disco, lounge, beach, pool, tennis court, horseback riding, game room, dive shop, rental cars, shops. AE, MC, V. Expensive.*

Dining and Lodging **Club Akumal Caribe & Villas Maya.** Accommodations at this resort (situated on the edge of a cove overlooking a small harbor) range from rustic but comfortable bungalows with red tile roofs and garden views (Villas Maya) to beachfront rooms in a modern three-story hotel building; all have air-conditioning, ceiling fans, and refrigerators. Also available are the more secluded one-, two-, and three-bedroom condominiums called the Villas Flamingo, on Half Moon Bay a half-mile from the beach. The bungalows and hotel rooms are cheerfully furnished in rattan and dark wood, with attractive tile floors; the high-domed condominium units, Mediterranean in architecture and room decor, have kitchens and balconies or terraces overlooking the pool and beach. The property began as a few thatched cottages built for CEDAM, the Mexican divers' organization, and it still emphasizes diving. The on-property dive shop offers resort courses, PADI certification, and cenote or cave diving, although all water sports, including snorkeling, windsurfing, kayaking, and deep-sea fishing, are available. As for the restaurant, dining here is about the fanciest experience you'll find anywhere along the coast. An optional meal plan includes breakfast and dinner. *Km 104, Carretera Cancún–Tulum, no phone. For reservations: Akutrame, Box 13326, El Paso, TX 79913, tel. 915/584–3552 or 800/351–1622. 40 bungalows, 21*

rooms, 4 villas, 3 condos. Facilities: restaurant (Moderate–
Expensive), snack bar, ice cream parlor, pizza parlor, bar,
pool, beach, dive shop, boutique, grocery. 3-night minimum
stay. AE, DC, MC, V. Expensive.

Bacalar **Rancho Encantado.** On the shores of Lake Bacalar, five min-
Lodging utes north of Chetumal, the Rancho comprises five little private *casitas* (cottages), each with its own patio and hammocks,
kitchenette, sitting area, and bathroom. Rustically decorated,
the property features native hardwood furniture and ceiling
fans, as well as beautifully landscaped grounds and a dining
room and bar. Included in the room rate are breakfast, dinner,
and tax. You can swim and snorkel off the private dock leading
into the lagoon. When traveling by car on Route 307, watch for
the road sign on your left. *For reservations: Turquoise Reef
Group, Box 2664, Evergreen, CO 80439, tel. 303/674–9615 in
CO or 800/538–6802 outside CO; fax 303/674–8735. 5 units. Facilities: restaurant, bar. No credit cards. Very Expensive.*

Boca Paila **Boca Paila Fishing Lodge.** This enclave of eight spacious
Lodging thatched cottages, situated on a narrow spit of land between
the Caribbean and the lagoons and flats of the Boca Paila peninsula, sits in the midst of the Sian Ka'an Biosphere Reserve.
Clean, bright, and cheerful accommodations include the basics:
bed, dresser, and nightstand within white walls and tile floors.
Catering principally to anglers, the lodge provides boats and
guides for fly-fishing (bonefish, tarpon, snook, and barracuda)
in the abundantly stocked lagoon channels, as well as for
billfishing off Cozumel; guests should bring their own tackle.
The staff also arranges six-day fishing packages and day trips
to the lagoons and flats at Ascensión Bay, 72 kilometers (45
miles) south. Guests who do not fish can participate in nighttime visits to the Sian Ka'an alligator farm and jaunts to Isla de
Pájaros, Cobá, Tulum, and the golf course at Puerto
Aventuras. Mayan specialties are served at mealtime. If you're
flying in from Cozumel or Playa del Carmen, arrange in advance for the lodge staff to pick you up; drivers are available for
day trips as well. *For reservations: Frontiers, Box 161, Wexford, PA 15090, tel. 987/21176, 987/20195 in Cozumel, or 800/
245–1950 outside Cozumel. 8 cottages. Facilities: restaurant,
fishing packages. Deposit required. No credit cards. Very Expensive.*

★ **Caphé-Ha.** Orginally built as a private home by an American
architect, this small guest house—located between a lagoon
and the ocean—is a perfect place to stay if you're interested in
bonefishing and birding. Rustic, comfortable, and relatively
new, Caphe-Ha combines local flavor and North American
standards, as evinced by the hand-built bentwood furniture
and Mexican leather chairs. A private two-bedroom house,
with a kitchen, private bath, and living room, and a two-unit
bungalow (with shared baths) are your choices; though neither
has fans or electricity, all the windows have screens to catch
the ocean breeze. A caretaker/chef from Mérida cooks meals
that are served in the solar-powered community palapa; he will
prepare vegetarian meals upon request. Fishing tackle and
snorkeling gear are available from the property's small dock,
but there's an extra charge for bonefishing. The room rates include breakfast and dinner; advance reservations must be accompanied by a 50% deposit, and a three-day or longer stay is
required during high season. Caphe-Ha is located 30 kilometers (19 miles) south of Tulum, on the road to Sian Ka'an, 5 ki-

lometers (3 miles) past the bridge at Boca Paila and around the next rocky point. *For reservations: tel. 99/213404 in Mérida or 212/219–2198 in NY. 1 villa, 1 bungalow. Facilities: fishing packages. No credit cards. Very Expensive.*

Casa Blanca Lodge. Punta Pájaros, on the southern side of Bahía de la Ascención, just across from Punta Allen at the tip of the Boca Paila peninsula, is reputedly one of the best places in the world for light-tackle saltwater fishing, to which this new, remote fishing resort provides unique access. The American-managed, all-inclusive lodge—just 100 feet from the ocean—is set on a rocky outcrop covered with palm trees. Bonefish and permit, which can be caught by wading or fishing from a poled skiff, swarm in the mangrove swamps, flats, and shallow waters. The lodge's seven large, modern guest rooms, painted white with turquoise trim, and with slatted windows and tile and mahogany bathrooms, provide a pleasant tropical respite at dusk. Furnishings include darkwood chairs but no desks or couches. An open-air thatched bar and a large living and dining area welcome anglers with drinks, fresh fish dishes, fruit, and vegetables at the start and end of the day. The lodge offers weekly fishing packages and shorter itineraries during June–July and October–December. Rates include three meals, fishing, and a round-trip charter flight from Cancún to the Punta Pájaros airstrip. Those coming by land must make the three-hour drive to Punta Allen and then take a one-hour boat trip across the bay. *For reservations: Frontiers, Box 161, Wexford, PA 15090, tel. 988/45891 in Cancún or 800/245–1950 outside Cancún. 7 rooms. Facilities: restaurant/bar, open-air bar, fishing packages. Prepayment required. No credit cards. Very Expensive.*

★ **Sol Pez Maya.** An idyllic fishing resort smack in the middle of the Boca Paila peninsula and the Sian Ka'an Biosphere Reserve, this property consists of only seven cabanas and a small restaurant. The simply furnished bungalows, with small patios, are set back slightly from the expanse of white beach, palm trees, and sea pines. This is the kind of place where you could spend hours in a beach chair, soaking up the sensual tropical climate. Unlike other beaches in Quintana Roo, this one has not been blighted by the lethal yellowing disease that has destroyed palm trees throughout the area: The proprietors treat their palms regularly with penicillin. Table fans are provided for morning and evening use, but the generator shuts down in the daytime and after 11 PM, when you must rely on the screen door to let in the sea breeze and keep out the fierce mosquitoes. Manager Nestor Erazo can arrange boat trips for bonefishing, fly-fishing, deep-sea fishing, birding, or exploring the savannah and the mangrove swamps and even an obscure Mayan ruin, Chunyaxché. Turtles come to the beach to lay their eggs between May and July. Sol Pez Maya is well worth the price, since fabulous fresh meals, daily fishing, and transfers to and from Cancún or Playa del Carmen are included. Follow the dirt road south of the Tulum ruins for about 24 kilometers (15 miles); the hotel is another kilometer (9/10 mile) beyond a small wooden bridge that cuts the peninsula in two. This road is very difficult to maneuver, and the trip takes about one hour. Call for restrictions. *For reservations: Box 9, Cozumel, Quintana Roo 77600, tel. 987/20072 or 800/336–3542; fax 987/21599. 7 bungalows. Facilities: restaurant, beach, fishing boats. No credit cards. Very Expensive.*

Chemuyil **Chemuyil.** This gorgeous little cove and coconut grove sur-
Dining and Lodging rounding a very quiet beach has its own campground, restaurant, and a soon-to-come hotel. Facilities include hammock
rentals (for sleeping under palm trees) and tiny open-air
palapas with mosquito netting and hammocks. The white, six-
unit hotel will offer kitchenettes and air-conditioning, with
breakfast and dinner included in the room rate. At Marco Polo,
the restaurant, you can sit at the bar or at a small table, or you
can lounge on a hammock under the palapa as you sip a delicious
freshly squeezed limonada. The cuisine is strictly seafood and
much the same as you'd find at any of a number of palapa
eateries in the area. Future plans include a dive shop and fishing and snorkeling packages. *Km 110, Carretera Cancún–Chetumal, no phone. 6 rooms. Facilities: restaurant (Moderate).
Inexpensive.*

Chetumal **La Cascada.** This hotel/restaurant specializes in regional cui-
Dining sine such as shellfish and chicken dishes as well as meat spe-
cials. To go along with your meal, select a domestic or imported
wine from the good-size list. The elegant La Cascada appeals to
Americans and Canadians. *Hotel Continental Caribe, Av. Héroes 171, tel. 983/21100. Expensive. AE, MC, V.*
Maria's. This informal, air-conditioned restaurant—formerly
Casablanca—has inherited the reputation of being the local
hangout. Overall, the food—mostly Mexican dishes—is good.
Av. Madero 293, tel. 983/22355. AE, MC, V. Moderate.
Restaurante del Caribe. People come here to enjoy the tranquil
view from the Boulevard Bahía and—incidentally—to order
lunch, snacks, and drinks. Chinese food and vegetarian dishes
are among the specialties served for lunch. *Blvd. Bahía 8 at Av.
Veracruz, no phone. AE, MC, V. Inexpensive.*
Sergio's. This popular pizza parlor is situated in a small, simply
decorated frame house. Other menu items include steak and
pasta. *Av. Alvaro Obregón 182 at Av. 5 de Mayo, tel. 983/22355.
AE, MC, V. Inexpensive.*

Lodging **Del Prado.** This hotel (formerly part of the Presidente chain) in
downtown Chetumal has seen better days. The modern, low-
rise structure feels like a motel with spacious rooms, but the
property experiences frequent problems with electricity and
plumbing. The decor tends toward mid-1970s nondescript; the
best thing about the Del Prado is the inner garden and pool
area. Ask for a room with a pool view. *Av. Héroes 138, Col.
Centro, 77000, tel. 983/20544 or 983/20542. 78 rooms, 2 suites.
Facilities: restaurant, bar, air-conditioning, satellite TV,
pool, shops, travel agency, car rental, parking. AE, DC, MC,
V. Moderate.*
Hotel Continental Caribe. The modern architecture sets the
tone for this downtown property, conveniently located across
the street from the municipal market. Highlighting the atrium
is a small fountain that gushes from the angular pool. Inside,
rooms are carpeted and decorated in a yellow and orange color
scheme. The hotel's restaurant, La Cascada—one of the best in
Chetumal—features international fare and bargain breakfasts. *Av. Héroes 171, Box 1, 77000, tel. 983/21100. 64 rooms, 10
suites. Facilities: restaurant, bar, air-conditioning, disco, cafeteria, minibar, TV, travel agency. AE, MC, V. Moderate.*
Príncipe. This relatively new (1986) three-star hotel in Chetumal is located some distance out of town, but the rooms are air-
conditioned, clean, and modern, and a pool and satellite TV are
planned for the near future. There is also a restaurant-bar on

the premises. *Av. Héroes 326, 77000, tel. 983/24799 or 983/ 25167. 52 rooms. Facilities: restaurant-bar, color TV, parking. AE, MC, V. Inexpensive.*

Cobá
Dining and Lodging

Villa Arqueólogica Cobá. This Club Med property, a three-minute walk from the entrance to the Cobá ruins, overlooks one of the region's vast lakes. Tastefully done in white stucco and red paint, with bougainvillea hanging from the walls and muse-um pieces throughout the property, the hotel has a clean, airy feel; corridors in the square, two-story building face a small pool and bar. Although the air-conditioned rooms are small, they feel cozy. A handsome library, housing books on the Maya and paperback novels, features a large VCR and a pool table. Piped-in medieval music adds to the ambience. Dining choices near the isolated Cobá ruins are quite limited, so the restau-rant here is an attractive option, though it should not be judged by the rather large, impersonal, and formal dining room. The food—if pricey—is very good. For regional fare, try the group-er, ceviche, lobster, chicken píbil, or enchiladas. On the more international side are spaghetti, entrecôte (boned rib steak), chicken with curry, and shish kebab. *For reservations: 800/ CLUB-MED. 40 rooms. Facilities: restaurant (Expensive), bar, pool, tennis court, gift shop. AE, MC, V. Moderate.*

Felipe Carrillo Puerto
Dining and Lodging

El Faisán y El Venado. Given the paucity of hotels in Felipe Carrillo Puerto, this one is your best bet. It's bare-bones, but you can choose between air-conditioned rooms or rooms with ceiling fans. The rooms also come with color or black-and-white TV and refrigerators. The pleasant restaurant does brisk busi-ness with locals at lunchtime because it is so centrally located. Yucatecan specialties such as poc chuc, *bistec a la yucateca* (Yucatecán-style steak), and pollo píbil are served in a simple but rustically decorated setting. *Av. Juárez 781, 77200, tel. 983/40043. 21 rooms. Facilities: restaurant (Moderate). No credit cards. Inexpensive.*

Playa del Carmen
Dining

Chicago Connection Sports Bar & Grill. As the name implies, this joint caters to the I-can't-leave-home-for-long-without-a-hamburger crowd. Replete with nautical decor, it makes a good show of re-creating an American-style eatery. This is a fun, in-formal place that especially hops when live music is played. *Av. 5a at Calle 6, tel. 988/21230, ext. 166. AE, MC, V. Expensive.*

Albatros. This beachfront palapa restaurant-bar is owned by Americans, and it rates high with compatriots who come to hang out as well as to sample the food. Suggestions for lunch include fish or sandwiches; breakfasts are also very good. *6 blocks north of ferry pier, no phone. MC, V. Moderate.*

Don Cipriano. On Sundays this simply decorated restaurant serves *carnita estilo Michoacán*, a dish featuring lamb from the faraway state of Michoacán and unique to the Mexican Ca-ribbean. Put in your order (based on the number of kilos) early in the morning (beginning at 8:30) and come back later in the day to sample the tasty barbecued meat. Don Cipriano also serves breakfast, freshly blended fruit juices, and Mexican snacks. *Av. 5a, opposite the bus station, no phone. No credit cards. Moderate.*

Limones. Probably the most romantic place in town, this res-taurant offers dining by candlelight, either alfresco in a court-yard or under the shelter of a palapa indoors. Candles atop tables, wine bottles hanging from the ceiling, and guitar music make this place all the more romantic. The owners hail from

Rome, and their cooking rates high for authenticity. House favorites include copious entrées such as fettuccine, lasagna, and lemon-sautéed beef scaloppini. Appetizers might be home-baked pizza bread or salads. *Av. 10a at Calle 2, 3 blocks north of the pier, no phone. AE, V. Moderate.*

Máscaras. The wood-burning brick oven here produces exceptionally good pizzas, pastas, and breads. Various beverages, including fresh-squeezed, sweetened lime juice, margaritas, and beer, help wash down the rich Italian fare. A broad selection of masks cover the walls of this Mexican- and Italian-style place. *Av. Juárez (on the beach), no phone. AE, MC, V. Moderate.*

Rick's Caribbean Dreams Café. Located upstairs at the Blue Parrot Inn, this trendy place with its excellent view was still being rebuilt in 1990 following the damage it sustained in the 1988 hurricane. Beach lovers thrive on the café's studiously hip, quasi-Caribbean ambience, and the food is decent if a bit overpriced. Japanese tacos (a seafood dish with flour tortillas); lobster, shrimp, and chicken kababs; burgers; and vegetarian dishes are on the menu, and so is breakfast. Come late in the day for a sandwich and coffee to this simply decorated, contemporary Mexican-style restaurant with white walls and bentwood furnishings. *7 blocks north of the pier, no phone. MC, V. Moderate.*

Chac Mool. Another simple palapa restaurant on the road to the airstrip, the Chac Mool serves good fresh fish, Yucatecán meals, and breakfast. *Along the road to the airstrip, no phone. No credit cards. Inexpensive.*

Doña Juanita. Juanita's daughter has now taken over the management of this simple, rustic restaurant on the outskirts of town. Fish dishes receive rave reviews for freshness, generous portions, and price. Try the fillet of red snapper. *Av. Juárez at Rte. 307, no phone. No credit cards. Inexpensive.*

Tacos al Pastor. Fans of these wickedly delicious little pork tacos frequent this stand opposite the Posada Sian Ka'an. *Av. 5a at Calle 2, no phone. No credit cards. Inexpensive.*

Lodging **Cabañas Playa Ojo de Agua.** Recently remodeled, this dive lodge, situated on a lovely beach just north of Puerto Morelos, books groups and individuals in hotel rooms or cabins and offers both American and European dining plans. All accommodations include ceiling fans and face the beach. A freshwater pool and a good restaurant that serves Yucatecán and American dishes (including fresh fish specials) are among the features here. *For reservations: Box 709, Mérida, tel. 99/215150. Facilities: restaurant, bar, pool, dive shop. No credit cards. Closed Sept. and Oct. Expensive.*

Las Palapas. Almost a dead ringer for the Shangri-La next door (the German Luebke family, who became rich from Cancún, own shares in both properties), this is one of the newer hotels (it opened in early 1990) north of Playa del Carmen. White cabanas with blue trim lend a rustic feel, and duplexes feature balconies or porches, palapas, and hammocks. The beach and pool are complemented by a shuffleboard area, clubhouse, beach bar, palapa bar, and attractive palapa restaurant, which features international cuisine as well as hamburgers, tacos, and other snacks. Probably because of the ownership, this place caters to German tour groups. *Km 292 on Rte. 307 (Box 116), Playa del Carmen, Quintana Roo, 77710, tel. 987/ 22977. 50 cabanas. Facilities: restaurant, 2 bars, pool, beach, in-room safes. 3-night minimum stay. AE, MC, V. Expensive.*

Shangri-La Caribe. Run by the locally known American Bilgore family, this tropical-village-like accommodation is far less intimate than are the Lafitte or Kai Luum properties owned by the same people. The white concrete walkways and large central pool reflect its relative newness (it was built in 1987). Its attractive whitewashed bungalows (some duplexes, some suites), capped with palapa roofs, have hammocks out front and ceiling fans inside; some of the larger cabanas also feature sitting areas. Music blares from the palapa-covered bar, where the French, German, and American clientele gather around the pool table. You can order American or Mexican food à la carte at the spacious restaurant. *On a dirt road (follow signs to Posada del Capitán Lafitte), off Rte. 307 and continue south a bit. For reservations: Turquoise Reef Group, Box 2664, Evergreen, CO 80439, tel. 303/674–9615 in CO or 800/538–6802 outside CO; fax 303/674–8735. 30 bungalows, 6 suites. Facilities: restaurant, bar, coffee shop, beach, pool, dive shop, water sports, gift shop, car rental. Land/air, scuba, and honeymoon packages available. All reservations (minimum 3 nights) must be prepaid; no credit cards. Closed around Sept. 1–Nov. 1. Expensive.*

★ **Albatros.** Owned and managed by Americans, the Albatros, which opened in late 1989, is a set of 18 homey thatched cabanas situated on the beach and complete with hammocks hanging on the patios. The one-, two-, and three-bedroom cabanas are gaily painted in pastel colors and have hot water and ceiling fans. Purified water is available from large demijohns, and extra care is taken to keep the premises free of insects. *6 blocks north of ferry pier; Box 31, Quintana Roo, 77710, no phone. 18 cabanas. Facilities: restaurant, bar, private boat. MC, V. Moderate.*

Blue Parrot Inn. This very cozy property is situated at the extreme northern end of the beach next to a hotel that's under construction. Room options vary from a one-story structure on the sand to private bungalows, some of which contain kitchenettes, mosquito nets, and purified water. Choose among two-story bungalows, palapas, or beachfront villas, all of which are decorated with rustic Mexican furnishings such as hammocks, bentwood, and stucco. *7 blocks north of pier; for reservations: Box 64, Quintana Roo, 77710, tel. 904/775–6660 or 800/364–3547; fax 988/44564. 9 palapas, 4 beachfront rooms, 3 bungalows, 1 beachfront villa. Facilities: restaurant, water-sports equipment. MC, V. Moderate.*

Campamento La Ruina. Named for the tiny Mayan ruin on the premises, this beachside campsite rents cabanas with one, two, or three cots; hammocks; and three sizes of tents. Facilities include washrooms and trailer hookups. Hot water is not available, however, so you'll have to make due with cold-water showers. *Calle 2 N, 3 blocks north of the pier, no phone. Facilities: restaurant. No credit cards. Inexpensive.*

Costa del Mar. Large, white, and a bit antiseptic, this hotel consists of a newly built (in 1990) two-story motel block, an older motel-like unit, and four bungalows. The rooms in all facilities are clean and functional and done in sandy white from the tile floors to the bedspreads and stucco walls. All the rooms but those in the bungalows have air-conditioning. *Calle Primera Norte, bis, between 10 and 12, tel. and fax 987/20231. 31 rooms, 4 bungalows. Facilities: restaurant, small pool. 3-night minimum stay. AE, MC, V. Inexpensive.*

Posada Lily. A nondescript, rather stark two-story motel painted deep blue, the Lily offers plain, overlit rooms with ceiling fans. A friendly ambience, low rates, and a convenient location right on the main street make this place a good bargain. *Av. Juárez, no phone. 15 units. AE, MC, V. Inexpensive.*

Posada Sian Ka'an. Located in town, 3 blocks north of the pier, the Posada features clean rooms with pine furnishings, plus kitchenettes, ceiling fans, and hot water, in a pleasant garden setting where you can hang up your own hammock. *For reservations: Box 135, Quintana Roo, 77710, tel. in Mérida, 992/ 97422. 11 rooms. No facilities. No credit cards. Inexpensive.*

Dining and Lodging **Las Molcas.** This large, pretty hotel (owned by Aviomar), situated in downtown Playa a half-block from the ferry pier and one block south of the plaza has a colonial-style lobby and hallways with red tile floors. Pleasant, attractive rooms face the pool, the sea, or the street. The modern, unremarkable hotel dining room, with some outdoor tables overlooking the plaza, is a safe bet for standard international fare, including sausage, tuna salad, spaghetti à la carbonara, steak, and *pollo al ajo* (chicken broiled with garlic). Other items you may find here are such local specialties as snapper, *pollo píbil* (chicken steamed in citrus juices), lime soup, and tacos. Breakfast is also served. *Box 79, Quintana Roo, 77710, tel. 987/21100 or 987/21200, ext. 109– 111; tel. 99/256990 in Mérida; 305/534–3716 for reservations. 35 air-conditioned rooms. Facilities: restaurant, bar, pool, gift shop. AE, MC, V. Expensive.*

Puerto Morelos **Los Pelícanos y las Palmeras.** If you're looking for good fresh
Dining fish—fried, grilled, or steamed—stop by these two small thatched huts on the beach. *Puerto Morelos, no phone. No credit cards. Inexpensive.*

Lodging **Posada Amor.** This small hotel near the ferry pier is family-run and a bit rustic. The rooms have ceiling fans, and hot water is available in the shared baths. *Near the ferry pier, no phone. 19 rooms. Facilities: restaurant. No credit cards. Inexpensive.*

Punta Bete **Xcalacocos.** This tranquil campsite at the southern end of
Lodging Punta Bete offers tents, RV hookups, 6 cabanas, showers, and rest rooms. A small restaurant is on the premises, and diving, snorkeling, and fishing gear can be rented. *At the Marlin Azul sign on Rte. 307, no phone. No credit cards. Inexpensive.*

Dining and Lodging **Posada del Capitán Lafitte.** Set on an invitingly long stretch of
★ beach just 10 kilometers (6 miles) north of Playa del Carmen at Punta Bete, this lodging wins hands down among the hotels on the Cancún–Tulum corridor for its genuinely chummy, unpretentious atmosphere. This is no luxury resort, but a simple cluster of two-unit cabanas, each with its own beachfront patio, private bath, and ceiling fan; the sea breeze will provide you with enough fresh air that you won't even miss the air-conditioning. Run by the Fuentes family for almost 20 years, the Capitán Lafitte has maintained its solitude: The only contact with the outside world is via radio to the hotel's Mérida office. Furthermore, breakfast, dinner, tax, and tips are included in the room rate, so you rarely need to carry money. The large palapa-covered restaurant emphasizes Yucatecán seafood specialties in an informal atmosphere where the company is quite gregarious. Abundant buffet dinners—accompanied by live music and entertainment—are served during the posada's weekly fiestas. In the evenings the European and American clientele congregates around a small but pretty pool/bar decorated with red tiles and coral-pink stucco. Guests at Lafitte can

dine at either Kai Luum (a three-minute walk) or Shangri-La,
properties with which it is loosely affiliated. Call for restrictions. *On a dirt road (follow the signs), 2⁹⁄₁₀ km (1⅘ mi) off Rte.
307. For reservations: Turquoise Reef Group, Box 2664, Evergreen, CO 80439; tel. 303/674–9615 in CO or 800/538–6802 outside CO; fax 303/674–8735. 39 rooms, 2-bedroom duplex cabin.
Facilities: restaurant (Moderate), bar, beach, pool, dive shop,
car rental. Land-air, scuba, and honeymoon packages available. All reservations (minimum 3 nights) must be prepaid; no
credit cards. Closed around Sept. 1–Nov. 1. Expensive.*

Kai Luum Camptel. Owned and managed by the locally known
Bilgore family, this "luxury" campground attracts a predomi-
nantly American clientele. Tents come with wooden platform
floors and gas lanterns and are covered with palapas; hammocks hang from the support poles; rest rooms are within an
easy walk from campsites. There is no electricity, so guests
spend the evening lounging in the beach chairs in the bar. During the day, you may opt for a massage or take a plunge in the
hot tub. The ecology-conscious owners also run tours to Belize,
Tikal, Palenque, and the major ruins of Yucatán. The restaurant—actually nothing but a palapa overhead and the sand
cushioning your feet underneath—is a stone's throw from the
beach. Diners sit at communal picnic tables and are served food
from a fixed—but surprisingly eclectic—menu that features
cuisine prepared by Mayan chefs. The restaurant ranks high
for warmth and informality, and large tables invite communal
dining with erstwhile strangers who quickly become chatty
companions. Breakfast and dinner are served, and tax and tip
are included in the rate. In many ways, Kai Luum Camptel is
comfortably reminiscent of a 1960s community: The bar—little
more than a palapa on the beach—runs on the honor system,
and the gift shop—housed in a palapa and filled with exquisite
handicrafts from throughout Mexico and Guatemala—has no
locks or doors. To afford guests an even richer experience, Kai
Luum—which had to be entirely rebuilt after the 1988 hurricane—shares some facilities with the Posada del Capitán Lafitte (a three-minute walk down the beach), as well as some
group activities, including snorkeling trips, scuba certification
and dives, fishing, and birding. Turtle eggs are carefully nur-
tured at a small hatchery on the beach between the Lafitte and
Kai Luum. Call for restrictions. *On a dirt road, 2⁹⁄₁₀ km (1⅘ mi)
off Rte. 307 (look for the Posada del Capitán Lafitte sign on the
left). For reservations: Turquoise Reef Group, Box 2664, Evergreen, CO 80439, tel. 303/674–9615 in CO or 800/538-6802 outside CO; fax 303/674-8735. 40 tents. Facilities: restaurant, bar,
beach, crafts shop, dive shop, hot tub. Land/air, scuba, and
honeymoon packages available. All reservations (minimum 3
nights) must be prepaid. No credit cards. Closed around Sept.
1– Nov. 1. Moderate.*

Tulum **Acuario.** Formerly El Faisán y El Venado, this modern hotel
Dining restaurant at the crossroads of Route 307 and the turnoff to the
Tulum ruins is more expensive than other places in the area.
However, it's well worth the price because the owner takes
pride in the preparation and quality of the food, which is more
than can be said of its competition. Although the diner-like setting is unimpressive, Acuario offers a menu that includes
above-average seafood, shrimp, soup, tacos, nachos, guacamole, and a really good coconut ice cream. Breakfast—beginning

at 6:30 AM—is quite satisfactory. *Km 127 Carretera Cancún–Chetumal, no phone. No credit cards. Moderate.*

El Crucero de Tulum. Another nondescript hotel restaurant, this one is covered with a palapa and sells take-out snacks and beer in addition to the seafood, tacos, nachos, and soups from the regular menu. *Carretera Cancún–Chetumal, no phone. No credit cards. Inexpensive.*

Lodging **Maya Tulum.** Located on Route 307 near the turnoff for the Tulum ruins, this modern, functional hotel offers 16 rooms with ceiling fans and hot water. Although the location makes it simple to find, this hotel tends to get noisier than some of the others set away from the road. *Tulum Pueblo, Domicilio Conocido, 77780, no phone. 16 rooms. Facilities: restaurant. AE, MC, V. Moderate.*

Acuario. This relatively new hotel (it opened in 1990), situated at the turnoff for the Tulum ruins, has small, clean rooms with satellite TV, screen windows, ceiling fans, and hot water. In addition to a pool with a swim-up bar, there is also a restaurant that specializes in seafood (*see* above). Future plans include a video bar and 11 more functional rooms. *Crucero de las Ruinas de Tulum, Km 127 Carretera Cancún–Chetumal, 77780, no phone. 11 rooms. Facilities: restaurant, bar, pool, parking, satellite TV. No credit cards. Inexpensive.*

Cabañas Tulum. This property, nicely situated in a coconut grove on a beach, is 7 kilometers (4 miles) south of the Tulum ruins on the dirt road leading to Boca Paila. Eighteen palapa bungalows with private bathrooms, and an indoor-outdoor restaurant, bar, and game room make a good package. *Tulum, 77780, no phone. 18 rooms. Facilities: restaurant, bar, game room. No credit cards. Inexpensive.*

Chac Mool. Situated just opposite the little guardhouse at the entrance to the Sian Ka'an Biosphere Reserve, this accommodation is also very near the Tulum ruins and Boca Paila. Chac Mool offers 20 palapa-covered units with beds and hammocks, as well as camping facilities. *Tulum, 77780, no phone. 20 units. Facilities: bar. No credit cards. Inexpensive.*

Xcaret **Restaurant Xcaret.** This small palapa restaurant, with walls
Dining lined with photos from diving expeditions, serves conch ceviche, lobster, poc chuc, and french fries. *Off Rte. 307, Xcaret, no phone. No credit cards. Inexpensive.*

Nightlife

There isn't much in the way of nightlife along the coast, unless you happen upon some entertainment in a luxury hotel bar. If you're staying in Akumal, try **Discoteca Akumal** at the Hotel Akumal; if you're in Playa del Carmen, try **Tequila**; in Chetumal visit **Antares** (Blvd. Bahía and 22 Enero) or **Escorpión** (Av. Juárez, between Othon P. Blanco and Carmen Ochoa).

7 Campeche

Introduction

The city of Campeche has a run-down but lovely feel to it: No self-conscious, ultramodern tourist glitz here, just an over-grown backwater town (population 220,000) content to rest on its staid old laurels. That good-humored, lackadaisical attitude is enshrined in the Spanish adjective *campechano*, meaning easygoing, hearty, genial, cheerful. The city gets only about 20,000 tourists a year, a number probably attributable to the relative paucity of attractions and to insufficient promotion.

Most of the State of Campeche is flat—never higher than 1,000 feet above sea level—but more than 60% of its territory is cov-ered by jungle, where the precious mahogany and cedar abound. The Gulf Stream keeps temperatures at about 26°C (78 °F) year-round; the humid, tropical climate is eased by eve-ning breezes. Campeche's economy is based on agriculture, fishing, logging, salt, tourism, and—more recently—hydro-carbons, of which it is the largest producer in Mexico. But most of the oil industry is concentrated at the southern end of the state, near Ciudad del Carmen.

Campeche's location on the gulf has played a pivotal role in its history. Ah-Kin-Pech (Mayan for "serpent chigger")—from which the Spanish name of Campeche is derived—was the capi-tal of an Indian chieftainship long before the Spaniards arrived in 1517. Earlier explorers had visited the area, but it was not until 1540 that the conquerors—led by Francisco de Montejo and, later, his son—established a real foothold at Campeche (originally called Salamanca), using it as a base for their con-quest of the peninsula.

Because Campeche was the only port and shipyard on the gulf, the Spanish ships, with their rich cargoes of plunder from the Mayan, Aztec, and other indigenous civilizations, dropped an-chor here en route from Veracruz to Cuba, New Orleans, and Spain. News of this wealth spread, and soon the shores were infested with pirates. From the mid-1500s to the early 1700s, such notorious corsairs as Diego the Mulatto, Lorencillo, Peg Leg, Henry Morgan, and Barbillas swooped down repeatedly from their base on Tris—or Isla de Términos, as Isla del Carmen was then known—pillaging and burning the city and massacring its people.

Finally, after appealing for years to the Spanish crown, the citi-zens of Campeche received funds that enabled them to build a protective wall (with four gates and eight bastions). For some time thereafter, the city thrived on its exports, especially *palo de tinte*—a dyewood used by the nascent European textile in-dustry—but also hardwoods, chicle, salt, and henequen. How-ever, when the port of Sisal on the northern Yucatán coast opened in 1811, Campeche's monopoly of the gulf traffic ended and its economy fell into decline.

The shape of modern-day Campeche is still defined by history. Remnants of the wall and other military structures divide it into two main districts, intramural (the old city) and extra-mural (the new). Because the city was long preoccupied with defense, colonial architecture is less developed here than elsewhere in Mexico. Churches are more somber; streets (still paved with cobblestones) are narrow because of the confines of the walls; houses are more practical than aesthetic in their design. Although the face of the city has altered over the centuries, as landfill was added and walls and bastions demolished to make room for expansion, it still retains a colonial tenor.

The state as a whole has a population of only about 613,000, most of it scattered through villages and small towns. Mayan traditions still reign in the countryside, which is dotted with windmills and fields of tobacco, sugarcane, rice, indigo, maize, and cocoa. Wildlife flourishes here, too: jaguars, tapirs, and armadillos roam free, while the sea provides fishing boats with shrimp, barracuda, swordfish, and other catch. Thousands of Guatemalan refugees now make their home in Campeche, where they have been settled into two camps, one of which was, until recently, involved in excavating the Mayan archaeological site of Edzná. Smaller, more obscure Mayan ruins exist throughout the state.

Essential Information

Important Addresses and Numbers

Tourist Information
The **main tourist office** is located at Plaza Moch Cohuo (Av. Ruíz Cortines, tel. 981/66068 or 981/66767), near the Baluarte San Carlos, and is open weekdays 8–2:30 and 4–9 during low season (September–May), and weekdays 8 AM–9 PM during high season (June–August). There are also **information modules** at the bus station (Av. Gobernadores s/n, tel. 981/60663 or 981/60419) and the airport (same phone). Modules are open daily 8–noon and 4–8 during low season, and weekdays 8–8 during high season.

Emergencies
Red Cross (Av. Resurgimiento s/n, tel. 981/60666 or 981/65202).

Police (Calle 12 between Calles 57 and 59, tel. 981/62111, 981/62329, or, in town, 06).

Medical Clinics
Hospital General (Av. Central at Circuito Baluartes, tel. 981/60920 or 981/64233) has a 24-hour emergency room.

Social Security Clinic (Av. Central at Circuito Baluartes, tel. 981/61855 or 981/65202) is open 24 hours for emergencies.

Late-night Pharmacies
Farmacia Ah-Kim-Pech (Calle Pedro Sainz de Baranda 100, Centro Comercial Ah-Kim Pech Local 113, tel. 981/68602) is open 24 hours and delivers to hotels.

Banks
Campeche banks are open weekdays 9–1:30; those where you can exchange money include **Banamex** (Calle 53 No. 15 at Calle 10, tel. 981/60730) and **Bancomer** (Av. 16 de Septiembre 120, tel. 981/66622).

Telephones
There are two public booths for making long-distance calls: one at Avenida Gobernadores s/n (open 8 AM–10 PM) and one at the corner of Calle 12 at Calle 59 (open 9 AM–10 PM).

Mail
The **post office** (Av. Pedro Saínz de Baranda s/n, between Calles 53 and 55; tel. 981/64390) is open Monday–Saturday 8–6 and Sunday 8–2.

Travel Agencies and Tour Operators
The major Campeche-based operators are **American Express/VIPs** (Prolongación Calle 59, Edificio Belmar, Depto. 5, tel. 981/11010 or 981/68333) and **Agencia de Viajes Campeche** (Calle 10 No. 339, tel. 981/65233 or 981/62844).

Arriving and Departing by Plane, Car, Train, and Bus

By Plane **Aeromexico** (tel. 800/237–6639) has daily flights from Mexico City and, via Mérida, from Houston, Los Angeles, Miami, New York, and Tucson.

By Car Campeche can be reached from Mérida in about 1½ hours along the 160-kilometer (99-mile) *via corta* (short way, Rte. 180). The alternative route, the 250-kilometer (155-mile) *via larga* (long way, Rte. 261), takes at least 3 hours but crosses the major Mayan ruins of Uxmal, Kabah, and Sayil. From Chetumal, take Rte. 186 west to Francisco Escarceja, where you pick up Rte. 261 north; the drive takes about 7 hours. Villahermosa is about 6 hours away driving inland via the town of Francisco Escárcega, but longer if you hug the gulf and cross the bridge at Ciudad del Carmen.

By Train The **Mexican National Railroad** (Av. Heroes del Nacozari, s/n, tel. 981/62009 or 981/61433) has routes to Campeche from Mérida and Mexico City, but the lines are not among those that have been recently upgraded. It may be difficult to book a sleeper on the Mexico City line (which is 24 hours long), so this journey is recommended only for the most stoic traveler. One train departs daily at 6 PM from Campeche for the seven-hour trip to Palenque.

By Bus There is generally a big difference between first- and second-class bus service throughout Mexico. The former offers fewer stops and more comfortable coaches, the price difference is negligible. **ADO** (Av. Gobernadores 289 at Calle 45, along Rte. 261 to Mérida, tel. 981/62802), a first-class bus line, runs service to Campeche from Coatzacoalcos, Ciudad del Carmen, Mérida every half-hour, and from Mexico City, Puebla, Tampico, Veracruz, and Villahermosa regularly, but less frequently. There is second-class service on **Autobuses del Sur** (tel. 981/63445) from Chetumal, Ciudad del Carmen, Escárcega, Mérida, Palenque, Tuxtla Gutiérrez, Villahermosa, and intermediate points throughout the Yucatán Peninsula.

Getting Around

By Bus The municipal bus system covers the entire system.

By Car Rental agencies include **Hertz** (Hotel Baluartes, Av. Ruíz Cortines s/n, tel. 981/63911 or 981/68848) and **AutoRent** (Ramada Inn, Calle 57 No. 1, tel. 981/62714 or 981/62233).

By Taxi Taxis can be hailed on the street, or—more reliably—commissioned from the **taxi stand** (Calle 8 between Calles 55 and 53, tel. 981/62366 or 981/65230).

Guided Tours

American Express/VIPs travel agency offers a half-day tour of the city including a stop at the Regional Museum, for about $13. For $14 you can tour Edzná, with a stop at a lookout point in town.

Exploring

Because it has been walled since 1686, most of historic Campeche is neatly contained in an area measuring just 5 blocks by 9 blocks. Today, for the most part, streets running north–south are even-numbered, and those running east–west are odd-numbered. The city is easily navigable—on foot, at least; the historical monuments and evocative name plaques above street numbers serve as handy guideposts.

At corners of Viejo Campeche stand *baluartes*, or bastions, in various stages of disrepair or reconstruction, hailing back to the hexagonal fortifications against the pirates who kept ransacking the city. They were completed; the pirates were driven away for good in 1717. Only short stretches of the wall, which once stretched 3 kilometers (2 miles), are extant. Two stone archways—one facing the sea, the other the land—are all that remain of the four gates that provided the only means of access to Campeche. There are also four outlying forts and 10 churches.

Campeche was one of few walled cities in North or Central America and was built along the traditional lines of defensive Spanish settlements, such as Santo Domingo (in the Dominican Republic), Cartagena (in Colombia), and Portobelo (in Panama). The walls also served as a class demarcation. Within them lived the ruling elite. Outside were the barrios of the Indians who aided the conquistadores, and whose descendants continued to serve the upper class. The mulattoes brought as slaves from Cuba also lived outside.

Campeche City

Numbers in the margin correspond to points of interest on the State of Campeche and Campeche City map.

Our Campeche City itinerary highlights attractions in town and detours briefly. While it may sound dauntingly ambitious to accomplish in one go, many of the sights described here can be seen in just a few minutes; two days, however, are better for the more leisure-minded visitor. Traveling throughout the State of Campeche could take from two to four days depending on how much time you devote to some of the towns that are farther off the beaten path.

❶ The **Centra de Informacíon de Turistica** (between Av. 16 de Septiembre and Av. Ruíz Cortines, tel. 981/66068 or 981/66767), housed in a modern building on the Plaza Moch Cohuo (after the *cacique*, or chief, responsible for the Spaniards' first defeat in Mexico, which took place in 1517 in nearby Champotón), is situated on a piece of landfill along the waterfront boulevard. Here you can pick up maps of the city and its environs.

❷ Across the way, what appears to be a flying saucer is actually the **Congreso del Estado,** the State Congress building, where government activities take place. Next door, notice the rather handsome neoclassical Municipal Palace, built in 1892.

❸ Continue southeast on Avenida 16 de Septiembre; on your left, where the avenue curves around and becomes Circuito Baluartes, you'll arrive at the first bastion, the **Baluarte San**

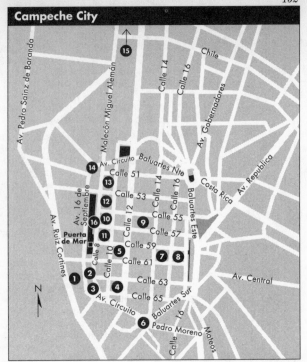

Carlos. Because this one contains only scale models of the original defense system, you may prefer to save your energy for some of the more elaborate installations. The dungeon, however, is interesting and can be visited. *Small admission fee. Open Tues.–Sat. 8–8, Sun. 8–1.*

One block east, occupying the full city block between Calles 10 and 12 and Calles 63 and 65, stands the **Ex-Templo de San José.** The Jesuits built this fine Baroque church in 1756, and today its facade stands as an exception to the rather plodding architectural style of most of the city's churches. Its immense portal is completely covered with blue talavera tiles and crowned by seven narrow, stone finials that resemble the roofcombs on many Mayan temples. The convent-school next door is now used for cultural events and art exhibitions. *Admission free. Open Tues.–Sat. 8–2 and 2:30–8, Sun. 9–1.*

Now head north on Calle 12 for 2 blocks, then turn right onto Calle 59, where you will pass the tiny **Iglesia de San Francisquito**, whose architecture and ambience do justice to the historic street's old-fashioned beauty. Behind the genteel lace curtains of some of the homes, you can glimpse equally genteel scenes of Campeche life, with faded lithographs on the dun-colored walls and plenty of antique furniture and clutter. Along Calle 59 once stood some of Campeche's finest homes, many of them two stories high, with the ground floors serving as warehouses and the upper floors as a residence. Geometric motifs decorated the cornices, and the windows were gaily adorned with iron latticework. The richest inhabitants built as close to the sea as possible, in case escape became necessary. Beneath the city a network of tunnels crisscrossed, linking the eight bastions and providing temporary refuge from the pirates.

6 Take Calle 10 south to Calle Bravo, home of the **Iglesia de San Román.** Generally, contemporary Campeche lacks the old city's character, but this exception—which sits just outside the intramural boundary in the barrio of the same name—suggests the old charm. San Román, with a bulbous bell tower typical of other Yucatán churches, was built to house the *naborios* (Indians brought by the Spaniards to aid in the Conquest and later used as household servants), and the barrio, like other neighborhoods, grew up around the church. Though it went up in the 16th century, the church became central to the lives of the Indians only when an ebony image of Christ, the "Black Christ," was brought in in about 1565. The Indians had been skeptical about the Christian saints, but this Christ figure came to be associated with miracles. The legend goes that a ship that refused to carry the tradesman and his precious statue was wrecked, while the ship that did take him on board reached Campeche in record time. To this day, the Feast of San Román—when the icon is carried through the streets as part of a colorful and somber procession—is the biggest such celebration in Campeche. People still come to see the black wood Christ mounted on a silver filigree cross. *Calle 10 s/n, no phone. Open Mon.–Sat. 7–noon and 4–8:30; Sat. Mass at 7:30 PM, Sun. Mass at 10 AM and 7:30 PM.*

Time Out   Stop for some fine *antojitos*, mouthwatering Mexican appetizers, at **La Bodega** (Calle 63, between Calles 12 and 14), a popular and inexpensive little restaurant.

7 One block beyond San Francisquito, at the corner of Calle 59 and Calle 14, is the **Museo Regional,** for which you should allow at least two hours. The museum occupies the former Casa del Teniente del Rey, or House of the King's Governor, who lived here between 1804 and 1811. His official's stature entitled him to build a house with architectural flourishes not permitted to less eminent citizens, including entrances flanked by columns or framed by portals, and the central atrium surrounded by Moorish archways leading off to numerous corridors and rooms. The ground floor comprises the archaeological museum, which is devoted primarily to the Maya. Jewels and jade masks from the tomb of Calakmul; figurines from Jaina; giant stone masks from Edzná; and plentiful illustrations, photographs, and models are on exhibit. The historical museum on the second floor covers the 18th century and includes religious art, weapons, manuscripts, and a superb carved ebony rudder shaped like a greyhound around which a serpent is entwined. *Admission free. Open Tues.–Sat. 8–2 and 2:30–8, Sun. 9–1.*

8 Old Campeche ends one block east of the museum at the **Puerta de Tierra,** the only one of the four city gates that still stands with its basic structure intact; the walls, arches, and gates were refurbished in 1987. This stone arch intercepts a long stretch of the partially crenelated wall, 26 feet high and 10 feet thick, that once encircled the city; looking through it, you can just barely see across town to its counterpart, the **Puerta de Mar,** through which all seafarers were forced to pass. Because the latter stands alone, without any wall to shore it up, the Puerta de Mar looks like the Arc de Triomphe. The wall that is standing today was demolished in 1893 and rebuilt in 1957.

9 Take Calle 55 back toward the waterfront and turn left on Calle 14; step inside the **Hotel Colonial** (*see* Dining and Lodging, below), a wonderful tiled mansion dating from the 1850s, when it belonged to another of the king's governors. The roof terrace affords a panoramic view of the city.

Walking one block farther west on Calle 55 will bring you to yet another exquisite mansion, this one highlighted by Moorish arcades. In 1865 Empress Carlotta, wife of the doomed Maximilian, stayed here briefly, but it was long enough for the town to celebrate her visit with all due pomp and circumstance. It was during the short-lived reign of Maximilian that Campeche, besieged by the French troops, was forced to become part of Yucatán; at his death it became an independent state.

10 Just opposite the mansion stands the **Parque Principal**, the southern side of which—Calle 57—is lined with several agreeable cafés and hotels; this is the focal point for the town's activities.

Time Out   **Café Literario El Murmillo**, a somewhat unusual, bohemian-style hangout along Calle 57, is the kind of starkly furnished and poorly lit gathering place that seems more typical of Paris or Madrid than of a backwater Mexican town. This café offers an amusing ambience in which to take some refreshment before continuing on.

11 Also situated along the plaza is the **Hotel Campeche** (*see* Dining and Lodging, below), a dilapidated but likable inn with colorful tile floors, an iron balustrade, and what must once have been a striking courtyard.

Along the north side of the plaza—on Calle 55 between Calles 8 and 10—is another exception to the generally somber architecture rule of colonial Campeche. The **Catedral,** right on the plaza, took two centuries (from 1650 to 1850) to build and incorporates Neoclassical and Renaissance elements. (The present cathedral occupies the site of Montejo's original church, which was built in 1540.) The simple exterior lines terminate in two bulbous towers rising to each side of the gracefully curved stone entrances, the fluted pilasters echoing those on the towers. Sculptures of saints set in niches recall the French Gothic cathedrals. The interior is no less impressive, with a single limestone nave, supported by Doric capitals and Corinthian columns, arching toward the huge octagonal dome above a black-and-white marble floor. The pièce de résistance, however, is the magnificent Holy Sepulcher, a carved-ebony, silver-encrusted urn.

13 Walk 1 block north of the cathedral to the corner of Calles 10 and 53, where you'll find the eclectic **Mansión Carvajal.** Built in the early 20th century by one of the wealthiest plantation owners in Yucatán, this structure did time as the Hotel Señorial before arriving at its present role as a sort of crafts-and-clothes bazaar/events hall/café/government office center. Take a stroll: The black-and-white tile floor, Art Nouveau staircase with Carrara marble steps and iron balustrade, and salmon-and-pale-green Moorish arcades speak volubly of the city's heyday when Campeche was the peninsula's only port. Also in the mansion are a gift shop and snack bar. *Calle 10 s/n, between Calles 53 and 55, no phone. Admission free. Open Mon.–Sat. 8–2:30 and 5–8:30. Closed Sun.*

Just a short block north on Calle 8 (which becomes Malecón
(14) Miguel Alemán) is the **Baluarte Santiago,** the last of the
bastions to be built (1704), which has been transformed into a
botanical garden where 250 plant species grow. It was demolished at the turn of the century but was rebuilt in the 1950s.
Architecturally this fort looks much the same as the others in
Campeche: a stone fortress with thick walls, watchtowers, and
gunnery slits. *Calle 8 at Calle 49, tel. 981/66829. Admission
free. Open Tues.–Sat. 9–1 and 4–8, Sun. 9–1.*

At this point, devotees of religious history may wish to venture
(15) 3 blocks north to the ruins of the **Iglesia de San Francisco**
(1546), the oldest church site in Campeche. Possibly more significant is that it marks the spot where—in 1517—the first
Mass on the North American continent was said. One of
Cortés's grandsons was baptized here, and the baptismal font
still stands.

Campeche has one other bastion museum that bears visiting:
(16) the **Baluarte de la Soledad,** otherwise known as the **Museo de
los Estelas.** The largest of the bastions, this one has comparatively complete parapets and embrasures that offer a sweeping
view of the cathedral, the municipal buildings, and the Gulf of
Mexico. Artifacts housed inside include 10 Mayan stelae and
other pieces from the Late Classical period (AD 600–900), such
as a sculpture of a man wearing an owl mask. *Calle 8, Circuito
Baluartes at Calle 57, no phone. Admission: P$500; free on
Sun. Open Tues.–Sun. 8–2 and 4–8.*

State of Campeche

After touring Campeche's churches and museums, you may
want to drive through the State of Campeche, stopping at some
of the archaeological sites and beaches. These attractions also
nicely break up a trip to Mérida, Villahermosa, or Chetumal.

*Numbers in the margin correspond to points of interest on the
Campeche State map.*

Along Route 180 The so-called short route to or from Mérida takes you past sev-
toward Mérida eral villages and minor archaeological sites. Although the pret-
(17) ty 15th-century town of **Hecelchakán,** 57 kilometers (35 miles)
north of Campeche, boasts a lovely church and ex-convent, it is
known primarily for the **Museo Arqueológico del Camino Real.**
This museum holds an impressive collection of clay figurines
from the island of Jaina and stelae from the Puuc region. It is
not possible to visit Jaina, because the archaeological zone is
being restored, so many of Jaina's intricate sculptures, most of
which have been removed from the island, are on display here.
*Rte. 180 to Hecelchakán, no phone. Admission: P$500; free on
Sun. Open Tues.–Sat. 8–2, Sun. 4–8; closed Mon.*

(18) Some 24 kilometers (15 miles) north, you'll come to **Calkiní** and
its fortress-monastery built by the Franciscans between 1548
and 1776. Inside the building is an exquisite cedar altarpiece on
which the four Evangelists have been carved, and the columns
and cornices adorning the convent have been painted in rich
gold, red, and black. The portal is plateresque (resembling fine
silverwork), while the rest of the structure is Baroque. Interestingly enough, the place itself dates back much earlier, to the
Ah-Canul dynasty. According to a local codex, the Ah-Canul
chieftainship was founded here in 1443 beneath a ceiba, a tree

*Golfo
de
Mexico*

Seybap

Siho

Chompo

Sabancuy

Isla Aguada

Puerto Real

**Isla del
Carmen**

Nuevo
Progresso   Atasta

Chekubul

Dieciocho
de Marzo

Pital

El Desecho

Felipe
Angeles

*Laguna
Términos*

El Vapon

Palizada

TABASCO

Villahermosa

El Naranjo

CAMPECHE
TABASCO

sacred to the Maya and frequently mentioned in their legends. The Ah-Canul was the most important dynasty at the time of the Conquest; the fighters rebelling against Montejo were put down in Mérida giving the coup de grace to the Maya spirit.

⑲ The neighboring village of **Becal** is noted for the famous *jipijapa* (Panama-style) hats made here by local Indians. The Indians weave reeds of the jipi plant or the huano palm in caves beneath their houses, because the humidity there keeps the reeds flexible. First produced in the 19th century by the García family, the hats have become a village tradition. Just across the Yucatán state line, in **Halachó,** townspeople weave motifs from **⑳** central Mexico into their baskets. The rest of the way to Mérida consists of relatively monotonous terrain, with the occasional clusters of white, thatched-roof huts, speed bumps, windmills, and spearlike henequen plants.

Along Route 261 This is by far the longer—and more interesting—way to reach **toward Mérida** the Yucatán capital. The first ruin, **Edzná,** deserves more fame **㉑** than it has. Archaeologists consider it one of the peninsula's most important ruins because of the crucial transitional role it played among several architectural styles. Its obscurity can be attributed to at least three factors: It is relatively difficult to reach; excavation began here only recently (in 1943); and at present there is no more money for the restoration work. Excavation, which had continued fitfully until 1987, stopped completely in early 1990, when international funding dried up. As a result, the refugees who worked the site—they live 23 kilometers (14 miles) southeast in the village of Quetzal-Edzná—have lost their major livelihood.

The site, occupied from 300 BC to AD 900, was discovered in 1927. The 6-square-kilometer (2-square-mile) expanse of savanna and occasional tall trees is situated in a broad valley prone to flooding and surrounded by low hills. It comprises two main complexes: the ceremonial center, which has been excavated, and the Grupo de la Vieja, which has not. Surrounding the site are vast networks of irrigation canals and moats, the remnants of a highly sophisticated hydraulic system that channeled rainwater into man-made *chultunes*, or wells.

Commanding center stage in the complex is the **Five-Story Pyramid,** which rises 102 feet over the Great Acropolis. The manmade platform consists of five stories, each narrower than the one below it, terminating in a tiny temple crowned by a roofcomb. The architecturally innovative roof of the gallery comprising each story functioned as a terrace for the story above. Hieroglyphs carved into the vertical face of the 15 steps between each story describe astronomy and history, while the numerous stelae depict the opulent attire and adornment of the ruling class—quetzal feathers, jade pectorals, and skirts of jaguar skin. Over the course of several hundred years, Edzná grew from a humble agricultural settlement into a major politico-religious center.

Carved into Building 414 of the Great Acropolis are some grotesque masks with huge and sinister protruding eye sockets, the effect of which is enhanced by the oversize incisors or tongues extending from the upper lips. Local lore holds that Edzná, which means the House of the Gestures, or Grimaces, may have been named for these images.

A variety of architectural styles have been discerned at this site. The Petén style of northern Guatemala and Chiapas is reflected in the use of acropoli as bases for pyramids, of low-lying structures that contrasted handsomely with soaring temples, and of corbeled arch roofs, richly ornamented stucco facades, and roofcombs. The Río Bec style, which dominated much of Campeche, can be seen in the slender columns and exuberant stone mosaics. The multistory structures, arched passageways, stone causeways, and hieroglyph-adorned stairways represent both the Chenes and Puuc styles. *Take Rte. 180 east for 44 km (27 mi) to Cayal and then Rte. 188 southeast for 18 km (11 mi). Admission: P$10,000. Open daily 8–5.*

㉒ Return to Route 180 and continue another 41 kilometers (25 miles) east to **Hopelchén,** the Place of the Five Wells. Noted for the lovely Franciscan church built in honor of St. Francis of Padua in 1667, this is a rich agricultural region where corn, beans, tobacco, fruit, and henequen are cultivated. From Hopelchén, you can travel either north or south, depending on which destination most appeals to you.

㉓ About 34 kilometers (21 miles) north, just short of the state line, lies **Bolonchén de Rejón,** named for the adjacent Cave of the Nine Wells, where legend says a distressed Maya girl took refuge from the vagaries of love. (In Mayan, the caves are called Xtacumbinxunán meaning "hidden lady.")

㉔ To the south of Hopelchén, off Route 261, are two small Mayan **㉕** ruins: **Hochob,** about 25 kilometers (16 miles) away, and **Dzibilnocac,** 61 kilometers (38 miles) away. Both are excellent examples of the Chenes architectural style, which peaked in the Classical period from about AD 200 to 900. Closely associated with the Puuc style and found throughout eastern Campeche and southern Yucatán, it is characterized by columns, ornamental friezes, frontal roofcombs, and multistory structures with sloping sides. Platforms, stairways, vaulted ceilings, and mounds are about all you will see, but if you have your own vehicle and a little time to spare, it can be fun to venture into this hinterland.

Route 180 to Villahermosa Heading south from Campeche, Route 180 hugs the coast, offering a wonderful view of the gulf. The deep green sea is so shallow that the continental shelf is almost visible at low tide, and because waves and currents are rare, the gulf resembles a lake more than the vast body of water that it is. The first **㉖** beach—presently under development—is near **Lerma** at Playa Bonita, which can be reached by public buses. The buses depart daily (6 AM–11 PM) from the market (Circuito Baluartes, between Calles 53 and 55). You would be better off, however, if **㉗** you continue south for 33 kilometers (21 miles) to **Seybaplaya,** a fishing port. A couple of kilometers beyond lies **Payucán,** a beach with fine white sand, moderate waves, palapas, and restaurants (but no dressing rooms). Off this beach, you can fish, dive, or take a boat trip out to sea. A little farther on Route 180 **㉘** is **Sihoplaya,** an attractive resort with one hotel operating and several others in the planning stages. Buccaneer Henry Morgan is said to have hidden here before attacking Campeche.

㉙ Traveling about 60 kilometers (37 miles) farther down, through a hilly region with curving roads, will bring you to **Champotón's** immensely satisfying vista of open seas. Champotón is a charming little town with a bridge, palapas right on the water, and plenty of swimmers and launches in sight. The Spaniards dubbed the outlying bay the *Bahía de la Mala Pelea* or Bay of the Evil Battle, because it was here that the Spanish conqueror and explorer Hernández de Córdoba's troops were trounced in 1517 by belligerent Indians armed with arrows, slingshots, and darts.

The 17th-century **Church of Nuestra Señora de las Mercedes** and the ruins of the **San Luis fort** still stand in Champotón. This area, ideal for fishing and hunting, teems with shad and bass as well as deer, wild boar, doves, and quail, and is sustained by an economy based largely on chicle, water coconut, sugarcane, bananas, avocados, corn, and beans.

30
31 Some 105 kilometers (65 miles) southwest, you'll come to **Isla Aguada**, surrounded by the Términos Lagoon. **Isla del Carmen,** a barrier island protecting the lagoon from the gulf, is the place the pirates who raided Campeche hid from 1663 until their expulsion in 1717. The island has served as a depot for everything from dyewoods and textiles to hardwoods, chicle, shrimp, and lately, oil. Its major development is at **Ciudad del Carmen,** on the eastern end, now connected by a bridge to the mainland.

There is a surprising variety of things to do on Isla del Carmen, which has several fine white-sand beaches with palm groves and shallow waters, excellent fishing (sailfish, swordfish, shrimp, oyster, and conch), water sports, restaurants, hotels, and even some nightlife. Catamarans regularly ply the inner canals, dolphins can be spotted at Zacatal, a Moorish 18th-century pavilion marks the center of Zaragoza Park, and the **Museum of Anthropology and History** (Av. Gobernadores 289, no phone) displays pre-Hispanic and pirate artifacts. Archaeological sites on the island include Xicalango, where Cortés's mistress, Malinche, eventually lived, and Itzankanac, where the last Aztec emperor, Cuauhtémoc, supposedly met his demise (although other sources place Itzankanac on the mainland, near Tabasco). Good bets for accommodations include the bare bones **Hotel Zacarias** (Calle 24 No. 58, tel. 938/20121) and the considerably pricier, five-star **Eurotel** (Call 22 No. 208, tel., 938/21030). The best beaches for swimming are **El Playon** and **Playa Benjamin.**

To Chetumal The vestiges of at least 10 little-known Mayan cities lie hidden
(off Route 186) off Route 186 between Francisco Escárcega and Chetumal, though in this section we cover only El Tigre. Four sites lie near the highway, but the others are more difficult to reach; a four-wheel-drive—and much enthusiasm—are required. The Campeche tourist office can recommend guides and direct you to the more obscure sites.

32 The ruins known as **El Tigre,** on the southern bank of the upper Río Candelaria near the Tabasco border, may have been the Postclassical site of Itzankanac, capital of the province of Acalán, where Spanish conquistador Cortés hanged Cuauhtémoc, the last Aztec emperor. This enormous site has barely been explored and is difficult to reach. Topographically, the region is unlike northern Campeche: Tall forests compete with dense jungle foliage, including hanging vines and orchids, and both are washed by waterfalls and the river (where boats can be rented to fish for haddock and bass or to watch the exotic water birds). El Tigre comprises a 656-foot-long ceremonial plaza closed in by three huge pyramid bases. Dozens of mounds crowd around smaller plazas and patios, and a 33-foot-wide *sacbe,* or white limestone causeway, leads off toward a swamp. *30 km (19 mi) southeast of Francisco Escárcega (on a dirt road). Admission: P$10,000. Open daily 8–2 and 4–8.*

Shopping

Folk art in Campeche is typical of the rest of Yucatán's handicrafts: tortoiseshell (now taboo for North Americans because the animals from which the shells come are an endangered species), basketry, gold and silver filigree, leather goods, embroidered cloth, and clay trinkets.

Shopping Districts/Malls The city has one large, modern shopping mall to its name: the **Plaza Comercial Ah-Kim-Pech** (between Calles 51 and 49), on the stretch of the waterfront boulevard known as Avenida Pedro Sáinz de Baranda. The variety of establishments here includes a supermarket, pastry shop, beauty salon, 24-hour pharmacy, money exchange, perfumery, sporting-goods store, and clothing shops. Visit the **municipal market** (Circuito Baluartes at Calle 53), at the eastern end of the city, for crafts and food.

Local Crafts For handicrafts, try **Artesanía Típica Naval** (Calle 8 No. 259, tel. 981/65708), where craftsman David Pérez's miniature boats and prize-winning regional costumes can be found. Another shop selling folk art, particularly wicker baskets, is **México Lindo** (Calle 57 No. 30, tel. 981/67206). Regional folk art is exhibited and sold at **Baluarte San Pedro** (Calle 51 at Calle 18, no phone), which was a prison during the Inquisition.

Sports

Hunting, fishing, and birding are popular throughout the State of Campeche. Contact the **Hotel Castelmar** (Calle 61 No. 2, tel. 981/65186) for information regarding the regulations and the best areas for each sport. Licenses and gun permits are required for big game, so make your inquiries well in advance.

Dining

There is nothing fancy about Campeche's restaurants, but its regional cuisine—particularly the fish and shellfish stews, shrimp cocktails, squid and octopus, crabs' legs, *panuchos* (tortillas stuffed with beans and diced dogfish), and Yucatecán specialties—is renowned throughout Mexico. Other unusual seafood delicacies include pompano wrapped in paper, red snapper in banana leaves, small-shark bread, and crayfish claws. *Botanas,* or canapés, include fried eggs, prunes in syrup with chile, *ceviche* (raw marinated fish), and *chicharrón* (fried pork rind). The addition of cumin, marjoram, bay leaf, cayenne pepper, and allspice imparts an exotic flavor to entrées. Fruits are served fresh, made into breads or liqueurs, or blended with rum or vinegar. Look for mango, papaya, *zapote* (sapodilla), mamey, guanabana, tamarind, watermelon, jícama, melon, pineapple, and coconut, to name only a few. Because regional produce is plentiful most restaurants—including those listed below—fall into the inexpensive (under $10 for an entrée, excluding drinks, service, and the 15% sales tax) category. Restaurants throughout Campeche have casual (no shorts) dress codes and do not require reservations.

For dining suggestions outside Campeche City, *see* Chapters 6 and 8.

Highly recommended restaurants are indicated by a star ★.

Campeche City

Barbillas. The relaxed atmosphere, accented by creamy white walls and tropical touches, makes this mostly seafood restaurant a good spot for a lunch break. Specializing in fish (pompano and snapper) and shellfish (shrimp, oysters, conch, and crabs' legs), this restaurant offers a real taste of Yucatecán fare. Located on the edge of town, Barbillas is somewhat out of the way, but the excellent service and extensive menu are worth the trip. *Av. Lázaro Cárdenas Fracc. 2000 at Av. López Portillo, no phone. AE. Closed dinner.*

Marganzos. This rustically furnished restaurant, conveniently situated on the corner of the plaza, serves tasty breakfasts featuring fried eggs and tortillas. Lunch and dinner menus include several seafood dishes as well as such specials as *pan de casón* (tortillas with chili peppers). Waitresses dressed in colonial Mexican–style skirts and embroidered blouses and wearing gold and coral accessories keep in step with Marganzos's regional theme. *Calle 8, no phone. AE (vouchers available at agency), V.*

Miramar. These two restaurants—one across from Hotel Castelmar and one near the town hall building—attract locals and foreign visitors with their fabulous *huevos motuleños* (fried eggs served on corn tortillas and topped with ham, beans, peas, and cheese), red snapper, shellfish, soups, and meat dishes. The wooden tables and chairs and the paintings of the coat-of-arms of the Mexican Republic give Miramar a colonial feel. *Calle 20 No. 8, tel. 981/20923; and Calle 8 No. 73, tel. 981/62883. MC, V.*

La Palapa del Paisa. There is nothing fancy about this restaurant, which is furnished with plastic chairs and metal tables, but it has a great location in town and a varied, hearty menu. Selections include such delectables as *pozole* (pork-hominy soup), *carnitas* (highly seasoned fried meat), *barbacoa* (steamed lamb covered with maguey leaves), *carne asada* (broiled steak), *menudo sinaloense* (tripe soup from the state of Sinaloa), *chilorio* (pork fried with chile, from the state of Sonora), and even Chinese food. *Av. Central 158, no phone. No credit cards.*

Restaurant Campestre. This Yucatecán-style restaurant offers little ambience, but it has good regional fare. Specialties include *antojitos* from the State of Jalisco, as well as pozole, barbacoa, *chicharrón* (fried pork rinds), *carnitas* (fried pork), and potatoes marinated in vinegar. *Av. Gobernadores s/n, tel. 981/62107. No credit cards.*

Lodging

Most of Campeche City's hotels are old (and several are in disrepair), reflecting the city's lackadaisical attitude toward tourism. Hotels tend to be either luxury accommodations along the waterfront, with air-conditioning, restaurants, and other standard amenities, or basic downtown accommodations offering only ceiling fans and a no-credit-card policy. Those in the latter category tend to be either seedy and undesirable or oddly charming with some architectural and regional detail unique to each.

For lodging suggestions outside Campeche City, *see* Chapters 6 and 8.

Highly recommended hotels are indicated by a star ★.

Category	Cost*
Expensive	over $40
Inexpensive	under $20

*All prices are for a standard double room, excluding service and the 15% tax.

Campeche City

Expensive **Baluartes.** The lackluster exterior—living up to its name, which translates as "bastion"—is matched by the rather garish interior decor. This four-story modern hotel overlooking the waterfront is a bit more personal, but less elegant, than the Ramada Inn next door. Still, the rooms have decent views of the bay or the city, and the numerous on-premises facilities offer convenience. *Av. Ruíz Cortines 61, tel. 981/63911. 120 air-conditioned rooms. Facilities: restaurant, cafeteria, snack bar, disco, pool, travel agency, car rental. AE, MC, V.*

Debliz. This new (opened in 1990) four-story hotel with elevator, is refreshingly decorated with cream color walls, beige carpets, dark wood furnishings, and paintings of flowers that adorn the walls. Room amenities include color TV, reading lamps, and double beds. The bar (open Thursday– Saturday) and garden are popular gathering places for hotel guests. *Av. Las Palmas, 55, tel. 981/10111; fax 981/61611. 120 rooms. Facilities: restaurant, cafeteria, bar, pool. AE, MC, V.*

★ **Ramada Inn.** A whitewashed, four-story modern hotel right on the seafront, the luxurious Ramada offers a relaxing pool area with greenery and a bar. Fairly large rooms, with all the necessary amenities, are decorated in blues with rattan furnishings; balconies overlook the pool or the bay. *Av. Ruíz Cortines 51, tel. 981/62233. 119 rooms. Facilities: restaurant, coffee shop, pool bar, gift shop, disco, pool, travel agency. AE, MC, V.*

Inexpensive **Campeche.** A classic run-down Mexican hotel with colorful tile
★ floors, thin mattresses, and peeling paint, this property has managed, in spite of it all, to retain its personality. The inner courtyard, trimmed with red tiles and iron balustrades, suggests the hotel's former loveliness. *Calle 57 No. 2, tel. 981/ 65183. 42 rooms. No facilites. No credit cards.*

Castelmar. Though modest, this hotel has certain colonial touches such as beautiful tiles and quasi-Moorish architecture. The rooms are huge, with high ceilings and ceiling fans, but they have peeling walls and smell of the sea. *Calle 61 No. 2, tel. 981/65186. 18 rooms. No facilities. No credit cards.*

Colonial. This building—the former home of a high-ranking army lieutenant—dates back to 1850 but was made over as a hotel in the 1940s, when its wonderful tiles were added. Pastel-colored rooms with ceiling fans, a roof terrace, and a very friendly staff make this place all the more inviting. *Calle 14 No. 122, tel. 981/62222 or 981/62630. 30 rooms. No facilities. No credit cards.*

Lopez. Pink, yellow, and white walls reflect the airy ambience found in this small, pleasant, two-story accommodation. Standard rooms include colonial-style desks and armoires, luggage stands, and easy chairs. Although the restaurant serves basic Continental fare, it's a convenient enough stop for breakfast, lunch, or dinner. *Calle 12 No. 189, tel. 981/62488. 39 rooms. Facilities: restaurant (closed Sunday). AE, MC, V.*

Nightlife

For entertainment, check out the sound-and-light show at the **Puerta de Tierra** (Calle 59 at Calle 18 and Circuíto Baluartes, no phone) every Friday evening at 9 (P$5,000). If you're in the mood to dance, try Campeche's one disco, **Atlantis,** in the Ramada Inn; or visit the bar at the Hotel Baluartes.

Campeche has two movie theaters: **Cine Estelar** (Malecón Miguel Alemán and Calle 49-B) and **Cine Selem** (Calle 12 and Calle 57), but both show only Spanish-language films.

8 Mérida and the State of Yucatán

Introduction

There is a marvelous eccentricity about Mérida. Fully urban, with maddeningly slow-moving traffic, Mérida also has a self-sufficient, self-contented air that would suggest a small town more than a state capital of some 600,000 inhabitants. Gaily pretentious turn-of-the-century buildings have an Iberian-Moorish flair for the ornate, yet most of the architecture is low-lying, so although the city sprawls, it is not imposing. Grandiose colonial facades adorned with iron grillwork, carved wooden doors, and archways conceal marble tiles and lush gardens; horse-drawn carriages hark back to the city's heyday as the wealthiest capital in Mexico.

Mérida is a city of subtle contrasts, from its opulent yet faded facades to its natives, very Spanish yet very Mayan. The Indian presence is unmistakable: People are short and dark-skinned, with sculpted bones and almond eyes; women pad about in *huipiles* (hand-embroidered sack-like white dresses), and craftsmen and vendors from the outlying villages come to town in their huaraches. So many centuries after the conquest, Yucatán remains one of the last great strongholds of Mexico's indigenous population. To this day, in fact, many Maya do not even speak Spanish, primarily because of the peninsula's geographic and hence cultural isolation from the rest of the country. Additionally, the Maya—long portrayed as docile and peace-loving—for centuries provided the Spaniards and the mainland Mexicans with one of their greatest challenges. As late as the 1920s and 1930s, rebellious pockets of Mayan communities held out against the outsiders, or *dzulobs*. Yucatecos speak of themselves as *peninsulares* first, Mexicans second.

The Mayan civilization—one of the great ancient civilizations—had been around since 1500 BC, but it was in a state of decline when the conquistadores arrived in AD 1517, burning defiant warriors at the stake, severing limbs, and drowning and hanging women. Ironically, Yucatán offered neither gold nor fertile land, but it became a strategic administrative and military foothold, the gateway to Cuba and to Spain. (Mérida still is the gateway to Cuba: Americans who cannot get to Cuba by other means take little-publicized charter flights.) Francisco de Montejo's conquest of Yucatán took three gruesome wars, a total of 24 years. "Nowhere in all America was resistance to Spanish conquest more obstinate or more nearly successful," wrote the historian Henry Parkes. In fact, the Maya were responsible for the deaths of more Spaniards than were any other tribe in the Americas—more than during the conquest of the Aztecs and the Incas combined. By the 18th century, huge maize and cattle plantations flourished throughout the peninsula, and the wealthy *hacendados* (plantation owners), left largely to their own devices by the viceroys in faraway Mexico City, accumulated fortunes under a semifeudal system. As the economic base shifted to the export of dyewood, henequen, and chicle, the social structure—based on Indian peonage—barely changed.

Insurrection came during the War of the Castes in the mid-1800s, when the enslaved indigenous people rose up with religious fervor and massacred thousands of whites. The United States, Cuba, and Mexico City finally came to the aid of the ruling elite, and between 1846 and 1850 the Indian population of

Yucatán was effectively halved. Those Maya who did not escape into the remote jungles of Quintana Roo or get sold into slavery in Cuba found themselves worse off than before under the dictatorship of Porfirio Díaz, who brought Yaqui prisoners to the peninsula as forced labor under the rapacious grip of the hacendados. Díaz's legacy is still evident in the precious French-style mansions that stretch along Mérida's Paseo de Montejo in Mérida.

Yucatán was then and still is a largely agricultural state, although oil, tourism, and the *maquiladora*, or in-bond industry (usually foreign-owned assembly plants), now play more prominent roles in the economy. Some 93 offshore platforms dot the continental shelf surrounding the peninsula, and soon there will be as many as 50 in-bond plants. The capital accounts for about half the state's population, but the other half lives a village life of subsistence, maintaining conservative traditions and lifestyles.

Physically, Yucatán too, differs from the rest of the country. Its geography and wildlife have more in common with Florida and Cuba—with which it was probably once connected—than with the central Mexican plateau and mountains. A mostly flat limestone slab possessing almost no bodies of water, it is riddled with underground cenotes, caves with stalactites, small hills, and intense jungle. Orchids grow in profusion, and vast flamingo colonies nest at swampy estuaries on the northern and western coasts, where undeveloped sandy beaches extend for 370 kilometers (230 miles). Deer, turkeys, boars, ocelots, tapirs, and armadillos flourish in this semitropical climate (the average temperature is 82°F, or 28°C).

But it is, of course, the celebrated Mayan ruins, Chichén Itzá and Uxmal especially, that bring most tourists to Mérida. The roads rank among the best in the country, and the local travel agencies are adept at running tours. At Chichén, visitors flock to see El Castillo pyramid, surrounded by recumbent stone figures of Chac Mool (the rain god); and the Puuc hills south of Mérida, where most of the ruins are situated, have more archaeological sites per square kilometer than anywhere else in the hemisphere. Yucatecán craftsmen also produce some of the finest crafts in Mexico, notably hammocks, filigree jewelry, huaraches, and huipiles. And small towns such as Progreso and Valladolid, while bereft of star-quality sightseeing attractions, charm visitors with their very unpretentiousness.

High season generally corresponds to high season in the rest of Mexico: the Christmas period, Easter week, and the month of August. Rains fall heaviest between May and October, bringing with them an uncomfortable humidity. Levels of service differ drastically between the high and low seasons, so you should be prepared for a trade-off.

Essential Information

Important Addresses and Numbers

Tourist Information The main **Tourist Information Center** (Teatro Peón Contreras, corner of Calles 60 and 57, tel. 99/249290 or 99/249389) is open daily 8–8 and will provide you with free information and brochures including "Yucatán Today," "Guía Turística Cultural

Yucatán,"and "Mayan View" (also available at many hotels). Kiosks, open 8–8, can be found at the airport (tel. 99/246764) and the ADO bus terminal (no phone), open Monday–Saturday 8–8, Sunday 8–2.

Consulates **United States** (Paseo de Montejo 453, tel. 99/255011, 99/258677, or 99/255409); **United Kingdom** (Calle 58, No. 450, at Calle 53, tel. 99/216799 or 99/283962); **Canada** (Calle 62, No. 309-D-19, tel. 99/256299).

Emergencies **Police** (tel. 99/252133); **Red Cross** (Calle 68, No. 583, at Calle 65, tel. 99/212445); **Fire** (tel. 99/249242).

Hospital **Hospital O'Horan** (Calle 59-A at Av. Itzaes, tel. 99/238711 or 99/213056).

Late-night **Farmacia Yza Aviación** (Calle 71 at Av. Aviación, tel. 99/
Pharmacies 238116); **Farmacia Yza Tanlum** (Glorieta Tanlum, tel. 99/ 251646); and **Farmacia Canto** (Calle 60, No. 513, at Calle 63, tel. 99/210106).

Banks If you need to exchange money, banks throughout Mérida are open weekdays 9–1:30. **Banamex** has its main offices in the handsome Casa de Montejo, on the south side of the main square, with branches in the Palacio del Gobierno (north side of the square) and at the airport. Several other banks can be found on Calle 65 between Calles 62 and 60.

Money There are two exchange houses: **Del Sureste** (Calle 56 at Calle
Exchange 57), open weekdays 9–5 and Saturday 9–1; and **Canto** (Calle 61 at Calle 52), open weekdays 9–1 and 4–7. On Sundays, for those who really need money, a man walks along Calle 60 wearing a placard announcing, "Money Exchange." Naturally, his exchange rate is far less favorable than at banks or hotels.

English-language **Librería Dante** has several branches around town (Calle 59 at
Bookstores Calle 68; Parque Hidalgo; in the Teatro Peón Contreras, at the corner of Calles 60 and 57; and on the main square, next to Pizza Bella), all of which carry a small selection of English-language books. **Libeco** (Calle 57, No. 500-5, at Calle 60) sells used books and magazines, some of them in English, and sets up a stall in Parque Santa Lucía on Sundays. For newspapers and magazines from Mexico City and the United States, visit **Discolibros Hollywood** (Calle 60, No. 496).

Travel Agencies Mérida's local agencies and operators include **Achach Ortíz**
and Tour Operators (Calle 60, No. 457, tel. 99/242290), **American Express** (Calle 56-A, No. 494, tel. 99/244222), **Buvisa** (Paseo de Montejo, No. 475, tel. 99/277922), **Ceiba Tours** (Calle 60, No. 495, tel. 99/ 244477 or 99/244499, fax 99/244588; Holiday Inn, tel. 99/256389 or 99/256877), **Intermar Caribe** (Prolong. Paseo de Montejo 74 at Calle 11, tel. 99/260037), **Turismo Aviomar** (Calle 60, No. 469, tel. 99/256990, fax 99/246887), **Turismo Planeta** (Calle 59, No. 501, Altos, tel. 99/281560, fax 99/233258; Hotel Calinda Panamericana, tel. 99/239111 or 99/239444; Hotel Maya Yucatán, Calle 58, No. 483, tel. 99/235146 or 99/235395).

Arriving and Departing by Plane

Airport The Mérida airport is 7 kilometers (4 miles) west of the city's
and Airlines central square, about a 20-minute ride. The following airlines serve Mérida: **Aeromexico** (tel. 800/237-6639) flies nonstop from Miami, Cancún, Mexico City, and Villahermosa. **Mexicana's** (tel. 800/531-7921) nonstops are from Cozumel,

Mexico City, and Havana. **Aerocozumel** (tel. 99/283057 in Mérida), a subsidiary of Mexicana, has flights from Cancún, Chetumal, Ciudad del Carmen, Minatitlán, Veracruz, and Villahermosa. **Aerocaribe** (tel. 99/230002) flies to Mérida via Cozumel from Miami and Dallas. **Avioteca** (tel. 99/264275), a Guatemalan carrier, flies from Houston, Los Angeles, San Jose, and Managua.

Between the Airport and City Center A private taxi costs about $5; collective service (usually a Volkswagen minibus), about $2. For both services, pay the taxi-ticket vendor at the airport, not the driver. If you're driving into town, take the airport exit road, make a right at the four-lane Avenida Itzaes (the continuation of Route 180), and follow it to the one-way Calle 59, just past El Centenario Zoo. Turn right on Calle 59 and go straight until you reach Calle 62, where you again turn right, and drive a block to the main square. (Parking is difficult here.) By bus, there is the irregular but inexpensive No. 79.

Arriving and Departing by Car, Bus, and Train

By Car Route 180, the main road along the Gulf Coast from the Texas border to Cancún, runs into Mérida. Mexico City lies 1,550 kilometers (960 miles) to the west; Cancún, 320 kilometers (200 miles) due east.

Driving from Cancún, you'll pass through Valladolid, Chichén Itzá, and numerous villages along the way. From Campeche, it takes less than two hours to reach Mérida via Route 180. This is the fastest route. Another option is the three-hour drive along Route 261 from Campeche, which passes the ruins of Uxmal and other ancient Mayan sites as well as present-day Mayan villages. From Chetumal, the most direct way—it takes approximately nine hours—is Route 307 to Felipe Carrillo Puerto, then Route 184 to Muna, continuing north on Route 261. These paved highways are in good shape.

By Bus The **main bus station** (Calle 69, No. 544, between Calles 68 and 70, tel. 99/249055) offers frequent first- and second-class service to Akumal, Cancún, Chichén Itzá, Playa del Carmen, Puerto Morelos, Tulum, Uxmal, Valladolid, and Xel-Há. It also serves Campeche, Felipe Carrillo Puerto, Palenque, Puebla, Veracruz, and Villahermosa. The **Progreso bus station** (Calle 62, No. 524, between Calles 65 and 67, tel. 99/248991) has departures for Progreso and Dzibilchaltún. Buses to Celestún, Izamal, Oxkutzcab, Sisal, Ticul, and Uxmal depart from the second-class station on Calle 50, No. 531, at Calle 67.

By Train What with the uncomfortable, inadequate train service and the high incidence of robberies, not even the tourist office recommends taking trains in Yucatán. All the same, you can get second-class train service (at Calle 55 between Calles 46 and 48, tel. 99/235944) to Mexico City via Campeche ($6) and to Valladolid (less than a dollar). The train to the capital takes about 36 hours—twice as long as the bus.

Telephones There are seven long-distance **Ladatel phone booths** around town: at the airport (open daily 8 AM–9 PM); at Avenida Reforma and Avenida Colón (open daily 9–1:30 and 5–10); Calle 57, No. 449 (open daily 8 AM–10 PM); Calle 59 at Calle 62 (open daily 8 AM–11 PM); Calle 63 at Calle 56 (open daily 8–8); the

ADO bus terminal (open daily 9–2 and 5:30–9:30); and at the Central Telmex, Calle 59 at Calle 66 (open daily 8 AM–10 PM).

Mail In addition to the **main post office** (Calle 65 at Calle 56, tel. 99/212561), there are branches at the airport (tel. 99/211556) and at the main bus station (Calle 70 between Calles 69 and 71, no phone).

Getting Around Mérida

By Bus Mérida's municipal buses run daily from 5 AM to midnight, but service is somewhat confusing until you master the system. In the downtown area, buses go east on Calle 59 and west on Calle 61, north on Calle 60 and south on Calle 62. You can catch a bus heading north to Progreso on Calle 56.

By Car Driving in Mérida can be hell because of the one-way streets (many of which end up being one-lane because of the parked cars), because there are so few prominent road signs, and because traffic is dense. But having your own wheels is the best way to take excursions from the city. There are almost 20 car-rental agencies in town, including **Avis** (Paseo de Montejo 500, tel. 99/289096), **Budget** (Hotel Misión, tel. 99/281750 or 99/272708), **Hertz** (Calle 86-B No. 621, no phone; or Calle 86-B Av. Aviación No. 546, tel. 99/238975), **National** (Calle 60, No. 486-F, tel. 99/218128, or at the airport, tel. 99/247068), and **Panam** (Hotel Montejo Palace, tel. 99/234097 or 99/247644; Av. Itzaes, No. 604, tel. 99/231392 or 99/231450; or Calle 41, No. 483-A, between Calles 52 and 54, tel. 99/238102 or 99/230730).

By Taxi Taxis are easy to find on the streets of Mérida, but you can also go to any of the 12 taxi stands or call the main taxi office (tel. 99/214347). Individual cabs cost between $4 and $5; collective service, about $1.

By Carriage Horse-drawn *calesas* (carriages) that drive along the streets of Mérida can be hailed along Calle 60. A ride to the Paseo de Montejo and back will cost about $7.

Guided Tours

There are more than 50 tour operators in Mérida, and they generally offer the same destinations. What differs is how you go—in a private car, a van, or a bus—and whether the vehicle is air-conditioned. A two- to three-hour city tour, including museums, parks, public buildings, and monuments, will cost between $5 and $16; or you can pick up an open-air sightseeing bus at Parque Santa Lucía. A day trip to Chichén Itzá, with guide, entrance fee, and lunch, runs approximately $20–$30. For about the same price you can see the ruins of Uxmal and Kabah in the Puuc region, and for a few more dollars you can add on the neighboring sites of Sayil, Labná, and the Loltún Caves. Afternoon departures to Uxmal allow you to take in the sound-and-light show at the ruins and return by 11 PM, also for $20–$30 (including dinner). If you want to combine archaeology and the seaside, take the six-hour tour of the ruins of Dzibilchaltún and the nearby beach town of Progreso; it includes an excellent seafood meal. There is also the option of a tour of Chichén Itzá followed by a drop-off in Cancún for about $35–$40. Most tour operators take credit cards (*see* Travel Agencies and Tour Operators, above).

Special-Interest Tours Several of the tour operators run overnight excursions to archaeological sites farther afield, notably Cobá, Tulum, Edzná, and Palenque. Fishing, diving, and golf packages are available as well. **Operadores Tortugas** (tel. 99/233672; in Progreso, tel. 99/350533) organizes tours to Dzibilchaltún, including a catamaran trip to the Yucalpetén lagoon or the Alacranes Reef and lunch in Progreso, for $45; two-hour lagoon trips cost $12.

Exploring

Mérida

Numbers in the margin correspond to points of interest on the State of Yucatán and Mérida maps.

Most streets in Mérida are numbered, not named, and most run one way. North–south streets have even numbers, which ascend from east to west; east–west streets have odd numbers, which ascend from north to south. Street addresses are confusing because they don't progress in even increments by blocks; for example, the 600s may occupy 2 or even 10 blocks. A particular location is therefore usually identified by indicating the street number and the nearest cross street, as in "Calle 64 at Calle 61" (the "at" may appear as "x") or "Calle 64 between 61 and 63."

❶ Begin at the **Plaza Principal**, which the Meridanos do *not* call the *zócalo* but rather the *plaza grande*. Ancient, geometrically pruned laurel trees and *confidenciales*—S-shaped benches designed for tête-à-têtes—invite lingering. The plaza was laid out in 1542 on the ruins of T'hó, the Mayan city demolished to make way for Mérida, and is still the focal point around which the most important public buildings cluster. The plaza is bordered to the east and west by Calles 60 and 62, and to the north and south by Calles 61 and 63. (Studying a map might be a good idea.)

❷ The pink stucco **Casa de Montejo** sits on the south side of the plaza, on Calle 63. Montejo—father and son—conquered the peninsula and founded Mérida in 1540; they built this stately palace 10 years later. The property remained with the family until the late 1970s, when it was restored by Agustín Legorreta (designer of the Hotel Camino Real in Mexico City) and converted into a bank. Built in the French style during Mérida's heyday as the world's henequen capital, it now represents the city's finest—and oldest—example of colonial plateresque architecture, which typically features elaborate ornamentation and *porfiriato* (refers to the reign of dictator Porfirio Díaz, and the architecture he inspired, which mimicked 19th-century French style in such traits as broad boulevards, heroic statues, mansard roofs, gilded mirrors, and the use of marble). A bas-relief on the doorway—which is all that remains of the original house—depicts Francisco de Montejo the younger, his wife and daughter, and Spanish soldiers standing on the heads of the vanquished Maya. Even if you have no banking to do, step into the building weekdays between 9 and 1:30 to glimpse the lushly foliated inner patio.

Continue around to the west side of the square, occupied by the ❸ 17th-century **Palacio Municipal** (Calle 62, between Calles 61 and 63)—the city hall—which is painted pale lavender and

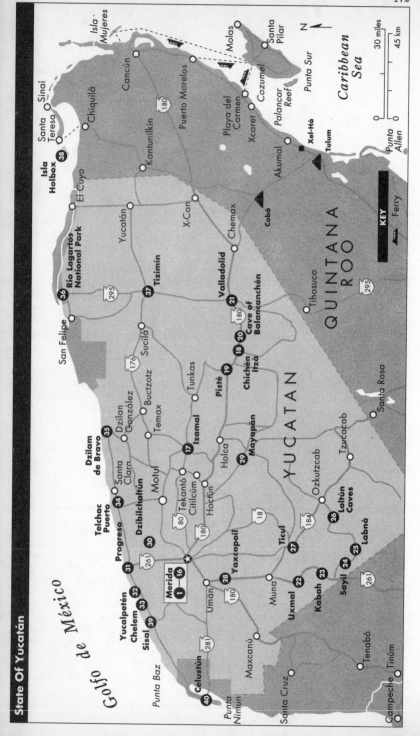

State Of Yucatán

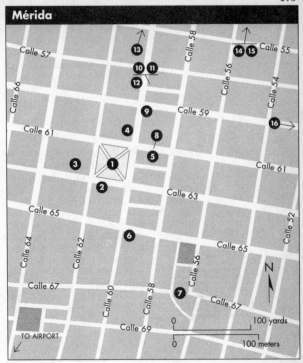

trimmed with white arcades, balustrades, and the national coat of arms. Originally erected on the ruins of the last surviving Mayan structure, it was rebuilt in 1735 and then completely reconstructed along colonial lines in 1928. It remains the headquarters of the local government.

4 Occupying the northeast corner of the square is the **Palacio del Gobierno** or Governor's Palace (Calle 61, between Calles 60 and 62), built in 1885 on the site of the Casa Real (Royal House). The upper floor of the Governor's Palace contains murals that depict the history of Yucatán, which Fernando Castro Pacheco painted in 1978. On the main balcony stands a reproduction of the Bell of Dolores Hidalgo, where Mexican independence was rung out on September 15, 1821. Every year on that date, the state governor tolls the bell to commemorate the great occasion.

Time Out Just to the left of the Governor's Palace is **Jugos California** (Calle 61 between Calles 60 and 62), a popular juice bar and hangout for locals and travelers, where you can get delicious tropical fruit concoctions.

5 The oldest **Catedral** on the North American mainland stands catty-corner from the Palacio del Gobierno. Begun in 1561, it took several hundred Mayan laborers, working with stones from the pyramids of the ravaged Mayan city, 36 years to complete. Designed in the somber Renaissance style by an architect who had worked on the Escorial in Madrid, its facade is stark and unadorned, with gunnery slits instead of windows, and faintly Moorish spires. Inside, the **Cristo de las Ampollas** (black Christ of the Blisters), now occupying the place of honor in the chapel next to the altar, is a replica of the original, which was destroyed during the Revolution (which was also when most of the gold that typically burnished Mexican cathedrals was carried off). According to legend, the Christ figure was carved from a tree that had burned all night yet appeared the next morning unscathed. A later fire left the statue covered with the blisters for which it is named. For those who are fond of near-superlatives, the crucifix above the main altar is reputedly the second largest in the world.

Continue 1½ blocks south from the cathedral along Calle 60 to Calle 65, Mérida's main shopping street. This bustling heart of the commercial quarter is lined with, among other businesses,
⑥ banks and perfumeries. Turn left to the **Mercado de Artesanías "García Rejón" market,** where you'll find local handicrafts and souvenirs. Shops selling dry goods, straw hats, and hammocks occupy both sides of Calle 65. A block farther east, between Calles 56 and 58, stand two picturesque 19th-century edifices housing the **main post office and telegraph buildings.**
⑦ Behind them sprawls the pungent, labyrinthine **Mercado Municipal,** where almost every patch of ground is occupied by Indian women selling chilies, herbs, and fruit. On the second floor of the main building is the **Bazar de Artesanías Municipales,** the principal handicrafts market, where you can buy jewelry, pottery, embroidered clothes, hammocks, and straw bags.

History lovers should stop in at the small but informative
⑧ **Museo de la Ciudad,** on Calle 61 between Calles 60 and 58. Once a hospital chapel for the only convent in the entire bishopric, it now houses prints, drawings, photographs, and other displays that recount the history of Mérida.

Calle 60, north of the square, features many noteworthy parks and historic buildings, including, only half a block away, the
⑨ small, cozy **Parque Hidalgo,** or Cepeda Peraza, as it is officially known. Dilapidated mansions-turned-hotels and sidewalk cafés stand at two corners of the park. Opposite, you'll find the **Café Express,** a gathering place that attracts primarily local men, though others are welcome.

⑩ Just north of the cathedral on Calle 60 is the Italianate **Teatro Peón Contreras,** designed in 1908 along the lines of the grand European turn-of-the-century theaters and opera houses. A restoration in the early 1980s retained the marble staircase and the dome with frescoes. Today, in addition to performing arts, the theater also houses temporary art exhibits and the main
⑪ **Centra de Información Turistica** (tel. 99/249290), which is located to the right of the lobby. The center distributes maps and can provide information about local attractions.

⑫ Opposite the theater, the arabesque **Universidad Autonoma de Yucatán** plays a major role in the city's cultural and intellectual life. The folkloric ballet performs on the patio of the main building (*see* Mérida for Free, below). A Jesuit college built in 1618 previously occupied the site; the present building, dating from 1711, recalls the Moorish style, with its scalloped, crown-like upper reaches and uncloistered archways.

⑬ Heading north on Calle 60, you'll pass the **Parque Santa Lucía** on your left, at Calle 55. The rather plain park draws crowds to its Thursday-night serenades, performed by local musicians.

The small church opposite the park dates from 1575 and was built as a place of worship for the African and Caribbean slaves who lived here; the churchyard functioned as the cemetery until 1821.

⑭ The 10-block-long street known as the **Paseo de Montejo** exemplifies the Parisian airs the city took on in the late 19th century, when wealthy plantation owners were building opulent, impressive mansions. The broad boulevard, lined with tamarinds and laurels, is sometimes wistfully referred to as Mérida's Champs-Elysées. Inside, the owners typically displayed imported Carrara marble and antiques, opting for the decorative and social standards of New Orleans, Cuba, and Paris over styles that were popular in Mexico City. (At the time there was more traffic by sea via the Gulf of Mexico and the Caribbean than there was overland across the lawless interior.) Although the once-stunning mansions fell into a disrepair from which few have recovered, their stateliness is still evident under the dowdiness.

⑮ The most compelling of these mansions, the white **Palacio Cantón,** presently houses the **Museum of Anthropology and History.** Its grandiose airs seem more characteristic of a mausoleum than a home, but in fact it was built for a general between 1909 and 1911 and was designed by Enrique Deserti, who also did the blueprints for the Teatro Peón Contreras. Marble shows up everywhere, as do Doric and Ionic columns and other Italianate Beaux-Arts flourishes. From 1948 to 1960 the mansion served as the residence of the state governor; in 1977 it became a museum. The seven-room museum now houses one of the finest Mayan collections in the country; bilingual legends accompany the displays. (Lengthier explanations, however, are in Spanish only; private guides are available for hire.) Exhibits explain the Mayan practice of dental mutilation and incrustation. A case of "sick bones" shows how the Maya suffered from osteoarthritis, nutritional maladies, and congenital syphilis. The museum also houses vivid, original mural paintings, reproductions of pyramids and sculptures, and various objects—such as conch shells, stones, and quetzal feathers—that were used as money. Other features include exhibits on Chichén Itzá, henequen production, and colonial religious art, and an excellent bookstore. *Calle 43 at Paseo de Montejo, tel. 99/ 230557. Admission: P$13,000. Open Tues.–Sun. 8–8; bookstore open weekdays 8–3.*

The Paseo de Montejo continues for a couple of kilometers, eventually becoming the road to Progreso. Before turning back from the museum, walk a few blocks north; you'll pass numerous restaurants and several hotels. To get back to the city center, you have your choice of buses, taxis, or walking.

Time Out If you're hungry, **Soberanis Montejo** (Paseo de Montejo 468, between Calles 39 and 37)—the uptown branch of a seafood restaurant chain—offers fish, conch, lobster, and shrimp at moderate prices in a more modern and attractive setting than the one downtown.

⑯ If you love Mexican crafts, you may want to trek several blocks east of the plaza, along Calle 59, to the **Museo de Arte Popular,** which is housed in a fine old mansion. The ground floor, devoted to Yucatecán arts and crafts, displays weaving, straw baskets, filigree jewelry, carved wood, beautifully carved conch shells, exhibits on huipil manufacture, and the like. The second floor focuses on the popular arts of the rest of Mexico. *Calle 59, between Calles 50 and 48, no phone. Admission: P$10,000. Open Tues.–Sat. 8–8.*

At the far south of the city, about 9 blocks south of the square, stands the **Ermita de Santa Isabel** (circa 1748), part of a Jesuit hermitage also known as the Hermitage of the Good Trip. A resting place in colonial days for travelers heading to Campeche, the restored chapel is an enchanting spot to visit at sunset and perhaps a good destination for a ride in a calesa. Next door there's a little garden with a waterfall and footpaths bordered with bricks and colored stones. *Calles 66 and 77. Admission free.*

Before leaving Mérida, there are a couple of small museums that may be of interest to you, including the **Gottdiener Museum** (Calle 59 between Calles 60 and 58), which presents masterpieces by the sculptor Enrique Gottdiener; and the **Juan Gamboa Guzmán State Painting Museum** (Calle 59 between Calles 60 and 58), where 19th-century oil paintings, colonial wood carvings, and photographs are displayed.

You can leave the city of Mérida by several routes: east toward Chichén Itzá and Valladolid; south to Uxmal; north to Progreso and the north coast; or west to Celestún.

To Chichén Itzá and Valladolid

Although it's possible to reach Chichén Itzá (120 kilometers/75 miles east of Mérida) along the shorter Route 180, it's far more scenic to follow Route 80 until it ends at Tekantó, then head south to Citilcum, east to Dzitas, and south again to Pisté.

Numbers in the margin correspond to points of interest on the State of Yucatán map.

Chichén Itzá attracts a large number of visitors who come for the famous ruins. For those traveling by car, the trip can be enhanced by stopping at several villages on the way. Route 80 passes through **Tixkokob,** a Mayan community famous for its hammock weavers. By cutting south at Tekanto and east again at Citilcum (the road has no number, and there are few road signs), you'll reach **Izamal,** nicknamed Ciudad Amarillo (Yellow City) for the painted earth-tone-yellow buildings. In the center of town stands an enormous 16th-century **Franciscan monastery** perched on—and built from—the remains of a pre-Columbian pyramid. One of the largest and oldest religious structures in Mexico, the church boasts a gigantic atrium and rows of 75 yellow arches. The pyramid, called Kinich Kakmó, is difficult to climb because of the crumbling steps, but once you're on top you'll have a wonderful view of the surrounding countryside, with its flat fields of maguey cactus and henequen broken only by occasional clumps of trees. On clear days it's even possible to spot Chichén Itzá.

Probably the best-known Mayan ruin, **Chichén Itzá,** the Maya-Toltec center, was the most important city in Yucatán from the 11th to the 13th century. The architectural mélange encapsulates one of the most compelling and typical themes of Mexican history: foreign domination and the intermingling of cultures. Founded in AD 432, then rediscovered in 964 by Maya-speaking

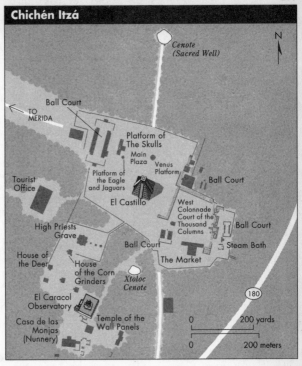

Chichén Itzá

*Cenote
(Sacred Well)*

N

Ball Court

TO
MERIDA

Platform of
The Skulls

Main
Plaza

Venus
Platform

Ball Court

Tourist
Office

Platform of
the Eagle
and Jaguars

El Castillo

West
Colonnade
Court of the
Thousand
Columns

Ball Court

High Priests
Grave

Ball Court

Ball Court

Steam Bath

House of
the Deer

House
of the Corn
Grinders

*Xtoloc
Cenote*

The Market

180

El Caracol
Observatory

Casa de las
Monjas
(Nunnery)

Temple of the
Wall Panels

0   200 yards

0   200 meters

Itzás (Chichén Itzá means "the mouth of the well of the Itzás")
from the Tabasco region, and again in 1185 by central-Mexican
Toltecs who abandoned it forever in 1224, Chichén was altered
by each successive wave of inhabitants. Francisco de Montejo
established a short-lived colony here in the course of his conquest of Yucatán. At the beginning of this century, U.S. Con-
sul General Edward Thompson carried out some of the earliest
excavations at the site, basing himself at a hacienda (now the
hotel Hacienda Chichén) and carting most of the treasure away
to the Peabody Museum at Harvard University.

The majesty and enormity of this site are unforgettable. An architectural hybrid, it incarnates much of the fascinating and
bloody history of the Maya, from the steep temple stairways
down which sacrificial victims were hurled, to the relentlessly
ornate beauty of the smaller structures. Its audacity and vitality are almost palpable. Chichén Itzá encompasses approximately 6 square kilometers (2 square miles), though only 20 to
30 buildings of the several hundred at the site have been fully
explored. These buildings include the often-photographed
Mayan pyramid, a sprawling colonnade evoking imperial
Rome, the largest ball-playing court in Mesoamerica, a sacrificial well once filled with precious offerings, and one of the only
round structures in the Mayan lands. Stone sculptures of the
feathered serpent god, reclining *Chac Mools* (rain gods, associated with human sacrifice), steam baths for ritual purifica-
tion, ruined murals, astronomical symbols, and broad *sacbeob*
(white roads) leading to other ancient centers endow the site

with nearly all the celebrated visual elements of the Mayan civilization.

Chichén Itzá is divided into two parts—Old and New—though architectural motifs from the classical period are found in both sections. A more convenient distinction is topographical, since there are two major complexes of buildings separated by a dirt path. The martial, imperial architecture of the Toltecs and the more cerebral architectural genius and astronomical expertise of the Maya are married in the 98-foot-tall pyramid called **El Castillo** (The Castle), which dominates the site and rises visible above all the other buildings.

Atop the castle is a temple dedicated to Kukulcán (known as Quetzalcóatl in central Mexico), the legendary leader-turned-deity who was incarnated by the plumed serpent. According to ancient lore, Kukulcán led the Toltecs on their migration to Yucatán, then disappeared to the east, promising to return one day; the Spaniards—whom the Toltecs mistook for gods—transformed that prophecy into a nightmarish reality. Four stairways, each facing a different cardinal point, provided access to the temple; only one is used today. Those who fear heights can hold on to a rusty chain running down the side. Each access way consists of 91 very steep and narrow steps, which, when one adds the temple platform itself, makes a total of 365 (one for each day of the Mayas' extraordinarily accurate solar calendar). Fifty-two panels on the sides stand for the weeks of the secular (as opposed to the religious) calendar, while the 18 terraces symbolize the months of the year. An open-jawed plumed serpent rests on the balustrade of each stairway, and serpents reappear at the top of the temple as sculptured columns.

At the spring and fall equinoxes (March 21 and September 21), the afternoon light and shadow strike one of these balustrades in such a way as to form a shadow representation of Kukulcán undulating out of his temple and down the pyramid to bless the fertile earth. The sound-and-light show in the evening is not as well done as the one at Uxmal, but the engineering is astounding and the colored lights that enhance the wall carvings of El Castillo provide after-dark entertainment. The accompanying narration is drawn from the works of Bishop de Landa—one of the first Spaniards to write about the Mayan religion and life—and from the few surviving Mayan texts, including the Books of Chilam Balam and Popul Vuh. Thousands of people travel to Chichén Itzá for the equinoxes, particularly in the spring when there is little likelihood of rain. Hotel reservations for the event should be made well in advance; a year ahead is not unreasonable (*see* Lodging, below). *Sound-and-light show in Spanish, P\$1,900, 7 PM; in English, P\$3,000, 9 PM.*

In 1937, archaeologists discovered a more ancient temple inside the Castillo. A humid, slippery stairway leads upward to an altar holding two statues: a Chac Mool and a bejeweled red tiger. The tiger wears a mosaic disc of jade and turquoise and is now housed in the Anthropology Museum in Mexico City. The inner temple is open to the public for only a few hours in the morning and again in the afternoon. Claustrophobes should think twice before entering: The stairs are narrow, dark, and winding, and there is often a line of tourists going both ways, making the trip somewhat frightening.

The temple rests on a massive trapezoidal square, on the west side of which is Chichén Itzá's largest **ball court,** one of seven on the site. Its two parallel walls are each 272 feet long, with two stone rings on each side, and 99 feet apart. The game was something like soccer (no hands were used), but it had religious as well as recreational significance. Bas-relief carvings at the court depict a player being decapitated, the blood spurting from his severed neck fertilizing the earth. Acoustics are so good that someone standing at one end of the court can hear the whispers of another person clearly at the other end. Sadly, the western wall of the court has been blackened by acid rain blown eastward from the oil fields on the Gulf of Mexico.

Between the ball court and El Castillo stands a **Tzompantli,** or stone platform, carved with rows of human skulls. In ancient times it was actually covered with stakes on which the heads of enemies were impaled. This Aztec motif was otherwise unknown in the Mayan region, though a similar platform was found at Tenochtitlán, the Aztec capital (modern-day Mexico City). The influence of the Toltecs, who preceded the Aztecs in the Valley of Mexico, is once again apparent.

The predilection for sacrifice was once believed to have come from the Toltecs, but recent research suggests that the pre-Toltec Maya had already been indulging in their own forms of the ritual. The **Sacred Well,** a cenote 65 yards in diameter that sits half a mile north of El Castillo at the end of a 900-foot-long sacbe, was used only for sacrifices; another cenote at the site supplied drinking water. Skeletons of men, women, and children were found in the first well; they were thrown in to placate the rain gods and water spirits. The slippery walls were impossible to scale, and most of the victims could not swim well enough to survive until noon, when those who did hang on were fished out to recount what they had learned. (Hunac Ceel, the notorious ruler of Mayapán in the 1450s, hurled himself into its depths to prove his divine ascendancy, and survived.) Thousands of gold, jade, and other artifacts, most of them not of local provenance, have been recovered from the brackish depths of the cenote. Long on display at Harvard's Peabody Museum, many of the finds have now been returned to the Mexican government. Trees and shrubs have washed into the well over the centuries, and their remains have prevented divers from getting to the bottom; because the cenote is fed by a network of underground rivers, it cannot be drained. More treasure undoubtedly remains. (The well's excavation launched the field of underwater archaeology, later honed by Jacques Cousteau.)

Returning to the causeway, on your left is the **Group of the Thousand Columns** with the famous **Temple of the Warriors,** a masterful example of the Toltec influence at Chichén Itzá. This temple so resembles Pyramid B at Tula—the Toltecs' homeland, north of Mexico City—that scholars believe the architectural plans must have been carried 800 miles overland. Indeed, they can cite no other case in the pre-Columbian world of identical temples built by two such distant tribes. Nonetheless, until more work is done at Chichén Itzá, controversy will continue as to whether the influence was exercised from Tula to Chichén Itzá or in the opposite direction. Masonry walls carved with feathered serpents and frescoes of vultures and jaguars consuming human hearts are among the unmistakably Toltec details. Using columns and wood beams instead of the Mayan arches and walls to divide space enabled the Toltec-Mayan architects to expand the interior and exterior spaces dramatically. Another anomaly is the murals of everyday village life and scenes of war: Such realism was rare in pre-Columbian art. The first artistic representation of the defeat of the Maya can be found on the interior murals of the adjacent **Temple of the Jaguar.**

To get to the less visited cluster of structures at Chichén Itzá—often confused with Old Chichén Itzá—take the main road south from the Temple of the Jaguar past El Castillo and turn right onto a small path opposite the ball court on your left. You'll pass several thatched huts (as well as young children and turkeys) en route. The ancient edifices here, overgrown with flowering vines, are as intriguing as the more visited ones, but the astronomical observatory dubbed **El Caracol** is the most impressive. The name, meaning "snail," refers to the spiral staircase at the building's core. Built in several stages, El Caracol is possibly the sole round building constructed by the Maya. Although definitely used for observing the heavens (judging by the tiny windows oriented toward the four cardinal points, and the alignment with the planet Venus), it also appears to have served a religious function, since the related Toltec cults of Kukulcán and the god of wind often involved circular temples.

After leaving El Caracol, continue south several hundred yards to the beautiful **Casa de las Monjas** (Nunnery) and its annex, which have long panels carved with flowers and animals, latticework, hieroglyph-covered lintels, and Chac masks (as does the nunnery at Uxmal). The Maya did not use it as such; it was the Spaniards who gave it the sobriquet.

At Old Chichén Itzá, located south of the remains of Thompson's hacienda, it is the "pure Mayan" style—a combination of Puuc and Chenes styles, with playful latticework, Chac masks, and gargoyle-like serpents on the cornices—that dominates. (This style also crops up at Uxmal, Kabah, Labná, and Sayil, among other sites.) Highlights include the Date Group (so named because of the complete series of hieroglyphic date inscriptions), the House of the Phalli, and the Temple of the Three Lintels. Mayan guides will lead you down the path by an old narrow-gauge railroad track to even more ruins, barely unearthed, if you ask. There are no restaurants at the site, but the parking lot has several soda, fruit, snack, and souvenir stands. *Admission to site and museum: P$10,000. Open daily 8–5.*

⑲ The town of **Pisté,** about 1 kilometer (⅜ mile) west of the ruins on Route 180, serves mainly as a base camp for travelers to Chichén Itzá. Hotels, campgrounds, restaurants, and handicrafts shops tend to be cheaper here than south of the ruins. At the west end of town are a Pemex station and a bank.

Time Out When in Pisté, ask a local to direct you to the **Carousel,** a palapa-covered restaurant that excels in Yucatecán cuisine and is reasonably priced.

From Chichén Itzá, drive east along Route 180 for about 4 kilometers (2½ miles), then turn left at the first dirt road you come to and continue for about ½ kilometer (³⁄₁₀ mile) to the ⑳ **Cave of Balancanchén.** This shrine, whose Mayan name translates as "hidden throne," remained virtually undisturbed from the time of the Conquest until its discovery in 1959. Within the shrine is the largest collection of artifacts yet found in Yucatán—mostly vases, jars, and incense burners once filled with offerings. You'll walk past tiers of stalactites and stalagmites forming the image of sacred ceiba trees until you come to an underground lake. The lake is filled with blindfish (small fish with functionless eyes), and an altar to the rain god rises above it. In order to explore the shrine you must take one of the guided tours, which depart almost hourly, but you must be in fairly good shape, because some crawling is required; claustrophobes should skip it, and those who go should wear comfortable shoes. Also offered at the site is a sound-and-light show that fancifully recounts Mayan history. *Caves can be also be reached by bus or taxi from Chichén Itzá. Admission to caves, including tour: P$10,000; show: P$11,500. Open daily 9–5; tours Mon.–Sat. 9–4, Sun. 8–11. Sound-and-light show in English, 11 AM, 1 and 3 PM; in Spanish, 9 and 10 AM, noon, 2 and 4 PM.*

Following Route 180 east for another 40 kilometers (25 miles) will take you to the second-largest city in the State of Yucatán, **Valladolid.** This picturesque, pleasant, and provincial town (population 50,000) is enjoying growing popularity among travelers en route to or from Río Lagartos (*see* below) who are harried by more touristy towns. Montejo founded Vallodolid in 1543 on the site of the Mayan town of Zací. The city suffered during the Caste War, when it was besieged by the rebellious Maya (who killed all the Europeans they could find), and again during the Mexican Revolution.

Today, however, placidity reigns in this agricultural market town. The center is mostly colonial, although it has many 19th-century structures. The main sights are the **colonial churches,** principally the large **cathedral** on the central square and the 16th-century **San Bernardino church and convent of Sisal,** 3 blocks southwest. The latter were pillaged during the insurrection.

A briny, muddy **cenote** in the center of town draws only the most resolute swimmers; instead, visit the adjacent **ethnographic museum** or the **Cenote Dzitnup** outside town. Cenote Dzitnup is dark and slightly forbidding, but you can swim here. Valladolid is renowned for its cuisine, particularly its sausages. Try one of the restaurants within a block of the square, which also has two very good and reasonably priced hotels. You can also find good buys on sandals, baskets, and the local liqueur, Xtabentún.

To Uxmal and the Puuc Route

If you opt for the southward journey from Mérida, follow Route 180 south and turn onto Route 261 at Umán; 80 kilometers (50 miles) farther south you'll reach **Uxmal.** If Chichén Itzá is the most impressive Mayan ruin in Yucatán, Uxmal is arguably the most beautiful. Where the former has a Toltec grandeur, the latter seems more understated and elegant—pure Maya. The architecture reflects the late classical renaissance of the 7th–9th centuries and is contemporary with that of Palenque and Tikal, among other great Mayan metropolises of the southern highlands. Although the name translates as "thrice built," the site was actually rebuilt, abandoned, and reoccupied in several stages, for reasons still unknown. Toltec (Itzá) invad-

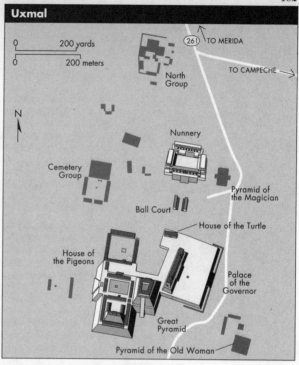

Uxmal

ers briefly occupied Uxmal in the 10th century; the site re-emerged as a Mayan ceremonial center in the postclassical era and was deserted for the last time some 90 years before the Conquest. When John Lloyd Stephens came upon Uxmal in 1840, it was owned by a descendant of the same Montejo family that had conquered Yucatán three centuries earlier.

In any case, the site is considered the finest and largest example of Puuc architecture, which embraces such details as ornate stone mosaics and friezes on the upper walls, intricate cornices with hooked noses, rows of columns, and soaring vaulted arches. Lines are clean and uncluttered, with the horizontal—especially the parallelogram—preferred to the vertical. Many of the flat, low, elongated buildings were built on artificial platforms and laid out in quadrangles. The cult of Chac, the elephant-snouted rain god whose image appears throughout Yucatán, became obsessive in this parched region. But the area lacks cenotes; though the Maya dug cisterns, called *chultunes*, for collecting rainwater, drought may be the reason that Uxmal was so often occupied and then abandoned. Phallic figures—rare in Mayan art—are abundant, too.

While most of Uxmal remains unrestored, three buildings in particular merit attention. The most prominent, the **Pyramid of the Magician**, is, at 92 feet high, the tallest structure at the site. Unlike most Mayan pyramids, which are stepped and angular, it has a strangely elliptical design. Built five times, each time over the previous structure, the pyramid has a stairway on its western side that leads through a monster-shaped doorway to two temples at the summit. The monster or mask motif is repeated on one side of the stairs. You get a magnificent panoramic view of Uxmal and the hills by climbing up to the top. According to legend, the pyramid derived its name from the magical dwarf who built it overnight; it is especially lovely at night, when its pale beige slope glows in the moonlight.

West of the pyramid lies the **Nunnery,** or Quadrangle of the Nuns. You may enter the four buildings; each comprises a series of low, gracefully repetitive chambers that look onto a central patio. The building on the southern side is broken by a tall corbeled arch that is formed by placing ceiling stones increasingly close to and on top of one another until they meet at a central supporting capstone. Elaborate decoration—in the form of stone latticework, masks, geometric patterns, representations of the classic Mayan thatched hut (*na*), coiling snakes, and phallic figures—blankets the upper facades, in contrast with the smooth, sheer blocks that face the lower walls.

Continue walking south; you'll pass the ball court before reaching the **Palace of the Governor,** which archaeologist Victor von Hagen considered the most magnificent building ever erected in the Americas. Interestingly, the palace faces east while the rest of Uxmal faces west. Archaeologists believe this is because the palace was used to sight the planet Venus. Covering 5 acres and rising over an immense acropolis, the palace lies at the heart of what must have been Uxmal's administrative center. Its 320-foot length is divided by three corbeled arches, which create narrow passageways or sanctuaries. Decorating the facade are intricate friezes (along the uppermost section), geometrically patterned carvings overlaid with plumed serpents, stylized Chac masks, and human faces. These mosaics required more than 20,000 individually cut stones.

First excavated in 1929 by the Danish explorer Frans Blom, the site served in 1841 as home to John Lloyd Stephens, who wrote of it: "The whole wears an air of architectural symmetry and grandeur. If it stood at this day on its grand artificial terrace in Hyde Park or the Garden of the Tuileries, it would form a new order . . . not unworthy to stand side by side with the remains of Egyptian, Grecian, and Roman art." Today a sound-and-light show recounts Mayan legends, including the kidnapping of an Uxmal princess by a king of Chichén Itzá, and focuses on the people's dependence on rain. The artificial light brings out details of carvings and mosaics that are easy to miss when the sun is shining—for example, the stone replicas of *nas*, which bear a remarkable resemblance to contemporary huts, on one facade of the nunnery. The show is performed nightly in Spanish and English and is one of the better such productions. *Admission to site and museum: P$10,000. Open daily 8–5. Sound-and-light show in Spanish, $1, 7 PM; in English, P$4,500, 9 PM.*

Four smaller Puuc sites near Uxmal are also worth visiting, and en route you pass through beautiful hilly jungles. **Kabah,** 23 kilometers (14 miles) south of Uxmal on Route 261, lies almost entirely in ruins; its mounded landscape has a soft, almost Grecian beauty. Linked to Uxmal by a *sacbe* (a road), at the end of which looms a great independent arch, is the 151-foot-long **Palace of the Masks,** so called because of the huge number of Chac masks with their hooked noses. Another 270 can be seen at the Codz-Poop temple, located on the east side of the road.

24 Five kilometers (3 miles) to the south you'll see the turnoff to **Sayil,** the oldest site of the group, renowned primarily for its majestic three-story **palace** with 100 rooms. The structure recalls Palenque in its use of multiple planes, its columned porticos and sober cornices, and in the play of its long, solid horizontal masses, heightened by colonnades. *Admission: P$10,000. Open daily 8–5.*

25 Another 9 kilometers (6 miles) beyond Sayil, on Route 261, rests the monumental arch at **Labná.** While most Mayan arches linked inner passageways at door height, this one is more characteristic of the great imperial arches of classical antiquity except for the corbels. It's further atypical of the Mayan style that this arch—adorned with lavish friezes, latticework, stepped frets, and, of course, the snouty Chac masks—dominates the entire facade. One of the curiosities of Mayan civilization is that the Maya never discovered the true, or curved, arch. *Admission: P$10,000. Open daily 8–5.*

26 Continue along the road from Labná for another 18 kilometers (11 miles) to the **Loltún Caves,** a 500-meter (⅗₀-mile) series of caverns containing Mayan and neolithic remains and stalactites and stalagmites. *Admission: P$11,500. Open Tues.–Sun. 9–5; guided tours at 9:30, 11, 12:30, 2, and 3.*

27 From Loltún, drive 10 kilometers (6 miles) northeast to **Oxkutzcab,** where, to the left, you can pick up Route 184. An additional 17 kilometers (10½ miles) will bring you into **Ticul,** where most of the Yucatecán pottery is produced, along with huipiles and shoes. Many descendants of the Xiu dynasty, which ruled Uxmal before the Conquest, still live here. One of the larger towns in Yucatán, Ticul boasts a handsome 17th-century church.

Time Out If you save your appetite for Los Almendros Restaurant, in Ticul, you'll be rewarded by what is considered the best regional restaurant in Yucatán.

From this point you can either head back to Mérida or continue on to Mayapán, about 49 kilometers (30 miles) to the east (*see* below).

28 If you wish to get back to Mérida, turn right at Muna (on Route 184) onto Route 261, and follow the road back. Along Route 261, about 62 kilometers (38 miles) north of Uxmal, you may want to stop at **Yaxcopoil,** a restored 17th-century hacienda that offers a nice change of pace from the ruins. The building, with its distinctive Moorish double arch out front, has been used as a film set and is the best-known henequen plantation in the region. Visit the museum inside, which displays archaeological pieces and machinery used in the processing of henequen. *Km 33, Rte. 261. Open Mon.–Sat. 8–sunset, Sun. 9–1.*

29 Those who are really enamored of Yucatán and the ancient Maya can detour at Ticul on Route 18 to the ruined city of **Mayapán,** the last of the great city-states on the peninsula. There have been few excavations here, however, so archaeological evidence of past glory is limited to a few fallen statues of Kukulcán, and today the site is mainly of historical interest. *Just before Telchaquillo, Mayapán is off the road to your left; follow signs.*

To Progreso and the North Coast

If you have decided to take the easterly course toward Progreso and the north coast, follow the Paseo de Montejo north out of Mérida, where it becomes Route 261. After 14 kilometers (9 miles) you'll come to the ruins of **Dzibilchaltún** ("the place where there is writing on flat stones"), which is thought to have been the capital of the Mayan states at one time. The site occupies more than 65 square kilometers (25 square miles) of land cluttered with thousands of mounds, low platforms, piles of rubble, plazas, and stelae. It was established around 2000 BC. Inhabited until shortly before the Conquest, it appears to be the oldest continuously occupied Mayan ceremonial center, but it is generally more impressive to archaeologists and historians than to tourists since much of it remains to be excavated.

For now, Dzibilchaltún's significance lies in the stucco sculpture and ceramics, from all periods of Mayan civilization, that have been unearthed here. The **Temple of the Seven Dolls** (circa AD 500), the only structure excavated on the site to date, is the only Mayan temple known to have windows. Low and trapezoidal, the temple exemplifies the late preclassical style, which predates such Puuc sites as Uxmal. The remains of stucco masks adorn each side, and there are vestiges of sculptures of coiled serpents. The stone cube atop the temple and the open chapel built by the Spaniards for the Indians are additional peculiarities. Twelve sacbeob lead to various groups of structures. The **Xlacah cenote**—at 144 feet one of the deepest in Yucatán—apparently supplied ceremonial as well as drinking water. Bones and ceremonial objects unearthed by divers from the National Geographic Society indicate that this cenote was used for sacrifices.

A small **museum** at the entrance to the site displays the seven vulcanized-rubber deformed male "dolls"—thought to be used against sickness—that were found deep inside the temple. The dolls, dating to the 13th and 14th centuries, are unusual because rubber is virtually unknown in the region, though the Lacandón Indians in Chiapas (descendants of the ancient Maya) make similar ones. The collection also includes thousands of figurines, bones, jewelry, and potsherds found in the cenote. There is a small refreshment stand. *Admission: P$10,000. Open daily 8–8.*

About 16 kilometers (10 miles) farther north on Route 261 is **Progreso,** the waterfront town closest to Mérida. Progreso, which is not particularly historical, is noisy with traffic and not at all picturesque. On weekdays during most of the year the town is deserted, but when school is out (Easter week, July, and August) and on summer weekends it becomes a popular vacation destination for families from Mérida. Progreso has fine sand and shallow waters that extend quite far out, making for nice walks, although its beaches are inferior to those of Quintana Roo. Because it is so close to Mérida and because its interest is limited, there is really no reason to spend the night here, but a couple of attractions in the small town may interest you.

The approach requires crossing some very foul-smelling swamps, and these remind you of Progreso's main raison d'être: It has been the chief port of entry for the peninsula since its founding in 1872, when the shallow port at Sisal, to the southwest, proved inadequate for handling the large ships that were carrying henequen cargo. In 1989 the 2-kilometer (1-mile) long pier was extended 7 kilometers (4 miles) out to sea to accommodate the hoped-for cruise-ship business and to siphon some of the lucrative tourist trade from Cozumel, but at the moment it looks as though all the millions invested have produced a white elephant because most cruise ships require deeper waters.

Progreso's attractions include its **malecón** (main square), Calle 19, which is lined with seafood restaurants. Fishermen sell their catch on the beach east of the city between 7 and 8 AM, so it's a good place to come for fresh fish. Some 120 kilometers (75 miles) offshore are the **Alacranes Reef,** where divers can explore sunken ships, and **Pérez Island,** which supports a sizeable population of sea turtles and seabirds. Sportfishing, for such catch as grouper, red snapper, dogfish, sea bass, and pompano, is popular at the **marina** in nearby Yucalpetén (*see* below).

For more information on the town and on guides who provide service to the reef, visit the **tourist office,** where representatives are friendly and helpful. *Calle 80, No. 176, at Calle 37, tel. 993/50104. Open Mon.–Sat. 9–1 and 3–7, Sun. 10–1.*

Three kilometers (2 miles) west of Progreso, at the end of the ㉜ narrow, marshy promontory, is **Yucalpetén.** Along the approach you'll pass a number of dead palm trees that were obliterated by the yellowing palm disease that has swept the peninsula in recent years. The harbor here dates only from 1968, when it was built to provide shelter for small fishing boats during the hurricane season. Little goes on here other than some activity at the yacht marina and the fancy Fiesta Inn, though more hotels are planned for the future. Just beyond ㉝ Yucalpetén is the even tinier village of **Chelem,** which has a few beachfront bungalow hotels.

A short drive (43 kilometers/27 miles) to the east of Progreso along the same road and past time-shares in progress, palm ㉞ groves, henequen fields, and tiny villages, sits **Telchac Puerto,** now known as Nuevo Yucatán—the state government's latest venture in tourism development. One reason for this location is its proximity to **Laguna Rosada,** where the flamingos come to nest; another is its lovely, empty (at least that's how they were at this writing) beaches. More and more foreigners are getting wind of the inexpensive rental homes in the nearby fishing village of **Chicxulub Puerto,** with its inviting beach and low winter rates.

If you continue east on the coastal road, eventually you'll get to ㉟ **Dzilam de Bravo,** where a better road—Route 281—heads back toward Mérida and points south. The pirate Jean Laffite supposedly lies buried just outside this village; at least there's a grave so marked, and two locals claim to be his descendants. Stop here for a swim in the gentle waters.

If you're a flamingo fan (flamingo season runs from April to May), take Route 281 13 kilometers (8 miles) to Dzilam González, then follow the unpaved road to Buctzotz, where you'll ㊱ pick up Routes 176 and 295 to Río Lagartos and **Río Lagartos National Park.** Actually a long estuary, not a river, the park was built with ecotourism in mind, though the alligators for which it and the village were named have long since been hunted into extinction. In addition to flamingos, birders can spot egrets, herons, ibis, cormorants, pelicans, and even peregrine falcons flying over these murky waters; fishing is good, too, and hawksbill and green turtles lay their eggs on the beach at night. **Hotel Nefertiti**—the only hotel in town—offers boat tours, or you can hire a boat from the docks near the hotel.

If you wish to extend this tour rather than return to Mérida, continue 104 kilometers (64 miles) south of Río Lagartos on Route 295 to Valladolid and then westward to Chichén Itzá (*see* above).

To return to Mérida, you'll have to take the same road back, but you may want to make a brief stop in two villages to break up the monotony of the drive. **Tizimín,** renowned as the seat of an indigenous messianic movement during the 1840s Caste War, is situated at the junction of Highways 176 and 295. The town boasts a 17th-century church dedicated to the Three Kings, who are honored here during a festival that is held December 15–January 15.

Motul, for which *huevos motuleños* are named, is the birthplace of the Indian rebel leader Felipe Carrillo Puerto, whose former house is now a museum containing displays on the life and times of the Socialist governor of Yucatán. *24 km (15 mi) south of Telchac Puerto along the road west toward Mérida. Open daily 8–noon and 4–6.*

Even farther afield is **Isla Holbox,** a tiny island (25 kilometers/ 16 miles long) at the eastern end of the Río Lagartos estuary and just across the Quintana Roo state line. A fishing fan's heaven because of the pompano, bass, barracuda, and shark thronging in its waters, the island also pleases seekers of tranquillity who don't mind rudimentary accommodations (two hotels, plus rooms and hammocks for rent) and simple palapa restaurants. Seabirds populate the air, the long sandy beach is strewn with seashells, and the swimming is good on the gulf side. To get there, take Route 176 to Kantunilkin, then head north on the unnumbered road for 44 kilometers (27 miles) to Chiquilá. Continue by ferry (schedules fluctuate but it runs twice daily; 1-hour crossing) to the island. Isla Holbox can also be reached from Valladolid.

Sisal and Celestún

Traveling westward from Mérida, take an hour-long drive on Route 25 to the town of **Sisal,** which gave its name to the henequen that was shipped from the port in great quantity during the mid-19th century. With the rise of Progreso, Sisal dwindled into little more than a fisherman's wharf. Today the attractions are few: There are a **colonial customs house** and the private 1906 **lighthouse.** Sisal livens up a bit in July and August when Méridanos come to swim and dine. **Hotel Felicidades,** a few minutes' walk up the beach east of the pier, caters to tourists during the vacation months and can be fun when a crowd arrives, although it is a bit dingy. **Club de Patos,** farther up the beach, is open only during the peak summer season. **Madagascar Reef,** one of three offshore reefs, offers excellent diving.

Take Route 180 southwest to Umán, then Route 281 for 92 kilometers (57 miles) to the backwater fishing town of **Celestún,** which sits at the end of a spit of land separating the Celestún estuary from the gulf on the western side of Yucatán. It is the only point of entry to the **Parque Natural del Flamenco Mexica-**

no, a 147,500-acre wildlife reserve with one of the largest colonies of flamingos in North America. From September through April clouds of pink wings soar over the pale blue backdrop of the estuary, which also features rocks, islets, cenotes, and mangroves, and make for stunning scenery; cormorants, ducks, and herons also fly overhead. There is good fishing in both the river and the gulf; and you can see deer and armadillo roaming the surrounding land.

Popular with Mexican vacationers, the park's sandy beach is pleasant during the day but tends to get windy in the afternoon, with choppy water and blowing sand. To see the birds, hire a fishing boat at the dock outside town. And take advantage of one of the several seafood restaurants on the beach strip.

Mérida for Free

Nearly every day of the week the Instituto de Cultura de Yucatán sponsors free performances of regional music and dance in the city parks, including the following:

Vaquerías, a traditional feast celebrated on regional haciendas after the cattle are branded. *In front of the Municipal Palace. Mon. 9 PM.*

Big Band music from North, Central, and South America. *Parque Santiago, Calles 59 and 72. Tues. 9 PM.*

Yucatecán folkloric ballet, with guitar trios and poetry. *Casa Cultural Mayab on Calle 63 between Calles 64 and 66. Wed. 8 PM.*

Yucatecán festivities, including music, song, poetry, and costumes at the Palacio de Gobierno. *Parque Santa Lucía. Thurs. 9 PM.*

University folkloric ballet. *Patio of the University of Yucatán's main building, Calles 60 and 57. Fri. 9 PM.*

Mérida en Domingo, comprising five separate special events: jazz, semiclassical, and folkloric music at 11 AM; Yucatecán music by the police orchestra, also at 11 AM, in Parque Santa Lucía (Calles 60 and 55); a traditional *mestizo* wedding celebration, performed by the city's folkloric ballet and the police orchestra at 1 PM in front of the Municipal Palace on the main square; marimba concerts on Sundays at 11:30 AM in Parque Hidalgo (Calles 60 and 59); and music and entertainment for children, at 10 AM in Parque de la Madre (Calle 60 between Calles 59 and 57).

What to See and Do with Children

El Centenario Zoological Park, Mérida's great children's attraction, is a large, somewhat tacky amusement complex consisting of playgrounds, rides (including ponies and a small train), a roller skating rink, snack bars, and cages with more than 300 marvelous native monkeys, birds, reptiles, and other animals, as well as pleasant wooded paths, a small lake where you can hire rowboats, and picnic areas. Come on Sundays if you enjoy the spectacle of people enjoying themselves. The French Renaissance–style arch (1921) commemorates the 100th anniversary of Mexican independence. *Av. Itzaes be-*

tween Calles 59 and 65 (entrances on Calles 59 and 65). Admission free. Open daily 9-6.

Parque Natural del Flamenco Mexicano (*see* Celestún in Exploring, above).

Museum of Anthropology and History (*see* Mérida in Exploring, above).

Museum of Popular Art (*see* Mérida in Exploring, above).

Shopping

Throughout the Exploring section we noted towns known for specific crafts, but for the most part Mérida is the best place in Yucatán to buy local handicrafts at reasonable prices. The main products include *hamacas* (hammocks), *guayaberas* (short, loose shirts), huaraches, huipiles, *ternos* (hand-embroidered dresses), baskets, *jipis* or Panama hats, leather goods, gold and silver filigree jewelry, masks, painted gourds, vanilla, and piñatas. A word about hammocks, one of the most popular craft items sold here: They are available in cotton, nylon, and silk as well as in the very rough and scratchy henequen fiber. Silk is unquestionably the best choice. Double-threaded hammocks are sturdier and stretch less than single-threaded ones, a difference that can be identified by studying the loop handles. Hammocks come in different sizes: *sencillo,* for one person; *doble,* very comfortable for one but crowded for two; *matrimonial,* which will decently accommodate two; and *familiares* or *matrimoniales especiales,* which can theoretically sleep an entire family. Unless you're an expert, avoid the hammocks sold by street vendors and head for one of the specialty shops (*see* Specialty Stores: Crafts, below).

Shopping Districts/Streets/Markets/Malls

On the second floor of the **central municipal market** (between Calles 65 and 56 and Calles 54 and 59) you'll find crafts, food, flowers, and live birds, among other items.

Sundays in Mérida, you will find an array of wares at three bazaars: the **Handicraft Bazaar,** in front of the Municipal Palace across from the main square, starting at 9; the **Popular Art Bazaar,** a flea market in Parque Santa Lucía, at the corner of Calles 60 and 55, also at 9; and the **Book Bazaar,** in the Callejón del Congreso, Calle 60, starting at 10.

Lining the streets north of the main square, especially **Calle 60,** are crafts and jewelry stores.

Mérida now has several shopping malls; the largest and newest is **Plaza Fiesta** (Calles 21 and 6), on the northeast edge of the city near the Jardines de Mérida, with about 75 shops.

Specialty Stores
Clothing

Fernando Huertas, a well-known Mexican clothing designer who cuts Mexican and Guatemalan handwoven cotton into exquisite (and high-priced) apparel, has two Mérida shops: a large one called Fernando Huertas (Calle 62, No. 492, between Calles 59 and 61) and the **Marie-Soleil Boutique** (Calle 59, No. 511, tel. 99/216035). Both shops also sell fine jewelry, masks, pottery, lacquerware, painted fish, and gourds.

Crafts **El Alcatraz** (Calle 58 between Calles 47 and 49, half a block from Parque Santa Ana) specializes in Oaxacan crafts. The best places for hammocks are **La Poblana** (Calle 65, No. 492) and **El Aguacate** (Calle 58, No. 492); for guayaberas, **Camisería Canul** (Calle 59 No. 496); and for jipis, **La Casa de los Jipis** (Calle 56, No. 526). Handicrafts are also on sale at the handicrafts market, **Bazar García Rejón** (corner of Calles 65 and 62); **Casa de las Artesanías** (Calle 63 between Calles 64 and 66); and **Artesanías Perla Maya** (Calle 60, No. 485, between Calles 55 and 57, near Parque Santa Lucía).

Galleries The **Teatro Daniel Ayala** (Calle 60 between Calles 59 and 61) and the **Galería del Ateneo Peninsular** (next to the Cathedral, between Calles 58 and 60) feature contemporary paintings and photography and are open weekdays 9–2 and 5–9, weekends 9–2. Local painters and sculptors also show their work at **Galería de Arte Art'Ho** (Calle 60, No. 477-A, between Calles 53 and 55).

Jewelry Probably the largest and finest selection of crafts—particularly silver jewelry—available is at **Sonrisa del Sol** (Calle 62, No. 500 Altos, between Calles 61 and 59, almost on the main square, tel. 99/281255). Good selections of earrings and onyx beads can be found at **El Paso** (Calle 59, No. 501) and **La Canasta** (Calle 60, No. 500), both under the same management.

Sports and Fitness

Participant Sports

Fishing Fishing has become an increasingly popular pastime as the passion for hunting declines because of the new concern for preservation. Those interested in sportfishing for such catch as grouper, red snapper, and sea bass, among others, will be sated in **Yucalpetén,** west of Progreso. **Río Lagartos** also offers good fishing in its murky waters. In the Parque Natural del Flamenco Mexicano in **Celestún,** you have your choice of river or gulf fishing. **Maya Tours** (Calle 60, No. 425, Mérida, tel. 99/242881 or 99/243022) arranges fishing trips (overnight or longer) to Cozumel, Isla Mujeres, Playa del Carmen, and other coastal locations.

Golf There is an 18-hole championship golf course (and restaurant, bar, and clubhouse) at **Club Golf La Ceiba,** 16 kilometers (10 miles) north of Mérida on the road to Progreso.

Hunting Hunting has always been popular in Yucatán, but as more species become endangered the sport is attracting fewer enthusiasts. The best hunting area is on the northwest coast around **Sisal,** 51 kilometers (32 miles) northwest of Mérida, and November–March remain the most successful months for hunting duck and other waterfowl. Other prizes include the small jungle deer, quail, and wild boar. The importation of firearms and other arrangements can be complicated, so it's best to go through a specialist and take part in a group expedition. **Ceiba Tours** (Holiday Inn, tel. 99/256389) is well versed at cutting through red tape and setting up expeditions, as is **Maya Tours** (*see* above).

Tennis **The Holiday Inn** (Av. Colón 498 at Calle 60, tel. 99/256877) has tennis courts, as do the **Club Campestre de Mérida** (Calle 30,

No. 500, tel. 99/71100 or 71700), the **Centro Deportivo Bancario** (Carr. a Motul s/n, Frac. del Arco, tel. 99/60500 or 99/77819), and the **Deportivo Libanés Mexicano** (Calle 1-G, No. 101, tel. 99/70669).

Spectator Sports

Baseball   Baseball is played with enthusiasm from February or March to July at the stadium in the **Kukulcán Sports Center** (Calle 14, No. 17), next to the Carta Clara brewery.

Bullfights   Bullfights are most often performed from December to March, or during other holiday periods at the **bullring** (Paseo de la Reforma), near Avenida Colón. Contact the travel desk at your hotel or one of the tourist information centers; prices range from $7–$11 for seats in the sun to $11–$17 for seats in the shade.

Dining and Lodging

Dining   Dining out is a pleasure in Mérida. The city's 50-odd restaurants offer a superb variety of cuisine—primarily Yucatecán, of course, but also Lebanese, Italian, French, Chinese, and Mexican—at very reasonable prices. Generally, reservations are advised for those places marked "Expensive," but only during the high season. Neat but casual dress is acceptable at all Mérida restaurants.

Pisté, the village nearest to Chichén Itzá, is not a gourmand's town: The food in most of its restaurants is simple, overpriced, and only fair. The hotel restaurants are your best bets. Most of the restaurants in town have been set up to handle tour-bus crowds and are empty the rest of the time. If you prefer to dine inexpensively, try one of the palapa-covered cafés along the main road. The small markets and produce stands can provide the makings for a modest picnic.

The restaurants near the ruins in Uxmal are nothing to write home about either. Stick to the hotel dining rooms. The exception is Los Almendros, in Ticul, which is well worth the 15-minute drive.

All restaurants are open for breakfast, lunch, and dinner unless otherwise noted. People who like eating with the locals might stop in at one of the many *loncherías* (diners) in Parque Santarina or Parque Santiago for panuchos, *empanadas* (meat-filled turnovers), tacos, or *salbutes* (which are like panuchos without the beans). As in Mérida, neat but casual dress is acceptable.

Highly recommended restaurants are indicated by a star ★.

Category	Cost*
Expensive	over $10
Moderate	$5–$10
Inexpensive	under $5

per person, excluding drinks, service, and sales tax (15%)

Lodging Outside of Mérida you'll find that accommodations fit the low-key, simple pace of the region. Internationally affiliated properties are the exception rather than the rule; instead, charmingly idiosyncratic old mansions offer visitors a base from which to explore the countryside and Mérida itself—which merits at least a two-day stay.

Mérida's 60-odd hotels offer a refreshingly broad range, from the chain hotels at the top end and the classic, older hotels housed in colonial or turn-of-the-century mansions (suffused with genteel charm and full of warm touches) to fleabags adequate only for the budget traveler unconcerned with creature comforts. As in the rest of Mexico, the facade rarely reveals the character of the hotel behind it, so check out the interior before turning away. Properties in Mérida have a 97000 postal code.

Location is very important in your choice of hotels: If you plan to spend most of your time enjoying Mérida, stay in the vicinity of the main square or along Calle 59; skip the rundown properties on the once-elegant Paseo de Montejo, which is a long haul from the center of the action. If you're a real stickler for hot water, test the faucets before renting a room. In general, the public spaces in Mérida's hotels are better maintained than the sleeping rooms. All hotels have air-conditioning unless otherwise noted.

Highly recommended hotels are indicated by a star ★.

Category	Cost*
Very Expensive	over $60
Expensive	$40–$60
Moderate	$30–$40
Inexpensive	under $30

All prices are for a standard double room, excluding 15% tax.

Chichén Itzá **Hacienda Chichén.** A converted 17th-century hacienda, this
Lodging hotel once served as the home of archaeologist Edward S. Thompson and later as the headquarters for the Carnegie expedition. The rustic cottages built for the expedition have been modernized, and all rooms, which are simply furnished in colonial Yucatecán style, have private bathrooms, ceiling fans, and verandas. An enormous old pool sits in the midst of the landscaped gardens. *Carretera Mérida–Cancún, Km 120, tel. in Mérida 99/248844 or 800/223–4084. 20 rooms. Facilities: restaurant, bar, pool. No air-conditioning. AE, DC, MC, V. Closed May–Oct. Very Expensive.*

★ **Mayaland.** The hotel closest to the ruins, this charming 62-year-old property belongs to the Barbachano family, whose name is practically synonymous with tourism in Yucatán. Accommodations include a wing and several bungalows set in a large garden on a 100-acre site. A rail track leads directly to Old Chichén Itzá; the observatory is visible from the alcoves on the road side of the hotel. Tucked into beautiful pathways overgrown with bougainvillea and trees are the bungalows, and the colonial-style rooms in the main building feature decorative tiles, ceiling fans, and mosquito netting; verandas overlook fountains, statues, and tropical gardens. At night musicians accompany dinner by the pool. *Carretera Mérida–Cancún, Km*

120, tel. in Chichén Itzá, 985/62777; in Mérida, Mayaland Tours, Av. Colón 502, tel. 99/252122 or 99/252133; fax 99/257022. 62 rooms. Facilities: restaurant, bar, pool. AE, MC, V. Very Expensive.

Misión. This two-story hotel, built around a central garden with pools, offers attractive rooms with tiling. *Zona Arqué ológica de Chichén Itzá, tel. 800/221–6509. 42 rooms. Facilities: restaurant, bar, pool, poolside bar. AE, DC, MC, V. Very Expensive.*

Pirámide Inn Resort and RV Park. This slightly tacky, American-owned two-story motel in Pisté features rooms with white walls, white tile floors, and modern furniture. The garden contains a small Mayan pyramid and a tennis court, and adjoining the inn are 30 RV hookups. *1 km before Chichén Hacienda, Box 433, Mérida, Yucatán (for reservations), no phone. 44 rooms. Facilities: restaurant, pool, satellite TV, lending library, tennis court. AE, MC, V. Moderate.*

Mérida
Dining
★

Alberto's Continental Patio. You can probably find this restaurant praised in just about every guidebook and it merits the kudos: The setting is romantic and the food is excellent. The building, which dates from around 1727, is adorned with such fine details as mosaic floors from Cuba, and the two beautiful dining rooms are tastefully furnished with dark wood trim and chairs, copper utensils, stone sculpture, and candles in glass lanterns on the tables. There is an inner patio where you can dine beneath the stars, surrounded by rubber trees. Most of the guests are tourists, but that need not detract from the surroundings or the food. If you order Lebanese food, your plate will be heaped with servings of shish kebab, fried kibi, cabbage rolls, hummus, eggplant, and tabbouleh, accompanied by pita bread, almond pie, and Turkish coffee. Black bean soup, enchiladas, fried bananas, and caramel custard make up the Mexican dinner; there are also a Yucatecán dinner, an Italian dinner, and à la carte appetizers and entrées. A gift shop sells handsome reproductions of ancient sculptures. *Calle 64, No. 482, at Calle 57, tel. 99/212298. Open daily 11–11. AE, MC, V. Expensive.*

Pancho's. The waiters in this steak and seafood restaurant— Mérida's version of the Carlos 'n' Charlie's chain—dress in what look like Hollywood's idea of "Bandito" costumes. The bar, with its fancy drinks, attracts the international singles set; dancing is possible some nights on the outdoor patio. *Calle 59, No. 509, between Calles 60 and 62, tel. 99/230942. AE, MC, V. Closed for lunch. Expensive.*

★ **Yannig.** Mérida's best French restaurant has moved to a new location on Avenida Pérez Ponce, quite a distance from the city center. However, the fare—prepared by a Breton chef—remains excellent. Onion soup, crepes, red snapper almandine, and beef bourguignon are among the specialties. Yannig boasts a good wine list and, for dessert, an array of ice cream sundaes including one topped with honey and a generous shot of tequila. The live music enhances the fine Gallic atmosphere. *Av. Pérez Ponce 105, tel. 99/270339. Open daily 6–midnight. AE, MC, V. Expensive.*

Los Almendros. Another Mérida classic, this chain restaurant credits itself with the invention of poc chuc, and though perhaps overrated, it does know how to cater to the tourists who frequently fill its chairs and tables to the limit. The two dining rooms have both ceiling fans and air-conditioning. The food tends to be on the greasy, oily side, and sometimes the taste of the food itself is all but drowned in wonderful local spices. Nonetheless, the restaurant provides a more than passable introduction to the variety of Yucatecán cuisine, including cochinita píbil, panuchos, pork sausage, papadzules, and *pollo ticuleño* (boneless, breaded chicken in tomato sauce, accompanied by fried beans, peas, red peppers, fried bananas, and ham and cheese), and all dishes are described in English on the paper menus. The sangria—with or without alcohol—washes it all down. *Calle 50-A, No. 493, between Calles 57 and 59, tel. 99/212851. AE. Moderate.*

La Casona. This pretty mansion-turned-restaurant near Parque Santa Ana has an inner patio, arcade, red tile roof, and ceiling fans. The accent is Italian, and the specialties include homemade pasta—ravioli, "straw and hay," manicotti, and linguine. Calzones stuffed with cheese or spinach, osso buco, chicken, fish, and píbil are other good bets. Vegetable soup accompanies most orders. The restaurant offers live music on weekends. *Calle 60, No. 434, between Calles 47 and 49, tel. 99/238348. Open daily 1–1. AE, MC, V. Moderate.*

Express. Young and middle-aged Méridano men in guayaberas spend hours in this plain café-style restaurant that reeks of Madrid café ambience (and of cigar smoke as well). That ambience is reinforced by the paintings of old Spain (or old Mérida) on the walls, the ceiling fans, and the old-fashioned globe lights. On the menu are broiled garlic chicken, sandwiches, shrimp, and red snapper. Service can be slow, but then Express is a place for lingering. *Calle 60, No. 502, at Calle 59, tel. 99/213738. No credit cards. Moderate.*

La Jungla. Sharing the second floor of a 400-year-old house with an immense crafts store, "The Jungle" is a strictly kitschy restaurant. The menu, featuring pizzas, spaghetti, sandwiches, garlic bread, fondue, and croissants, appeals to Americans who have had their fill of pollo pibil and seafood. *Calle 62, No. 500 Altos, tel. 99/281255. Open daily 11:30–11:30. MC, V. Moderate.*

Pizza Bella. This pizza place on the main square next to Librería Dante also serves Mexican and American breakfasts, espresso, and cappuccino. Checkered tablecloths atop wooden tables and an eclectic collection of posters (maps to beer advertisements) adorning the walls add atmosphere to this otherwise pizza-joint-style restaurant. *Calle 61, No. 500, Depto. E-2, tel. 99/236401. No credit cards. Moderate.*

Pórtico del Peregrino. The name means "pilgrim's porch," and this colonial-style restaurant has the decor to match: A red tile floor, iron grillwork, and copious plants set the tone in both the indoor and outdoor patio sections. The menu features lime soup, baked eggplant with chicken, shrimp, chicken píbil, shish kebob, mole enchiladas, seafood stew, chicken liver brochettes, and spaghetti. For dessert, try the coconut ice cream with Kahlúa. *Calle 57, No. 501, tel. 99/216844. AE, MC, V. Closed for breakfast. Moderate.*

Siqueff. The restaurant's 12 tables are spaced around a capacious dining room, which encloses an inner courtyard framed by Moorish arches and brick walls. Siqueff specializes in Lebanese and Yucatecán dishes, offering a *menú árabe* (eggplant, garbanzo beans, kafta, meat, kibi, salad) and a *menú turístico* (lime soup, chicken píbil and *pollo ticuleño* and dessert). Argentine-style beef, shellfish, and paella are also served, as are daily specials. *Calle 59, No. 553, between Calles 68 and 70, tel. 99/*

249287 or 99/247465. Open Mon.–Sat. 7:30–7:30; Sun. 9:30–5:30. MC, V. Moderate.

Ananda Maya Ginza. One of a handful of vegetarian restaurants in town, this one is light on the decor, which includes wood tables, white walls, and stone floors, and heavy on the health drinks, made mostly with local vegetables, fruit, and herbs. The terrace of this old historic home provides a quiet dining atmosphere beneath a big tree. *Calle 59, No. 507, between Calles 60 and 62, tel. 99/282451. Open Mon.–Sat. 10–10; closed Sun. No credit cards. Inexpensive.*

Café Louvre. Catty-corner from the main square, this café is very popular, though tiled walls and floors give it something of a chilly ambience. The service tends to be indifferent, but that doesn't seem to bother the locals, who come here for the sandwiches, huevos motuleños, hot cakes, fried bananas with cream, and iced tea (an unusual beverage in Mexico). *Calle 62, No. 499-D, at Calle 61, tel. 99/213271. No credit cards. Inexpensive.*

Cafetería Pop. A favorite with the student crowd (the university is across the street), this place—with some 12 white-linoleum-covered tables—resembles a crowded American diner. The busiest time is 8 AM–noon, but for late risers the breakfast menu can be ordered à la carte all day. In addition, sandwiches, hamburgers, spaghetti, chicken, fish, beef, and tacos are featured. Beer, sangria, and wine are served only with food orders. *Calle 57, No. 501, at Calle 62, tel. 99/216844. MC, V. Inexpensive.*

Carnitas de Michoacán. If you have a hankering for tacos with broiled meats—the ever-popular Mexican specialty (though it's not very common in Yucatán)—check out this no-frills place outside of town. Lamb, chicharrón (fried pork rind), tacos *à la gringa* (flour tortillas topped with pork and cheese and cooked on a spit), and the *Gabriel especial* (flour tortillas covered with pork, cheese, and mushrooms) get high ratings. *Calle 58-A, No. 499, Prolongación Paseo de Montejo, near the Monumento a la Patria, no phone. Open 10–2. No credit cards. Inexpensive.*

Nicte-Ha. Metal chairs and tables with plastic tablecloths sit under an arcade right on the main square, making this modest eatery a fine place for people-watching. A good selection of Yucatecán fare—soups, huevos motuleños, poc chuc, seafood, *antojitos* (appetizers), and a combination platter—is offered at budget prices. Afterward, stop in at the *sorbetería* next door for a sherbet. *Calle 61, No. 500, at Calle 60, tel. 99/230784. No credit cards. Inexpensive.*

Lodging **Calinda Panamericana.** This internationally affiliated property is far more elegant on the outside and in its vast public spaces than in its guest rooms, which have clearly seen better days. The management is on the indifferent side, but the Calinda is still a grand old Mexican hotel in the Spanish tradition, from the rococo fountain in the cavernous atrium to the black-and-white tile floors, Corinthian columns, and intricately carved hardwood portals. The room fixtures are old, and the rooms, although large, are rather plainly furnished. The pool area, including a bar and restaurant, is lovely and old-fashioned; off-key musicians and folkloric dancers perform there nightly. Because it's located right on Calle 59—2 blocks from the plaza—with an adjacent parking lot, the Calinda is convenient for travelers with cars. *Calle 59, No. 455, tel. 99/239111, 99/239444 or*

800/228–5152; fax 99/286–5679. 110 rooms. Facilities: restaurant, bar, disco, travel agency. AE, MC, V. Very Expensive.

Casa del Balam. This very pleasant hotel on well-heeled Calle 60 (opposite the Opera House) was built 60 years ago as the home of the Barbachano family, pioneers of Yucatán tourism. Today the hotel—owned and managed by Carmen Barbachano—has a lovely courtyard ornamented with a fountain, arcades, ironwork, and a black-and-white tile floor; rocking chairs in the hallways impart a colonial feeling, as do the mahogany trimmings and cedar doorways. The rooms are capacious and well maintained, featuring painted sinks, wrought-iron accessories, and minibars. The suites are especially agreeable, with large bathrooms, tiny balconies, arched doorways, and mahogany bureaus. *Calle 60, No. 488, Box 988, tel. 99/248844, 99/248130 or 800/624–8451; fax 99/245011. 54 rooms. Facilities: restaurant, 2 bars, minibar, pool, sun deck, travel agency, car rental, gift shop. AE, MC, V. Very Expensive.*

Holiday Inn. A deluxe, modern hotel at the fashionable north end of the Paseo de Montejo—too far from the center if you are on foot, fine if you have a car—this is Mérida's only five-star hotel, but wholly Americanized, with probably the only king-size beds in town. Rooms are decorated in typical Holiday Inn fashion and include simple, functional furnishings. Mexicans hold business meetings and conventions here. *Av. Colón 498 at Calle 60, tel. 99/256877 or 800/465–4329. 214 rooms. Facilities: 3 restaurants, 4 bars, disco, minibars, pool, lighted tennis court, shops, parking. AE, DC, MC, V. Very Expensive.*

Misión. Part of the city's landscape for decades (in its earlier incarnation it was the Hotel Mérida), the Misíon has two major assets: an excellent location in the heart of downtown and a genuine colonial ambience, with archways, patios, fountains, and pool, and furnishings that include chandeliers and wood beams. Handsome public areas make it a pleasure to spend time here; it is not just a place to retire for the night. *Calle 60, No. 491, tel. 99/239607, 99/239407, or 800/221–6509. 139 rooms. Facilities: restaurant, nightclub, snack bar, pool, travel agency, gift shop. AE, DC, MC, V. Expensive.*

Montejo Palace. Although the seven-story Montejo Palace—situated only a block from the Anthropology Museum—is perfectly adequate and functional, it is a bit short on character; this wouldn't be a first-choice selection, but should be considered as a backup if other hotels are filled. The rooms have white walls with paintings of Mérida and curved wood doorways, colonial-style furniture, and balconies; the carpets, curtains, and bedspreads are a bit faded. Convenient additions to the otherwise unimpressive hotel include the rooftop nightclub and a few shops next door. *Paseo de Montejo 483-C, tel. 99/246046 or 800/221–6509; fax 99/280388. 88 rooms. Facilities: restaurant, cafeteria, bar, nightclub, pool, travel agency, gift shop. AE, DC, MC, V. Expensive.*

★ **Casa Mexilio.** One would never guess that behind the drab exterior of this guest house sits the most exquisitely decorated bed-and-breakfast in all Mérida, if not the entire country. Two partners—one Mexican, one American—have brought the best of their respective architectural and decorating traditions to bear on this small house with five guest rooms (one on each floor), which is being restored to something beyond its original splendor. From the dark entrance you approach a tiny pool adjacent to a charming kitchen, painted as extravagantly as the kitchen that belonged to Frida Kahlo, the celebrated Mexican painter and the wife of the even more famous muralist Diego Rivera. At the top of the narrow stairs is a sun deck laden with cacti; one entire wall of the house is covered with vines. Middle Eastern wall hangings, French tapestries, colorful tile floors, black pottery, tile sinks, rustic furniture, loft beds, and white walls make up the eclectic decor, which reaches its pinnacle in an immensely cozy sitting room on the second floor, complete with hammock, stereo, TV, and bookshelves. The price includes breakfast. *Calle 68, No. 495, tel. 99/214032; for reservations tel. 303/674–9615 or 800/538–6802; fax 303/674-8735. 5 rooms. Facilities: restaurant, pool. AE, MC, V. Moderate.*

Del Gobernador. A modern stucco exterior and simple air-conditioned lobby match the clean rooms painted in white, cream, and light pinks of this 10-year-old, three-star downtown property. Wood furniture, carpets, and hanging plants add comfort to the units, and most rooms have balconies. *Calle 59, No. 535, tel. 99/237133; fax 99/281590. 61 rooms. Facilities: restaurant/ bar, pool, travel agency. AE, MC, V. Moderate.*

Caribe. The Caribe was being remodeled at press time, but it already possessed all the makings of an authentic colonial hotel, including tile floors, and dark wood furniture, and a large inner courtyard with arcades. It's located on Parque Hidalgo, but only one room has a plaza view; the others overlook the inner courtyard. Air-conditioned rooms cost slightly more, but all rooms are pleasant, if lacking in warmth. Amenities include guest privileges at the Mérida golf club. *Calle 60, No. 500, tel. 99/249022; fax 99/248733. 56 rooms. Facilities: restaurant, outdoor cafeteria, pool, travel agency, parking. AE, DC, MC, V. Inexpensive.*

★ **Gran Hotel.** Cozily situated on Parque Hidalgo, this 1894 hotel is the oldest in the city, and it still lives up to its name. The five-story neoclassical building, with an art-nouveau courtyard complete with wrought-iron bannister, variegated tile floors, Greek columns, and a myriad of potted plants, exudes charm. High ceilings in rooms drenched in cedar provide a sense of spaciousness. All units have balconies and some have air-conditioning. Ask for a room overlooking the park. Porfirio Díaz, Fidel Castro, and Sandino stayed in sumptuous Room 17, and Room 12½ has an enormous sitting room. TVs are available upon request. The Patio Español restaurant, although separately owned, is situated in the hotel. *Calle 60, No. 496, tel. 99/ 247622 or 99/283784; fax 99/247730. 24 rooms. Facilities: restaurant, sun roof. MC, V. Inexpensive.*

Maya Yucatán. Yet another modern, characterless hotel, this six-story property features pale salmon arcades, a lobby bar where music is played, and plain hallways. The newer colonial-style section extends over the small pool. The rooms are bare but functional. *Calle 58, No. 483, tel. 99/235395 or 99/235215; fax 99/234642. 78 rooms. Facilities: lobby bar, disco, pool, travel agency. AE, MC, V. Inexpensive.*

Posada Toledo. This slightly musty inn occupies a beautiful old colonial house with high ceilings, floors of patterned tile, and old-fashioned carved furniture that evoke its former elegance. The dining room, where breakfast is served, is particularly fine, with stained-glass door frames. Antiques clutter the halls, along with warm, faded portraits of 19th-century family life, so that one feels more like a personal guest of the establishment than another nameless hotel client. The rooms have the same bright tile floors; glass doors on the dining room cabinets reveal family heirlooms; and the inner patio—with marble columns enclosing a tropical garden—is a study in Mexican refinement. You have a choice of a ceiling fan or air-conditioning. *Calle 58 No. 487, at Calle 57, tel. 99/231690 or 99/232256. 20 rooms. No facilities. MC, V. Inexpensive.*

Trinidad. Eccentricity holds sway at this impossibly original, slightly ramshackle, bizarre little hotel, nearly unidentifiable unless you are looking specifically for it. In its previous lives it has been a hacienda, an auto rental shop, and a furniture store, but in the late 1980s owner Manuel Ribero Cervera made it into a hotel. An adjacent and still browsable gallery houses leftovers from the Trinidad's days as a furniture store. The large, chaotic lobby is filled with plants, a fountain, and yellow wicker furniture; making your way through the maze that is the rest of the hotel, you'll encounter painted wooden angels, curved columns, and even a green satin shoe mounted on a pedestal. The rooms are small and equally odd. *Calle 62, No. 464, tel. 99/213029 or 99/232033. 17 rooms. Facilities: pool. AE, MC, V. Inexpensive.*

Progreso
Dining

Capitán Marisco. This large and pretty restaurant-bar on the malecón features a nautical motif, with a ship's rudder in the center of the main dining room and a fountain adorned with seashells. The house specialty is *filete a la hoja de plátano* (fish fillet—usually grouper, sea bass, or pompano—cooked in a banana leaf), but the entire menu is dependable. For a superb view of the sea, visit the outdoor terrace on the second floor. *Malecón between Calles 10 and 12, tel. 993/50639. AE, MC, V. Expensive.*

El Cordobés. Located right on the square, this large if nondescript restaurant is popular with old salts from the United States who have learned of this place by word-of-mouth. People come here to converse for hours and pick from a menu that features sandwiches, soup, fish, shellfish, meat, and eggs. *Calle 31, No. 150, no phone. No credit cards. Moderate.*

Lodging

Fiesta Inn Mérida Beach. This unlikely luxury chain hotel and time-share (affiliated with Posadas de México) sits in Yucalpetén, a tiny fishing village 35 kilometers (22 miles) north of Mérida and very close to Progreso. The attractive two-story pastel stucco exterior and lobby are complemented in the rooms by teal carpets, orange curtains, and coral-and-oyster-white walls. Some rooms have sofa beds; all have balconies. The pretty pale-green-and-purple cafeteria features a nautical decor. The pool—alongside which mariachis play on weekends—is right on the beach, which is separated from the property by a small lawn. The inn surrounds a little harbor filled with boats, and the jetty leads to a tiny lighthouse. Most guests are traveling on a package tour with Adventure Tours (Canada). *Calle 19, No. 91, Col. Reparto Costa Azul, Progreso 97320, tel. 800/FIESTA–1, 993/50300, or 993/50222; fax 993/50699. 88 rooms. Facilities: cafeteria, pool bar, cable TV, 2 pools, 4 tennis courts, surfing, marina, gift shop, bicycle rental, beauty salon. AE, DC, MC, V. Very Expensive.*

Sian Ka'an. These four whitewashed, thatched-roof, two-story villas, right on the beach in Chelem (just west of Yucalpetén and near Progreso) all come with kitchenettes, ceiling fans, and terraces that overlook the water. Decorated in rustic Mexican-Mediterranean style, the suites feature handwoven bedspreads, *equipales* (leather chairs from Jalisco), and hand-blown glassware. Prices include breakfast. *Calle 17, s/n, tel. in Mérida, 99/273525, fax 99/281355; in Chelem, tel. 993/51243. 8* *suites. Facilities: restaurant, beach, pool. AE, DC, MC, V. Very Expensive.*

Paraíso Maya. This brand-new five-star hotel was one of the first to open (1990) in the new development of Nuevo Yucatán, otherwise known as Telchac Puerto. Part of the Yucatecán hotel chain Amigoteles, the hotel is big, and it has been nicely done in Mexican pastel stucco and dark wood. The rooms have kitchenettes (with burners on top of the refrigerators) and balconies; ask for one with a sea view. There are also suites, condominiums, and time-share units. The hotel plans to add another 400 rooms by 1992. 79 km (49 mi) northeast of Mérida. *Calle 62, No. 515, Mérida 97000 (for reservations), tel. 99/281351, 99/280211, or 800/458–6888; fax 99/232700 or 714/494–5088. 163 rooms. Facilities: satellite TV, fans, air-conditioning, pool, beach, water sports, car and motorcycle rental, 2 restaurants, disco, travel agency, gift shops. AE, MC, V. Moderate.*

Progreso. This clean, modest-but-tasteful three-star hotel in the heart of Progreso opened in 1990. The rooms, some with balconies, are furnished in pine, with arched window frames and tiled baths. *Calle 29 at Calle 28, tel. 993/50039. 9 rooms. Facilities: air-conditioning or ceiling fans. MC, V. Inexpensive.*

Uxmal
Dining
★

Los Almendros. Located in Ticul, a small town 28 kilometers (17 miles) east of Uxmal (turn left at Santa Elena), this restaurant offers fresher and juicier foods than do the other members of the Los Almendros chain. Although the interior is simple and clean, with whitewashed walls, the scenery behind the restaurant gives you a real taste of Yucatán: It's not unusual to see old Mayan women in their huipiles and baseball hats patting corn tortillas by hand. As for the menu, the prices are the same as in the other branches, and poc chuc and cochinita píbil are good choices. This is one place, however, where you should make reservations, especially during high season. *Calle 23, No. 196, no phone. MC, V. Moderate.*

Lodging

Hacienda Uxmal. The oldest hotel at the site, built in 1955 and still owned and operated by the Barbachano family, this pleasant colonial-style building has lovely floor tiles, ceramics, and iron grillwork. The rooms—all with ceiling fans and air-conditioning—are tiled and decorated with worn but comfortable furniture. Inside the large courtyard are a garden and pool. Across the road and about 100 yards south you'll find the ruins. *Within walking distance of the ruins, tel. in Uxmal, 99/247142; in Mérida, Mayaland Tours, Av. Colón 502, tel. 99/252122 or 99/252133, fax 99/257022. 80 rooms. Facilities: restaurant, bar, pool, gift shop. AE, DC, MC, V. Very Expensive.*

Villa Arqueológica Uxmal. The hotel closest to the ruins is this two-story Club Med property built around a large Mediterranean-style pool. The functional rooms have cozy niches for the beds, tiled bathrooms, and powerful air conditioners. Mayan women in traditional dress serve well-prepared French cuisine in the restaurant, and large cages located around the hotel contain tropical birds and monkeys. For a fee, day-trippers can use the pool, then dine in the restaurant. *Within walking distance of the ruins, tel. 99/247053; in the U.S., tel. 800/CLUB–MED. 44 rooms. Facilities: restaurant, bar, pool, tennis court, gift shop. AE, MC, V. Expensive.*

Valladolid
Lodging

El Mesón del Marqués. This building, on the north side of the main square, is a well-preserved, very old hacienda built around a lovely courtyard. The old-fashioned yellow rooms—some with air-conditioning, some with ceiling fans—are attractively furnished with rustic and colonial touches. Unusually large bathrooms boast bathtubs—a rarity in Mexican hotels. As an added draw, El Mesón features a pool, a crafts shop, and a restaurant that serves local specialties. *Calle 39, No. 203, tel. 985/62073. 25 rooms, plus 9 suites. Facilities: restaurant, bar, gift shop, pool. MC, V. Inexpensive.*

The Arts and Nightlife

The Arts

Mérida Mérida enjoys an unusually active and diverse cultural life, including free government-sponsored music and dance performances nightly in local parks (*see* Mérida for Free, above). For information on these and other performances, consult the tourist office, the local newspapers, or the billboards and posters at the Teatro Peón Contreras (Calle 60 at Calle 57) or Café Pop (Calle 57 between Calles 60 and 62).

Among a variety of performances presented at the **Teatro Peón Contreras** is "The Roots of Today's Yucatán," a combination of music, dance, and theater presented by the Folkloric Ballet of the University of Yucatán. *Admission: $7. Tues. 9 PM.*

Another theater that regularly hosts cultural events is the **Teatro Daniel Ayala** (Calle 60 between Calles 59 and 61).

Nightlife

Mérida Downtown movie theaters include **Cine Aladino** (Calle 60, No.
Film 514), **Cine Apolo** (Calle 60, No. 487), **Cine Fantasio** (Calles 59 and 60), **Cine Mérida** (Calle 62), **Cine Rex** (Calle 57, No. 553).

Events The **Hotel Calinda Panamericana** (Calle 59, No. 455, tel. 99/239111 or 99/239444) stages folkloric dances most nights by the pool. **Tulipanes** (Calle 46, No. 462-A, tel. 99/272029), a restaurant and nightclub built over a cenote, stages a folkloric ballet and "Mayan ritual" performance that ends with a "sacrifice" nightly at 8.

Music A number of restaurants feature live music and dancing, including **El Tucho** (Calle 60, No. 482, between Calles 55 and 57, tel. 99/242323), **La Prosperidad** (Calle 53 at Calle 56, tel. 99/240764), and **Pancho's** (Calle 59 between Calles 60 and 62, tel. 99/230942).

Discos There are discos that appeal to both locals and tourists at the **Holiday Inn** (Av. Colón, No. 498, at Calle 60), **Hotel Calinda Panamericana** (Calle 59, No. 455), and **Montejo Palace** (Paseo de Montejo, No. 483-C) hotels. **Bin Bon Beach** (Carretera Progreso–Chicxulub) has the reputation for being the hottest disco in town, even though it's actually in Monterreal, 20 minutes north by car/taxi from downtown Mérida. **Excess** (Prolongación Paseo de Montejo), Mérida's newest and most exclusive disco, is in the conspicuous lavender building.

State of Yucatán Both Chichén Itzá and Uxmal offer elaborate nighttime sound-and-light shows accompanied by narrations of Mayan legends (*see* Exploring, above).

Spanish Vocabulary

Note: *Mexican Spanish differs from Castilian Spanish.*

Words and Phrases

	English	Spanish	Pronunciation
Basics	Yes/no	Sí/no	see/no
	Please	Por favor	pore fah-**vore**
	May I?	¿Me permite?	may pair-**mee**-tay
	Thank you (very much)	(Muchas) gracias	(**moo**-chas) **grah**-see-as
	You're welcome	De nada	day **nah**-dah
	Excuse me	Con permiso	con pair-**mee**-so
	Pardon me/what did you say?	¿Como?/Mánde?	pair-**doan/mahn**-dey
	Could you tell me?	¿Podría decirme?	po-**dree**-ah deh-**seer**-meh
	I'm sorry	Lo siento	lo see-**en**-toe
	Good morning!	¡Buenos días!	**bway**-nohs **dee**-ahs
	Good afternoon!	¡Buenas tardes!	**bway**-nahs **tar**-dess
	Good evening!	¡Buenas noches!	**bway**-nahs **no**-chess
	Goodbye!	¡Adiós!/¡Hasta luego!	ah-dee-**ohss/ah**-stah-**lwe**-go
	Mr./Mrs.	Señor/Señora	sen-**yor**/sen-**yore**-ah
	Miss	Señorita	sen-yo-**ree**-tah
	Pleased to meet	Mucho gusto	**moo**-cho **goose**-to you
	How are you?	¿Cómo está usted?	**ko**-mo es-**tah** oo-**sted**
	Very well, thank you.	Muy bien, gracias.	**moo**-ee bee-**en**, grah-see-as
	And you?	¿Y usted?	ee oos-**ted**?
	Hello (on the telephone)	Bueno	**bwen**-oh
Numbers	1	un, uno	oon, **oo**-no
	2	dos	dos
	3	tres	trace
	4	cuatro	**kwah**-tro
	5	cinco	**sink**-oh
	6	seis	sace
	7	siete	see-**et**-ey
	8	ocho	**o**-cho
	9	nueve	new-**ev**-ay
	10	diez	dee-**es**
	11	once	**own**-sey
	12	doce	**doe**-sey
	13	trece	**tray**-sey
	14	catorce	kah-**tor**-sey
	15	quince	**keen**-sey
	16	dieciséis	dee-es-ee-**sace**
	17	diecisiete	dee-**es**-ee-see-**et**-ay
	18	dieciocho	dee-**es**-ee-**o**-cho
	19	diecinueve	**dee-es**-ee-new-**ev**-ay
	20	veinte	**vain**-tay
	21	veinte y uno/veintiuno	**vain**-te-oo-no

30	treinta	**train**-tah
32	treinta y dos	train-tay-**dose**
40	cuarenta	kwah-**ren**-tah
43	cuarenta y tres	kwah-**ren**-tay-**trace**
50	cincuenta	seen-**kwen**-tah
54	cincuenta y cuatro	seen-**kwen**-tay **kwah**-tro
60	sesenta	sess-**en**-tah
65	sesenta y cinco	sess-**en**-tay **seen**-ko
70	setenta	set-**en**-tah
76	setenta y seis	set-**en**-tay **sace**
80	ochenta	oh-**chen**-tah
87	ochenta y siete	oh-**chen**-tay see-**yet**-ay
90	noventa	no-**ven**-tah
98	noventa y ocho	no-**ven**-tah **o**-cho
100	cien	see-**en**
101	ciento uno	see-en-toe **oo**-no
200	doscientos	doe-see-**en**-tohss
500	quinientos	keen-**yen**-tohss
700	setecientos	set-eh-see-**en**-tohss
900	novecientos	no-veh-see-**en**-tohss
1,000	mil	meel
2,000	dos mil	dose meel
1,000,000	un millón	oon meel-**yohn**

Colors	black	negro	**neh**-grow
	blue	azul	ah-**sool**
	brown	café	kah-**feh**
	green	verde	**vair**-day
	pink	rosa	**ro**-sah
	purple	morado	mo-**rah**-doe
	orange	naranja	na-**rahn**-hah
	red	rojo	**roe**-hoe
	white	blanco	**blahn**-koh
	yellow	amarillo	ah-mah-**ree**-yoh

Days of the Week	Sunday	domingo	doe-**meen**-goh
	Monday	lunes	**loo**-ness
	Tuesday	martes	**mahr**-tess
	Wednesday	miércoles	me-**air**-koh-less
	Thursday	jueves	who-**ev**-ess
	Friday	viernes	vee-**air**-ness
	Saturday	sábado	**sah**-bah-doe

Months	January	enero	eh-**neh**-ro
	February	febrero	feh-**brair**-oh
	March	marzo	**mahr**-so
	April	abril	ah-**breel**
	May	mayo	**my**-oh
	June	junio	**hoo**-nee-oh
	July	julio	**who**-lee-yoh
	August	agosto	ah-**ghost**-toe
	September	septiembre	sep-tee-**em**-breh
	October	octubre	oak-**too**-breh
	November	noviembre	no-vee-**em**-breh
	December	diciembre	dee-see-**em**-breh

Useful phrases	Do you speak English?	¿Habla usted inglés?	**ah**-blah oos-**ted** in-**glehs**?

I don't speak Spanish	No hablo español	no **ah**-blow es-pahn-**yol**
I don't understand (you)	No entiendo	no en-tee-**en**-doe
I understand (you)	Entiendo	en-tee-**en**-doe
I don't know	No sé	no **say**
I am American/ British	Soy americano(a)/ inglés(a)	soy ah-meh-ree-**kah**-no(ah)/ in-**glace**(ah)
What's your name? My name is . . .	¿Cómo se llama usted? Me llamo . . .	**koh**-mo say **yah**-mah oos-**ted**? may **yah**-moh
What time is it?	¿Qué hora es?	keh **o**-rah es?
It is one, two, three . . . o'clock.	Es la una; son las dos, tres	es la **oo**-nah/sone lahs dose, trace
Yes, please/No, thank you	Sí, por favor/No, gracias	**see** pore fah-**vor**/no **grah**-see-us
How?	¿Cómo?	**koh**-mo?
When?	¿Cuándo?	**kwahn**-doe?
This/Next week	Esta semana/ la semana que entra	es-tah seh-**mah**-nah/lah say-**mah**-nah keh en-trah
This/Next month	Este mes/el próximo mes	es-tay mehs/el **proke**-see-mo mehs
This/Next year	Este año/el año que viene	es-tay **ahn**-yo/el **ahn**-yo keh vee-**yen**-ay
Yesterday/today/ tomorrow	Ayer/hoy/mañana	ah-**yair**/oy/mahn-**yah**-nah
This morning/ afternoon	Esta mañana/tarde	es-tah mahn-**yah**-nah/**tar**-day
Tonight	Esta noche	es-tah **no**-cheh
What?	¿Qué?	keh?
What is it?	¿Qué es esto?	keh es **es**-toe
Why?	¿Por qué?	pore **keh**
Who?	¿Quién?	kee-**yen**
Where is . . .? the train station? the subway station? the bus stop? the post office? the bank? the . . . hotel? the store?	¿Dónde está . . .? la estación del tren? la estación del Metro? la parada del autobús? la oficina de correos? el banco? el hotel . . .? la tienda . . .?	**dohn**-day es-**tah** la es-tah-see-**on** del **train** la es-ta-see-**on** del **meh**-tro la pah-**rah**-dah del oh-toe-**boos** la oh-fee-**see**-nah day koh-**reh**-os el **bahn**-koh el oh-**tel** la tee-**en**-dah

the cashier?	la caja?	la **kah**-hah
the . . . museum?	el museo . . . ?	el moo-**seh**-oh
the hospital?	el hospital?	el ohss-pea-**tal**
the elevator?	el ascensor?	el ah-**sen**-sore
the bathroom?	el baño?	el **bahn**-yoh
Here/there	Aquí/allá	ah-**key**/ah-**yah**
Open/closed	Abierto/cerrado	ah-be-**er**-toe/ ser-**ah**-doe
Left/right	Izquierda/derecha	iss-key-**er**-dah/ dare-**eh**-chah
Straight ahead	Derecho	der-**eh**-choh
Is it near/far?	¿Está cerca/lejos?	es-**tah sair**-kah/ **leh**-hoss
I'd like . . .	Quisiera . . .	kee-see-**air**-ah
a room	un cuarto/una habitación	oon **kwahr**-toe/ **oo**-nah ah-bee- tah-see-**on**
the key	la llave	lah **yah**-vay
a newspaper	un periódico	oon pear-ee-**oh**- dee-koh
a stamp	un timbre de correo	oon **team**-bray day koh-**reh**-oh
I'd like to buy . . .	Quisiera comprar . . .	kee-see-**air**-ah kohm-**prahr**
cigarettes	cigarrillo	ce-gar-**reel**-oh
matches	cerillos	ser-**ee**-ohs
a dictionary	un diccionario	oon deek-see-oh- **nah**-ree-oh
soap	jabón	hah-**bone**
a map	un mapa	oon **mah**-pah
a magazine	una revista	**oon**-ah reh-**veess**-tah
paper	papel	pah-**pel**
envelopes	sobres	**so**-brace
a postcard	una tarjeta postal	**oon**-ah tar-**het**-ah post-**ahl**
How much is it?	¿Cuánto cuesta?	**kwahn**-toe **kwes**-tah
It's expensive/ cheap	Está caro/barato	es-**tah kah**-roh/ bah-**rah**-toe
A little/a lot	Un poquito/ mucho . . .	oon poh-**kee**-toe/ **moo**-choh
More/less	Más/menos	mahss/**men**-ohss
Enough/too much/too little	Suficiente/de- masiado/muy poco	soo-fee-see-**en**-tay/ day-mah-see-**ah**- doe/**moo**-ee **poh**-koh
Telephone	Teléfono	tel-**ef**-oh-no
Telegram	Telegrama	teh-leh-**grah**-mah
I am ill/sick	Estoy enfermo(a)	es-**toy** en-**fair**-moh(ah)

Please call a doctor	Por favor llame un médico	pore fa-**vor ya**-may oon **med**-ee-koh
Help!	¡Auxilio! ¡Ayuda!	owk-**see**-lee-oh/ ah-**yoo**-dah
Fire!	¡Encendio!	en-**sen**-dee-oo
Caution!/Look out!	¡Cuidado!	kwee-**dah**-doh

On the Road

Highway	Carretera	car-ray-**ter**-ah
Causeway, paved highway	Calzada	cal-**za**-dah
Route	Ruta	**roo**-tah
Road	Camino	cah-**mee**-no
Street	Calle	**cah**-yeh
Avenue	Avenida	ah-ven-**ee**-dah
Broad, tree-lined boulevard	Paseo	pah-**seh**-oh
Waterfront promenade	Malecón	mal-lay-**cone**
Wharf	Embarcadero	em-bar-cah-**day**-ro

In Town

Church	Templo/Iglesia	**tem**-plo/e-**gles**-se-ah
Cathedral	Catedral	cah-tay-**dral**
Neighborhood	Barrio	**bar**-re-o
Foreign Exchange Shop	Casa de Cambio	**cas**-sah day **cam**-be-o
City Hall	Ayuntamiento	ah-yoon-tah-mee **en**-toe
Main Square	Zócalo	**zo**-cal-o
Traffic Circle	Glorieta	glor-e-**ay**-tah
Market	Mercado (Spanish)/ Tianguis (Indian)	mer-**cah**-doe/ tee-**an**-geese
Inn	Posada	pos-**sah**-dah
Group taxi	Colectivo	co-lec-**tee**-vo
Group taxi along fixed route	Pesero	pi-**seh**-ro

Items of Clothing

| Embroidered white smock | Huipil | whee-**peel** |
| Pleated man's shirt worn outside the pants | Guayabera | gwah-ya-**beh**-ra |

Leather sandals	Huarache	wah-**ra**-chays
Shawl	Rebozo	ray-**bozh**-o
Pancho or blanket	Serape	seh-**ra**-peh

Dining Out

A bottle of . . .	Una botella de . . .	**oo**-nah bo-**tay**-yah deh
A cup of . . .	Una taza de . . .	**oo**-nah **tah**-sah deh
A glass of . . .	Un vaso de . . .	oon **vah**-so deh
Ashtray	Un cenicero	oon sen-ee-**seh**-roh
Bill/check	La cuenta	lah **kwen**-tah
Bread	El pan	el pahn
Breakfast	El desayuno	el day-sigh-**oon**-oh
Butter	La mantequilla	lah mahn-tay-**key**-yah
Cheers!	¡Salud!	sah-**lood**
Cocktail	Un aperitivo	oon ah-pair-ee-**tee**-voh
Dinner	La cena	lah **seh**-nah
Dish	Un plato	oon **plah**-toe
Dish of the day	El platillo de hoy	el plah-**tee**-yo day oy
Enjoy!	¡Buen provecho!	bwen pro-**veh**-cho
Fixed-price menu	La comida corrida	lah koh-**me**-dah co-**ree**-dah
Fork	El tenedor	el ten-eh-**door**
Is the tip included?	¿Está incluida la propina?	es-**tah** in-clue-**ee**-dah lah pro-**pea**-nah
Knife	El cuchillo	el koo-**chee**-yo
Lunch	La comida	lah koh-**me**-dah
Menu	La carta	lah **cart**-ah
Napkin	La servilleta	lah sair-vee-**yet**-uh
Pepper	La pimienta	lah pea-me-**en**-tah
Please give me	Por favor déme	pore fah-**vor** **day**-may
Salt	La sal	lah sahl
Spoon	Una cuchara	**oo**-nah koo-**chah**-rah
Sugar	El azúcar	el ah-**sue**-car
Waiter!/Waitress!	¡Por favor Señor/Señorita!	pore fah-**vor** sen-**yor**/sen-yor-ee-**tah**

Menu Guide

English	*Spanish*
Full-service restaurant	Restaurante
Coffee shop	Cafetería
Small café serving local dishes, often found in marketplaces	Fonda
Snack bar or stand, usually for stand-up eating	Taquería
Fixed-price menu	Comida corrida
Special of the day	Menú del día
Drink included	Bebida incluida
Local specialties	Platillos típicos
Made to order	Al gusto
Extra charge	Extra
In season	De la estación

Breakfast

Toast	Pan tostado
Bread	Pan
Corn tortillas	Tortillas de maíz
Jam	Mermelada
Honey/syrup	Miel
Soft-boiled egg	Huevo tibio
Bacon and eggs	Huevos con tocino
Ham and eggs	Huevos con jamón
Eggs with chili tomato sauce over tortillas	Huevos rancheros
Fried eggs	Huevos estrellados
Scrambled eggs	Huevos revueltos
Eggs scrambled with vegetables	Huevos mexicanos
Omelet	Tortilla de huevos/omelet
Eggs scrambled with tortilla strips, cheese and chile sauce	Chilaquiles
Hard rolls	Bolillos
Sweet rolls or bread	Pan dulce
Whole-wheat bread	Pan de trigo
Yogurt	Yogurt/búlgaro

Snacks

Appetizer or snack	Antojitos
Appetizers	Botanes
Filled flour tortilla	Burrito
Sweet potato candy	Camote
Boat-shaped meat-filled corn cakes	Chalupas
Meat-filled turnovers	Empanadas
Fried rolled tacos	Flautas
Thick meat-filled corn cakes	Gorditas
Fried meat-filled corn cakes	Garnaches
Salted roasted pumpkin seeds	Pepitas
Flour tortillas filled with melted cheese	Quesadillas
Puffy fried bread	Sopapillas
Small corn pancakes topped with	Sopes

beans and cheese

Tortillas filled with meat, beans, cheese, etc., cooked over an open fire	Tacos
Tortillas topped with pork cooked on a spit	Tacos al pastor
Sandwiches on hard rolls	Tortas
Flat fried tortillas topped with meat, beans, etc.	Tostadas

Starters

Spicy sausage	Chorizo
Pork sausage	Salchicha de puerco
Cold cuts	Carnes frías/Fiambres
Assorted appetizers	Botana surtida
Fried pork rinds	Chicharrones
Croquettes (fish, fowl or meat)	Croquetas (de pescado, ave o carne)
Smoked mussels	Mejillones ahumados
Smoked oysters	Ostiones ahumados
Marinated seafood or fish	Ceviche
Cheeses	Quesos
Fried tortilla strips (corn chips)	Totopos

Soups

Soup of the day	Sopa del día
Vegetable soup	Sopa de verduras
Chicken soup	Sopa de pollo
Broth, consommé—beef or chicken	Caldo
Light soup with beef and vegetables—beef broth	Caldo de res
Onion soup	Sopa de cebolla
Garlic soup	Sopa de ajo
Lentil soup	Sopa de lentejas
Cold vegetable soup	Gazpacho
Tortilla soup	Sopa de tortilla, sopa azteca
Spicy chicken-vegetable soup	Caldo tlalpeño
Piquant pork-hominy soup	Pozole
Tripe soup	Menudo
Lima bean soup	Caldo de habas
Egg soup	Sopa de huevo
Noodle soup	Sopa de fideos
Meatball soup	Sopa de albóndigas
Avocado soup	Sopa de aguacate
Tomato soup	Sopa de jitomate
Cream of . . .	Crema de . . .

Vegetables

Olives	Aceitunas
Swiss chard	Acelga
Avocado	Aguacate
Garlic	Ajo
Artichokes	Alcachofas
Celery	Apio
Eggplant	Berenjena
Beet	Betabel
Zucchini	Calabacita
Winter squash, pumpkin	Calabaza
Chayote squash, vine pear	Chayote

Peas	Chícharos
Chilis	Chiles

Mild–medium: ancho, pasilla, poblano, verde, güero
Hot (picante): jalapeño, chipotle, pequín, mulato, serrano, habanero

Cabbage	Col
Cauliflower	Coliflor
Green beans	Ejotes
Corn on the cob	Elote
Asparagus	Espárragos
Spinach	Espinaca
Squash flower	Flor de calabaza
Red beans	Frijoles colorados
Pinto beans in seasoned sauce	Frijoles de olla
Black beans	Frijoles negros
Refried beans	Frijoles refritos
Broad beans	Habas
Mushrooms	Hongos
Mushroom fungus from corn	Huitlacoche
Jicama, a root vegetable with an apple-potato taste	Jícama
Red tomato	Jitomate
Lettuce	Lechuga
Corn	Maíz
Turnip	Nabo
Prickly pear pad	Nopal
Cucumber	Pepino
Sweet pepper	Pimiento dulce
Green pepper	Pimiento verde
Radish	Rábano
Green pepper strips	Rajas
Green tomato	Tomatillo/tomate verde
Tomato	Tomate
Carrot	Zanahoria

Dairy Products

Cream	Crema
Sour cream	Crema agria
Milk	Leche
Butter	Mantequilla
Cheese	Queso
Fresh farmer's cheese	Queso fresco

Potatoes, Rice, and Noodles

Rice	Arroz
White rice	Arroz blanco
Yellow rice	Arroz a la mexicana
Rice with greens	Arroz verde
Pilaf	Sopa seca
Spaghetti	Espagueti
baked with cheese	al horno
Noodles	Fideos
Macaroni	Macarrón(es)
Pasta, noodles	Pastas
Potatoes	Papas
mashed	puré de papas
french fries	papas fritas en aceite

Fish and Seafood

Abalone	Abulón
Tuna	Atún
Cod	Bacalao
Squid	Calamares
in their own ink	en su tinta
Shrimp	Camarones
Crab	Cangrejo
Red snapper	Huachinango
Crab	Jaiba
Lobster	Langosta
Prawns, crayfish	Langostinos
Octopus	Pulpo
Small saltwater fish	Mojarras
Haddock	Róbalo
Pompano	Pámpano
Sardines	Sardinas
Salmon	Salmón
Shark	Tiburón
Sea turtle	Tortuga
Trout	Trucha

Methods of preparation

Smoked	Ahumado
In garlic	Al ajillo, Al ajo, Al mojo de ajo
Baked	Al horno
Baked with tomato sauce and olives	A la veracruzana
Grilled	A la parrilla
Breaded	Empanizado
Marinated	En escabeche
Fried	Frito

Meat

Meatballs	Albóndigas
Steak	Bistec/biftec de lomo
Goat	Cabrito
Lamb, mutton	Carnero
Beef	Carne de res
Beef stew with vegetables	Carne guisada con verduras
Fried pork	Carnitas
Cutlet	Chuleta
Ribs	Costillas
Steak strips	Fajitas
Fillet steak	Filete
Liver	Hígado
Loin strip steak	Filete de lomo
Shoulder	Hombro
Pork loin	Lomo
Dried, shredded beef	Machaca
Breaded veal	Milanesa de ternera
Leg	Pierna
Pork	Puerco
Sausages	Salchichas
Veal	Ternera

Methods of preparation

Grilled	A la parrilla
Charcoal-broiled	A las brasas
Baked	Al horno
Roasted	Asada
Well done	Bien cocida
Stewed	En cazuela
Au jus	En su jugo
Fried	Frita
Very rare	Media cruda
Medium	Término medio

Game and Poultry

Rabbit	Conejo
Chicken, hen	Gallina
Turkey	Guajolote
Wild hare	Liebre
Duck	Pato
Turkey	Pavo
Chicken breast	Pechugas de pollo
Chicken	Pollo
Venison	Venado

Typical Dishes

Chicken with rice	Arroz con pollo
Steamed meat wrapped in leaves	Barbacoa
Slow-steamed goat or lamb with mild chile flavor	Birria
Broiled beef with vegetables	Carne asada
Fried pork	Carnitas
Sweet peppers stuffed with beef filling in cream and nut sauce	Chiles en nogada
Stuffed mild green chiles fried in batter	Chiles rellenos
Tortillas with filling and served in a sauce	Enchiladas
chicken	de pollo
cheese	de queso
chicken-filled with cream sauce	Suizas
Red mole sauce with meat, fowl, and fruit	Manchamanteles
Rice with seafood, meat, and vegetables	Paella
Spicy ground-beef mixture with raisins	Picadillo
Chicken steamed in citrus juices	Pollo píbil
Hash	Salpicón
Filled cornmeal wrapped in corn leaf	Tamal
Pork with smoky tomato sauce, potatoes, and avocado	Tinga

Sauces and Preparations

Red chile marinade	Adobo
Avocado sauce/dip	Guacamole
Spicy sauce of chile, chocolate, sesame, and almonds	Mole

Green tomato and nut sauce	Mole verde
Spicy sesame-seed sauce	Pipián
Béchamel sauce	Salsa bechamela
Uncooked or slightly cooked tomato, onion, chile sauce	Salsa cruda/mexicana
Red chile tomato sauce	Salsa de chile rojo
Tartar sauce	Salsa tártara
Green tomato, chile, coriander sauce	Salsa verde

Fruits and Nuts

Almond	Almendra
Hazelnut	Avellana
Chestnut	Castaña
Peanut	Cacahuate
Apricot	Chabacano
Cherimoya, vanilla-flavored fruit	Chirimoya
Plum	Ciruela
Prune	Ciruela pasa
Coconut	Coco
Date	Dátile
Peach	Durazno
Strawberry	Fresa
Dried Fruit	Frutas seca
Pomegranate	Granada
Passion fruit	Granadilla
Soursop	Guanábana
Guava	Guayaba
Fig	Higo
Lime	Limón
Large tropical fruit, related to mango	Mamey
Tangerine	Mandarina
Mango	Mango
Cantaloupe	Melón
Honeydew melon	Melón verde
Orange	Naranja
Walnut	Nueces
Raisin	Pasas
Papaya	Papaya
Pear	Pera
Green apple	Perón
Pineapple	Piña
Pine nut	Piñón
Watermelon	Sandía
Tamarind	Tamarindo
Grapefruit	Toronja
Cactus pear	Tuna
Grape (green or red)	Uva (verde o roja)

Nonalcoholic Beverages

Coffee	Café
black	*negro*
American	*americano*
with cream	*con crema*
with milk	*con leche*
decaffeinated	*descafeinado*
cappuccino	*capuchino*

espresso	*exprés/solo*
Chocolate corn gruel	Champurrada
Mexican hot chocolate	Chocolate
Lemonade	Limonada preparada
Mineral water	Agua mineral
carbonated	*con gas*
noncarbonated	*sin gas*
Fruit ade	Agua de . . .
Hibiscus flower drink	*jamaíca*
Bottled soft drink	Refresco
Fruit-flavored corn gruel	Atole
Cold drink flavored with seeds, coconut, fruit or oatmeal	Horchata
. . . juice	Jugo de . . .
Milk	Leche
Malted milk	Leche malteada
Pureed fruit drink	Licuado
Tea	Té
Herb tea	Té de hierbas
Chamomile tea	Té de manzanilla

Alcoholic Drinks

. . . straight	Copa de . . .
On the rocks	En las rocas
With water	Con agua
Rum and Coke	Cuba libre
Tequila with Triple Sec and lime juice	Margarita
Red wine with fruit	Sangría
Beer	Cerveza
light/dark	*clara/oscura*
Champagne	Champaña
Sugarcane brandy	Chicha
Hard cider	Sidra
Cognac, brandy	Coñac
Strong Mexican brandy (firewater)	Aguardiente
Liqueur	Licor
Agave liquor	Tequila
Agave liquor with a worm in the bottle	Mezcal
Fermented agave drink	Pulque
Alcoholic eggnog liqueur	Rompope
Rum	Ron
Whiskey	Wisky

Index

Personal Itinerary

Departure *Date*

Time

Transportation

Arrival *Date*   *Time*

Departure *Date*   *Time*

Transportation

Accommodations

Arrival *Date*   *Time*

Departure *Date*   *Time*

Transportation

Accommodations

Arrival *Date*   *Time*

Departure *Date*   *Time*

Transportation

Accommodations

Personal Itinerary

Arrival *Date*   *Time*

Departure *Date*   *Time*

Transportation

Accommodations

Arrival *Date*   *Time*

Departure *Date*   *Time*

Transportation

Accommodations

Arrival *Date*   *Time*

Departure *Date*   *Time*

Transportation

Accommodations

Arrival *Date*   *Time*

Departure *Date*   *Time*

Transportation

Accommodations

Personal Itinerary

Arrival *Date*   *Time*

Departure *Date*   *Time*

Transportation

Accommodations

Arrival *Date*   *Time*

Departure *Date*   *Time*

Transportation

Accommodations

Arrival *Date*   *Time*

Departure *Date*   *Time*

Transportation

Accommodations

Arrival *Date*   *Time*

Departure *Date*   *Time*

Transportation

Accommodations

Personal Itinerary

Arrival   *Date*   *Time*

Departure   *Date*   *Time*

Transportation

Accommodations

Arrival   *Date*   *Time*

Departure   *Date*   *Time*

Transportation

Accommodations

Arrival   *Date*   *Time*

Departure   *Date*   *Time*

Transportation

Accommodations

Arrival   *Date*   *Time*

Departure   *Date*   *Time*

Transportation

Accommodations

Personal Itinerary

Arrival   *Date*   *Time*

Departure   *Date*   *Time*

Transportation

Accommodations

Arrival   *Date*   *Time*

Departure   *Date*   *Time*

Transportation

Accommodations

Arrival   *Date*   *Time*

Departure   *Date*   *Time*

Transportation

Accommodations

Arrival   *Date*   *Time*

Departure   *Date*   *Time*

Transportation

Accommodations

Addresses

Name

Address

Telephone

Name

Address

Telephone

Name

Address

Telephone

Name

Address

Telephone

Name

Address

Telephone

Name

Address

Telephone

Name

Address

Telephone

Name

Address

Telephone

Name

Address

Telephone

Name

Address

Telephone

Name

Address

Telephone

Name

Address

Telephone

Name

Address

Telephone

Name

Address

Telephone

Name

Address

Telephone

Name

Address

Telephone

Addresses

Name

Address

Telephone

Name

Address

Telephone

Name

Address

Telephone

Name

Address

Telephone

Name

Address

Telephone

Name

Address

Telephone

Name

Address

Telephone

Name

Address

Telephone

Name

Address

Telephone

Name

Address

Telephone

Name

Address

Telephone

Name

Address

Telephone

Name

Address

Telephone

Name

Address

Telephone

Name

Address

Telephone

Name

Address

Telephone

Notes

Fodor's Travel Guides

U.S. Guides

Alaska
Arizona
Boston
California
Cape Cod, Martha's
  Vineyard, Nantucket
The Carolinas & the
  Georgia Coast
The Chesapeake
  Region
Chicago
Colorado
Disney World & the
  Orlando Area
Florida
Hawaii

Las Vegas, Reno,
  Tahoe
Los Angeles
Maine, Vermont,
  New Hampshire
Maui
Miami & the
  Keys
National Parks
  of the West
New England
New Mexico
New Orleans
New York City
New York City
  (Pocket Guide)

Pacific North Coast
Philadelphia & the
  Pennsylvania
  Dutch Country
Puerto Rico
  (Pocket Guide)
The Rockies
San Diego
San Francisco
San Francisco
  (Pocket Guide)
The South
Santa Fe, Taos,
  Albuquerque
Seattle &
  Vancouver

Texas
USA
The U. S. & British
  Virgin Islands
The Upper Great
  Lakes Region
Vacations in
  New York State
Vacations on the
  Jersey Shore
Virginia & Maryland
Waikiki
Washington, D.C.
Washington, D.C.
  (Pocket Guide)

Foreign Guides

Acapulco
Amsterdam
Australia
Austria
The Bahamas
The Bahamas
  (Pocket Guide)
Baja & Mexico's Pacific
  Coast Resorts
Barbados
Barcelona, Madrid,
  Seville
Belgium &
  Luxembourg
Berlin
Bermuda
Brazil
Budapest
Budget Europe
Canada
Canada's Atlantic
  Provinces

Cancun, Cozumel,
  Yucatan Peninsula
Caribbean
Central America
China
Czechoslovakia
Eastern Europe
Egypt
Europe
Europe's Great Cities
France
Germany
Great Britain
Greece
The Himalayan
  Countries
Holland
Hong Kong
India
Ireland
Israel
Italy

Italy 's Great Cities
Jamaica
Japan
Kenya, Tanzania,
  Seychelles
Korea
London
London
  (Pocket Guide)
London Companion
Mexico
Mexico City
Montreal &
  Quebec City
Morocco
New Zealand
Norway
Nova Scotia,
  New Brunswick,
  Prince Edward
  Island
Paris

Paris (Pocket Guide)
Portugal
Rome
Scandinavia
Scandinavian Cities
Scotland
Singapore
South America
South Pacific
Southeast Asia
Soviet Union
Spain
Sweden
Switzerland
Sydney
Thailand
Tokyo
Toronto
Turkey
Vienna & the Danube
  Valley
Yugoslavia

Wall Street Journal Guides to Business Travel

Europe

International Cities

Pacific Rim

USA & Canada

Special-Interest Guides

Bed & Breakfast and
  Country Inn Guides:
  Mid-Atlantic Region
  New England
  The South
  The West

Cruises and Ports
  of Call
Healthy Escapes
Fodor's Flashmaps
  New York

Fodor's Flashmaps
  Washington, D.C.
Shopping in Europe
Skiing in the USA &
  Canada

Smart Shopper's
  Guide to London
Sunday in New York
Touring Europe
Touring USA